I0760996

International acclaim for **Outsmart the MBA Clones**

I was glued to Dan's book. With best practice, common sense and extraordinary intelligence throughout, **just when I was thinking it can't get any better, I realized there was still more than half the book to go.**

> Ren Spiteri, Director
> Bulldog, Malta
> *www.virtualbulldog.com*

The only thing scarier than your competition already reading this book, is how they may be applying it in the market that could have been yours. If you're serious about having an unfair advantage, **you'd be foolish to pass up the wisdom and tools within these pages**

> Ray Podder, Brand and Competitive Strategy Development
> Grow, Los Angeles
> *www.growbrand.com*

In an era where consumers are fed up by similar products and brands, to create an "unfair competitive advantage" may be the only way to succeed. The book is **definitely a branding and marketing "Eureka!"** for the present market and consumer realities in emerging economies such as the BRIC countries as well as in developed ones. This book will bring out the best in managers and foster successful differentiation of companies in the market by furthering differentiation in the behavior of managers.

> Paula Limena, Marketing and Branding Consultant
> Executive Director, Imageneer Consulting, São Paulo, Brazil
> *www.imageneer.com.br*

Dan Herman's new marketing paradigm is all about competing successfully. It offers new laws of marketing and quite a different mindset. He challenges the MBA clones and their old marketing gurus who fail to provide the answers to changing circumstances. **His concepts are original yet very accessible to the reader.** Reading the book is a true pleasure for practicing marketers and brand builders who love their profession.

> Leo van Sister, Founder and CEO
> BrandCustodians, Amsterdam
> *www.merkcommissarissen.nl*

This book is the new ultimate truth in competitive strategies, marketing and branding.
The methodology is brilliantly explained, AND I can attest to its real life effectiveness.

      Andris Romanovskis, Creative director

      Rhino Design Agency, Riga

      www.rhino.lv

This insightful book is a practical guide to breaking out of the typical corporate/institutional frame of mind that limits the thinking of so many of today's executives. Some business people prefer to swim in a sea of sameness but **this book helps you to create and surf the waves of success.**

      Jonas Bergvall, Managing Partner

      Coco's Brand Concept, Strängnäs, Sweden

      www.cocosbrandconcept.com

They say history is a bad motorist because it hardly ever signals when it's taking a turn. Watch out! **Dan's new book will make marketing history turn a new page.** What will emerge is an immense opportunity for businesses around the world to continuously create unfair advantages and keep making their competition irrelevant. I strongly recommend this book. It is a must-read for executives and for business and management students.

      Gaurav Bahirvani, Brand Futurist

      Founder & Principal, BRANDTEGIST, Mumbai

      www.brandtegist.com

With expertise and authority Dan Herman finally did away with the rigid military sense of "competitive strategy" to show us how it takes presence and effect in the psyche of customers. Like an optometrist providing you with the right lenses for your eyeglasses enabling you to see immediately a lucid image so Dr. Herman makes you see anew today's markets and consumers in a way which all of a sudden makes perfect sense. Singlehandedly he created a new vocabulary for marketing and branding that represents new horizons of thinking and acting. **It is a wonderful and brilliant book that reads like an adventure novel.**

      Edvin Jurin, Special Projects–Executive Director

      McCann Erickson Croatia, Zagreb, Croatia

      Director, FESTO (Croatian Advertising Festival)

      www.mccann.hr/eng/emce.htm

Outsmart the MBA Clones

The Alternative Guide to Competitive Strategy, Marketing, and Branding

Dr. Dan Herman

Translation from the original text in Hebrew by
Eetta Prince-Gibson, Ephrat Abisror, and Dan Herman

Paramount Market Publishing, Inc.

Paramount Market Publishing, Inc.
950 Danby Road, Suite 136
Ithaca, NY 14850
www.paramountbooks.com
Telephone: 607-275-8100; 888-787-8100   Facsimile: 607-275-8101

Publisher: James Madden
Editorial Director: Doris Walsh

This publication is designed to provide accurate and authoritative information in regard to the subject matter covered. It is sold with the understanding that the publisher is not engaged in rendering legal, accounting, or other professional services. If legal advice or other expert assistance is required, the services of a competent professional should be sought.

All trademarks are the property of their respective companies.

Cataloging in Publication Data available
ISBN 978-0-9786602-8-4

To Laura, the wonderful love of my life,
and to my dear Robby, the most amazing boy in the world.

*"The secret of success is to know something
nobody else knows."*

—Aristotle Onassis

*"If everyone has to think outside the box,
maybe it is the box that needs fixing."*

—Malcolm Gladwell

Contents

part 1

1 Introduction: MBA Clones Are All Around You   1

2 What is an Unfair Advantage?   8

3 Some Surprising Insights about Strategy   20

4 The Three Myths about Competitive Advantage   34

5 The Great Secret of Differentiation that No One Imitates   45

6 Strategy Development: How Will You Know What's Next?   55

part 2

7 An Overview of O-Scan: How to Identify, Invent, and Maximize Opportunities   68

8 Some O-Scan Methods: Obtaining Insight about Consumers and Their Future Desires   86

9 Some More O-Scan Methods: Identifying Opportunities Using the Consumption Process Analysis   105

10 Still More O-Scan Methods: Identifying Opportunities through Self-Analysis and Competitive Analysis   116

part 3

11 Inside Information from the Consumer's Mind   136

12 The Real Reasons for Brand Success   157

13 How Do You Create a Brand that is More than the Product?   172

14 Satisfying Marketing Vs. Electrifying Marketing   193

15 How Are Marketing Hits Developed?   207

16 How to Drive Consumers Crazy for Your Brand   232

Index   254

About the Author   261

part 1

An alternative understanding of competitive strategy, competitive advantage, and how to achieve it

1

Introduction:
MBA Clones Are All Around You

Go with the Flow

This book may be irrelevant in five years, but that shouldn't concern you. If you use the tools that it offers you, in five years you'll be very wealthy. Today, a five-year period is the "long term." In fewer than five years, Nokia was transformed from a local Finnish company to the world leader in the cell phone market. By the end of those same five years, the same brilliant strategy that led to this amazing achievement had become, just as amazingly, dated and non-competitive.

We live in an accelerated world. Not only does change take place faster, it occurs more frequently. In this world, the old type of marketing innovation just isn't enough. In this world, no achievements are final and durable. Today's achievement isn't in the bag tomorrow. There's no way to conquer a share of the market, because market shares constantly shift from competitor to competitor. So it's not relevant anymore to talk about your market share in terms of something you possess. It is an indicator of how well you are doing at a given point in time. It is not property. The important criterion these days is your *average market share* over, let's say, a given year.

In this world, there are no more long-term strategies from which you may never digress. Over the past decade or so, champion long-term strategists and huge global companies such as IBM, McDonald's, Coca-Cola, Levi Strauss, Mercedes, and Disney learned that lesson and were forced to adopt new strategies. Long-term strategies have been replaced by *strategies that are constantly adapting and changing* as new market opportunities are identified and maximized.

Another sad truth (or not, depending on which side you're on) is that there are no more long-term competitive advantages. The vast availability of manufacturing and marketing resources, coupled with the consumers' unprecedented openness to try new products and brands, have turned every advantage into a temporary one. The mission now is to obtain a *renewable competitive advantage*.

In this new reality, there are no more "launch-and-forget" brands, like Marlboro, that zealously maintain their visual identity and advertising style over many years. Brands and their symbols now change at a very rapid pace, and that is a good thing, not a fault of management.

Most of the rules of strategy, marketing, and branding that you learned are no longer relevant. They were created for the long term, but the long term is dying. The way to succeed over the long term is to succeed in the short term, time after time. That's one topic that this book is about.

The MBA Clones

In this book, you'll encounter new terminology and numerous approaches and methods that you didn't previously know. Not only that, you'll also discover many views and recommendations that completely contradict what you heard or read in the past about strategy, innovation, marketing, and branding. This book presents a new approach to achieving growth and a competitive advantage, complemented by a new method for developing and managing brands. Many CEOs today attend the same MBA programs, study the same books, and go to the same workshops, and all of them can quote Porter, Kotler, Aaker, and Ries. There are others too, but with your permission, I'll use this quartet to represent common wisdom.

What's wrong with MBA-graduate managers who apply the professional knowledge and skills they have learned? Look what's happening: Copernicus Marketing Consulting, an American company, recently published a research report whose very title should shake you up: *The*

Commoditization of Brands. Its research shows that brands are turning into commodities—undifferentiated merchandise like sugar or corn. The brands are too similar, so much so that most consumers are unable to tell them apart. In the past, much was made of the idea that products are becoming similar and branding was supposed to supply us with the differentiation. Well, I have bad news for you. Our brands have come to resemble one another for the same reasons our products began to resemble one another: because marketers themselves have become virtually indistinguishable.

All those managers who are supposed to compete with one another and create the differentiation that gives consumers a good reason to prefer one product over another are using the same data; they conduct the same focus groups and the same surveys, analyze the data with the same tools, and use the same concepts and approaches in order to create distinctive products and brands. The result? Most products, and even most brands, appear the same to the consumer. These managers are not playing me-too. Even without consciously imitating each other, they achieve the same results, simply because they think the same way. In other words, they are "MBA clones."

This fair competition is styled after athletics, not war. Everyone starts at the same point. Everyone has the same information. Everyone is talented. Everyone is full of initiative. Everyone is creative and everyone knows Porter, Kotler, Aaker, and Ries. So everyone gets to exactly the same place.

How about winning over competitors by unfair advantage? What do you think about getting to know the thought biases of your competitors and taking advantage of them for your own benefit? What do you think about adopting different business thinking that will give you an advantage? This book will provide you with exactly this opportunity.

Not every MBA graduate becomes an MBA clone. But MBA graduates are definitely an at-risk population. This book offers you an alternative form of business thinking that can help you avoid becoming an MBA clone. This moment can be the start of your unfair advantage (a term with a specific meaning, which will become clear in Chapter 2).

Skepticism Pays Off

You might say that if Porter, Kotler, Aaker, and Ries are the marketing gods who epitomize truth, then contradictory approaches might lead you into an abyss. In response, I have three things to say:

1. Porter, Kotler, Aaker, and Ries *were* largely right. Past tense. Many things have changed, as I mentioned. These changes, in the market and in consumer behavior, have made the well-known rules of do and don't obsolete. As a result, following these rules might lead you to failure. The gurus of the past have not kept up with the changes in the world around them, and those who are always quoting the books they wrote in the 1970s, 1980s, and even 1990s—the previous century—certainly haven't kept up. On some topics, the gurus were *never* right. Ries, for example, contended that positioning is a process that allows you to appropriate a concept to your brand, usually in the form of an adjective implying a benefit to the consumer (such as "leading" or "prestigious"). Ries was unaware that consumers may perceive more than one brand as "prestigious." BMW and Mercedes are both prestigious, and consumers have no problem with that.

2. The rules of do and don't are intended for technicians who don't have any deep psychological or business understanding of what is really going on. These technicians sometimes discover that these rules don't apply, and then their conclusion is that there aren't any rules.

   Engineers, unlike technicians, understand the rationale behind these simplistic rules. Therefore, they are able to decide when the rules apply, when they don't, and when it would be advantageous to do the exact opposite. They understand the laws of nature. Engineers are also able to devise alternative paths to the same goals. Something similar happens in our field, too. The principles introduced in this book are based on this kind of understanding.

3. Theoretical concepts are tools for thinking about reality. They are not reality itself. No one has ever smelled *brand values* or tasted *positioning*. When these terms are useful, use them. But when they are not, think about the situation differently. Your point of view determines your action options, and the better you are at examining many points of view, the more creatively and flexibly you will act to suit the situation at hand. This book offers you fresh concepts that enable you to view reality in a new light and discover new directions for action.

I'll give you an example. How many times have you heard a marketer ask, "Is this a niche product, or a mass-market product?" He learned to ask that question in business school. He learned that in a competitive market, it's better to segment the consumers and gain control over a portion of the market. Philip Kotler said that there are riches in niches. He stated this as an absolute truth. What a mistake! In most cases, that initial question narrows your thinking. Anyone who automatically thinks "niche" also thinks about burrowing inside and defending it. But what if there isn't any niche?

A niche is a limited and constrained potential market. A niche is a group of consumers with specific needs, for example, eyeglass wearers when we're talking about vision-correction procedures. Anything else isn't a niche. Whenever possible, I prefer to replace the question about niches with a different one: "How many consumers can our product or brand turn on?" Business people who thought that way about "niche products" turned them into mass-market products and turned themselves into billionaires.

The Jacuzzi, for example, began as a medical niche product, until someone suddenly said, "It doesn't only cure you, it makes you feel good. Maybe more people will buy it." So, at first, it really was a product for the rich only—a niche product. Then someone suggested making a cheaper version and expanding the market potential. Now Jacuzzi is almost a mass-market item. The same thing has happened to many other prestigious products.

Other types of products that began as niche items now belong to the wider market. 4X4s were once used only by soldiers and wilderness freaks. Today, most 4X4 owners (many of them women) wouldn't take them anywhere near the wilderness for fear of getting them dirty. How many people can get excited about a 4X4 vehicle, anyway? A lot, it turns out. We've now got the urban 4X4, the luxury 4X4, and so forth. All of a sudden, marketers discovered that many people love driving in comfort, high above others on the road.

Once upon a time, cellular phones were a business-sector niche product. And then the prices of both phones and service dropped. It's still more expensive than a land-line in many parts of the world, but it's a price many can afford. The moment we took our heads out of the niche, how many people got interested in cell phones? It's happened to many technological products. You can see how much the niche question can limit you. The same holds true for many concepts that the much-admired marketing gurus taught us.

Common Practice or an Unfair Advantage — The Choice is Yours

This book is about how to achieve an unfair advantage over your competitors. You create this unfair advantage because you are not competing in the same ways your competitors are. An unfair advantage will pull you out of the rat race. You'll be safe from the competition and your competitors will become much less relevant. In some cases, you will even be able to create your own private monopoly.

This is very different from everything you've learned. This is new territory, and I'm sure that some of you are beginning to feel this is a risky venture. Expertise and professionalism, not conservatism, are my responses to risk. In today's business world, conservatism is dangerous. More than two decades ago, two young stars at McKinsey & Co., the Vatican of conservatism wrote *In Search of Excellence,* one of the most successful management books of all time. In it, they listed the 43 most successful American companies. Within five years, two-thirds of those companies had crashed. One of these marketers, Tom Peters, later became an outspoken critic of McKinseyism.

One of the classic ways to shield yourself from different thinking is to say, "That's very theoretical. In practice, it doesn't work that way." That idiotic statement does contain a grain of truth. A new possibility, by virtue of its newness, is not common practice. It becomes praxis for those who understand the potential, go for it, and grab the winnings. Practical people will always be left behind. An unfair advantage belongs to the quick and open-minded. This book not only tells you to be different, it *shows* you how to be profitably different. It could be the beginning of your unfair advantage.

One more short comment, before we dive in.

This book deals primarily with competitive strategy. It also touches upon subjects related to the development of brands, with *branding* seen as one aspect of contemplating and realizing a competitive strategy. The book will not teach you how to build a brand, step-by-step. Another book I wrote, *Just-on-Desire Branding,* already a bestseller in Israel and Russia (and soon to be available in English and other languages), does precisely that.

If you're interested in any of my other writings and services, visit my websites, *www.advantigizers.com* and *www.danherman.com.*

2

What is an Unfair Advantage?

A Price-Driven Market? There's No Such Thing

I know that most of you don't even have a common competitive advantage at the moment, and you may be convinced that in your market you'll never have one. Perhaps you think yours is just a "price-driven" market in which consumers consider only the price when they make their purchasing decisions. You probably know that your competitors will imitate every successful move you make. It's so frustrating, and I agree completely. A common competitive advantage is almost impossible to achieve and it isn't even worth striving for. The old style of competitive advantage is victory by points, and by nature it's temporary. It's an ordinary advantage achieved through fair competition: you're smarter and faster, you try harder, and then presto—you're better. Your process is more efficient and economical. Your last product, advertising campaign, or promotion—what a success! For a month or a year, you have an advantage. But your competitors aren't stupid, and they're going to close the gap, one way or another.

I suggest that you go for *an unfair advantage*. But first, let's explore the idea of price-driven markets a bit further to give you some food for thought in case that concept is dragging you down. Often, a price-driven market is an illusion. You and your competitors create it yourselves, unintentionally. All competitors are convinced that the only criterion that interests consumers is price, and all of their messages to consumers, therefore, are about price: discounts, promotions, low-price-every-day, and so forth. The result will come as no surprise: consumers really do become interested only in price, and in ever-increasing numbers they gravitate toward the lowest prices (or toward whoever manages to create the impression of offering the lowest prices—and I personally hate cheaters in the market or anywhere else). This behavior, of course, reinforces the marketers' belief that the market really is "price-driven," as they had always suspected. It's a vicious circle. But is price really the only thing that interests consumers? I dare say: almost never. And the proof is that there are very few product categories in which most consumers buy the cheapest brand.

How about another angle? The same consumer who, in relation to your product or service, is "price-driven," has no trouble spending high prices for other products and services. Am I right? I want to propose a different perspective. The market isn't price-driven and neither is the consumer. It's the marketers who are price-driven. If that's what you're selling, why should it come as a surprise that that's what they're buying? In many formerly price-driven markets, there's a competitor who one day stopped talking about price and began offering an added value, the kind that turns consumers on. And do you know what happened? He won. One day, someone is going to do that in your market. Who knows? It may be you.

Double Immunity to Competition

An unfair advantage is not a common advantage and it is certainly not an advantage based on low price. When you have an unfair advantage, you are very successful and, at the same time, immune to competition. You have an unfair advantage when your competitors are helpless, when they can't take your clients or even a portion of the sales away from you. Sound impossible? Several companies manage to do this, or at least come close. I'll give some examples soon. But first, it's important to understand that an unfair advantage has two characteristics which, taken together, provide you with double immunity to competition.

1. An unfair advantage means that there is a group of consumers who truly believe that you cannot be replaced. You'll have a hard time convincing Belvedere Vodka drinkers to even sip the super-premium vodka made by Absolut, especially if the Belvedere is served with Tsar Imperial Beluga. Try to talk to a true cigar aficionado about something other than Habanos made *totalmente a mano*, such as the Cohiba Esplendidos brand. A Ferrari lover will explain to you, as if he were talking to an inexperienced child, that a Porsche just isn't the same thing. If you'd like to hear the same story about brands that are a bit more familiar to everyday folk, I'll do that in a moment. Meanwhile, it's important to clarify the principle: an unfair advantage means that you essentially have a private monopoly—one you can't get from the government, only from the consumers.

2. An unfair advantage means that you have a clear and significant differentiation that none of your competitors wants to imitate. I'm repeating this, so it will be clear. The second characteristic of an unfair advantage is that it's highly unlikely your competitors will want to imitate what you're doing, despite the fact that you're really succeeding. How can this be? Take, for example, The Body Shop chain. This is a completely commercial enterprise in the field of toiletries and self-care that has hoisted the flag of realism (most women don't look like supermodels) and promoted activism on behalf of both the world's disadvantaged and the environment. The company is tough on its suppliers, prohibiting them from performing experiments on animals or harming the environment. It motivates its workers to volunteer and contribute. It's special. It succeeds, and no one is copying it. Why? It has managed to hoodwink the MBA clones and act according to its own way of thinking. There's a secret here, and I'm devoting Chapter 5 to disclosing it.

Black, Bitter, and Exciting

Here's a brand with an unfair advantage: Guinness Beer. Against all odds, this brand of beer has many devoted admirers throughout the world. This is the story: In December 1759, a young, energetic man named Arthur Guinness took over a failing brewery on James Street in Dublin, signing a lease for no less than 9,000 years (at the excellent rate of 45 Irish pounds per year!) In those days, the local beer was quite bad, and the Irish preferred whiskey and gin. In order to create a differentiation for himself that would also allow him to daringly penetrate the English market, Guinness decided to make a strong, thick beer (the technical name is Stout) from roasted rye, which gave it that darker-than-charcoal color and deep, rich, bitter taste. Today, you can get a Guinness in more than 150 countries, and it is one of the most successful global beer brands. Guinness die-hards wouldn't drink any other beer. "God's nectar," they call it. The competitors didn't jump at the idea of producing another black, bitter beer. Bingo! A private monopoly.

But let me tell you something: it's not because of the 198 calories a pint (similar to American light beer and fewer than a pint of squeezed orange juice). Guinness succeeds because it's an acquired taste—something you have to get used to. It's the ultimate male experience. All male experiences, I'll have you note, are based on overcoming something unpleasant, dangerous, or difficult. It's clear that the benefit of drinking Guinness is psychological; it reinforces self esteem. But drinking it in a pub is also a sign of group affinity and a declaration of who you are and what you're made of. The ability to drink Guinness is an entrance ticket to the Men-Who-Can-Drink-Guinness Club. But wait, this is more than a club. It's a cult. These men have an immediate rapport, and that—the social value—is no less important than the taste.

Brands with an unfair advantage like Guinness still need to renew and update their relevance. Two important steps taken by a Guinness' owner, Diageo, are worth noting. The first is the Extra Cold campaign that Guinness launched in 1999. After investing millions of dollars in research and development, Guinness took out a patent on a clever cork that jets a combination of nitrogen and carbon dioxide to cool the beer immediately when the bottle is opened. This new invention keeps Guinness on the minds of clubbers who want to drink their beer but take time out for dancing. Another novelty is the Guinness Storehouse, which opened in Dublin in 2000. This isn't just a museum presenting the history and manufacturing process of black gold. It is a training center for employees and a conference center. Primarily, however, it's an active and exciting entertainment spot that includes an art gallery, restaurants, coffee shops, bars, and event facilities. If you have the chance to visit, I highly recommend that you buy a drink at the charming Gravity Bar that offers a spectacular 360-degree view of Dublin.

Beauty is on the Feet of the Beholder

Birkenstock is another brand that has enjoyed an unfair advantage for many years. In 1897, Konrad Birkenstock had a great idea: to design the internal part of the shoe to fit the arch, sole, and other parts of the foot that would step into it. Konrad, born into a family of shoemakers, developed insoles for shoes, which were just beginning to be mass manufactured. His son, Carl, improved on his father's invention and even copyrighted the term Footbed Support. But it was *his* son, Karl, who in 1954 established the company that we know today. Every morning, he awoke with excitement at the prospect of producing the most comfortable shoes in the world. And he succeeded. In 1966, Margot Fraizer from Santa Cruz, California, bought herself a pair of Birkenstocks while visiting her native Germany. When the chronic foot pain from which she had been suffering for years suddenly disappeared, she was thrilled. She thought that many other Americans might be equally pleased, and she became the U.S. distributor for Birkenstock.

The rest is history. The Birkenstock brand—ugly sandals and clogs with clumsy soles—became known as amazingly comfortable. Since the 1960s, the American version, Footprints, has marketed closed clogs that cover the toes and even shoes. The main point is that Birkenstock is an expert in comfort, and let fashion and style be damned. People who wear Birkenstocks, all day or only in their leisure time, enjoy their comfort, but their Birkenstocks are also a means of telling the world, "When it comes to my comfort, I don't give a damn about how it looks." Birkenstock is the look because it is the anti-look. Hippy students wear Birks. Cool young people wear Birks. The rich and beautiful wear Birks. Birkenstock has a clear identity: ugly and comfortable. The fact that the company is committed to protecting the environment and using only recyclable materials doesn't hurt, either. For their clients, Birkenstock is a cult. "Birkenstockers" connect immediately. Only a few marginal companies have tried to imitate the style, because who wants to manufacture ugly sandals? It's a classic unfair advantage.

A typical MBA clone will tell you that Birkenstock is a niche brand. But you already know better. The Birkenstock market is as big as its ability to turn more and more consumers on to the concept that comfort is more important than beauty and style.

A few years ago, Birkenstock decided to forego its unfair advantage. Its thinking went something like this: Everyone already knows that Birkenstocks are comfortable, so why not make shoes, clogs, and sandals that look good, too?

Designer Yves Béhar was commissioned to head the revolution. Immediately, he created the philosophy for the new approach: "We make the shoe from the inside out, we don't start with appearance," he said. Since the clumsy sole was still the base of the shoe, the result was stylish, but different. The company dubbed the series Urban Design, also referring to it as The Architect Collection. That was smart. The series resonated with people who appreciate comfort and are open to unusual design. This smart shoe company has walked away with gold medals at several design competitions. And it all began in 2002.

By 2003, Birkenstock had developed an appetite. This time, it hired supermodel Heidi Klum to help design a series that was truly fashionable and exciting. What happened? More and more shoe manufacturers around the world began to think about making the inside soles of their shoes more comfortable. For example, the prestigious brand Cole Haan began to offer amazingly attractive (and not the least bit clumsy) shoes with Nike Air soles. Within several years, the entire shoe industry had moved in this direction, using various forms of technology. Birkenstock is losing its differentiation. Its addicted clients are starting to feel that wearing Birkenstock isn't very special any more. The company could become just another shoe manufacturer, lacking any special advantage in the rat race.

Perhaps the Birkenstock people know something I don't know. Perhaps consumers who want everything here and now (we'll talk about them later) really have taken over the market, and there just aren't enough people left who want comfortable and ugly. Maybe. Whatever the case, Birkenstock is losing its unfair advantage.

Desire Creates a Monopoly—But What Creates Desire?

Brands with a private monopoly are brands whose buyers crave them— no less. Two factors affect a consumer's feelings about a brand.

The first factor determines the strength of the emotions. Consumers develop strong feelings only toward brands that provide them with some benefit that is both significant and rare. A significant benefit has a considerable effect on the consumer's well-being, quality of life, and general happiness. A rare benefit is one the consumer cannot easily obtain elsewhere. Please note: When I say elsewhere, I'm not necessarily referring to a product in the same category and brand that competes head-on with yours. If the consumer can obtain a similar benefit from a totally different product, that's okay. So, since we're seeking to make your product distinctive, we'll have to look for a benefit that is both significant and rare.

The second factor determines the direction of the emotions—positive (desire) or negative (disappointment, rejection). Consumers desire a product when they trust and think highly of the brand that promises them the significant and rare benefit—in other words, when they can rely on the product to consistently supply the promised benefit. The good thing about this second factor is that any good manager can assure it. It's just a matter of good management. The first factor is a much tougher challenge.

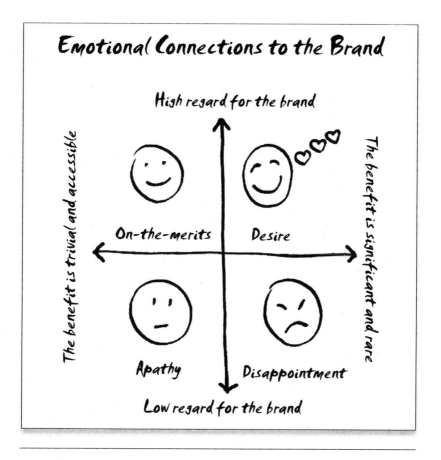

Two central factors influence a consumer's emotional connection to a brand. The first is the extent to which the benefit is important and rare (not provided by competing brands). The second is the extent to which the consumer believes that the brand can provide that benefit adequately and consistently (evaluation of the brand).

Loyalty Creates a Monopoly—But What Creates Loyalty?

You have a monopoly when you have a very high level of customer loyalty. This situation is rare. Even lower-level loyalty is rapidly nearing extinction. The data on this have been conclusive for quite some time. We'll expand on this topic in Chapter 15. I want to reassure you right now and tell you that you don't have to achieve customer loyalty in order to succeed. But if you want a private monopoly, then a high level of loyalty is a must. So what creates it?

It's not incidental that the factors that influence customer loyalty to a specific brand are similar to the factors that influence the strength of the emotional connection to the brand. There are two such factors:

The first is customer satisfaction or, better still, delight. Many believe that a high level of customer satisfaction alone will lead to loyalty. This would be great if it were true. Why? Good managers know how to manage their companies in ways that will bring about customer satisfaction. But does satisfaction beget loyalty? Despite what common sense seems to dictate, the answer is "not exactly." A high level of satisfaction, even enthusiasm, is a pre-requisite of loyalty, but neither satisfaction nor even enthusiasm ascertain loyalty.

The second factor, just as necessary but much more important, is effective differentiation. Consumers know there's something they can get only from you (differentiation) and that something is very important to them (effectiveness). You can't escape it. And so, in Chapter 5, we will deal extensively with the techniques for developing effective differentiation for your products, the kind that your MBA-clone competitors won't want to imitate.

The two central factors that affect consumer loyalty are the extent to which the benefit is unique (differentiation) and the extent of customer satisfaction with the brand. Essentially, we can discuss loyalty in only one case (and even then it is not exactly the same as loyalty between people): when consumer satisfaction is high and the product benefit is unique.

You Need a Strategy

I've already said that customer desire and loyalty, together with the low likelihood that your competitors will try to imitate you, create a private monopoly. I've discussed the two main factors that influence desire, and the two main factors that influence loyalty. I've said that they are similar but not identical. "High esteem for the brand" is similar to "high level of satisfaction." "Important and rare benefit" is similar to "effective differentiation."

I've emphasized that two of these factors, "high esteem for the brand" and "high level of satisfaction" are completely manageable. That is, any good manager can guarantee them. The other two are different. "Significant and rare benefit" and "effective differentiation" are a matter of strategy.

By definition, strategy is the way you plan to achieve your goals. In a competitive environment, your goal is for your customer to buy from you and not from your competitors. Therefore, strategy is the way in which you plan to achieve an advantage over your competitors, in the consumers' eyes. Differentiation is almost always a pre-condition for achieving such advantage. You must do something differently from your competitors so that you provide certain consumers with a good reason for preferring *you*. If you are really a great strategist, you can lead your customer to want you only, and thus create your own private monopoly.

To understand differentiation in more depth, you must realize that the only uniqueness that counts is the one that the consumer perceives and cares about. There are three types of differentiation, and only one is really strategic. There is temporary differentiation, the kind that a successful new product, or even a promotion, might achieve. For a moment, or perhaps over a period of time, the consumers will have a good reason to prefer you.

The second form of differentiation, which exists only under certain conditions, is circumstantial. Examples are a historical monopoly, a consumer's personal familiarity with one of your workers, or the store's proximity to the consumer's home. Don't underestimate circumstantial differentiation! From the consumer's point of view, the fact that his aunt works at a certain bank makes that bank distinctive. Categories such as banks, insurance companies, and even various retail outlets are often based on this kind of differentiation. The third form that we have yet to discuss is strategic differentiation. This is the differentiation that gives you the most competitive advantage possible across various purchasing situations.

How do you develop this kind of a strategy? That will be discussed in more detail in upcoming chapters. The general approach I'm about to present is known as the Advantagizing Approach: the masterful creation of competitive advantages.

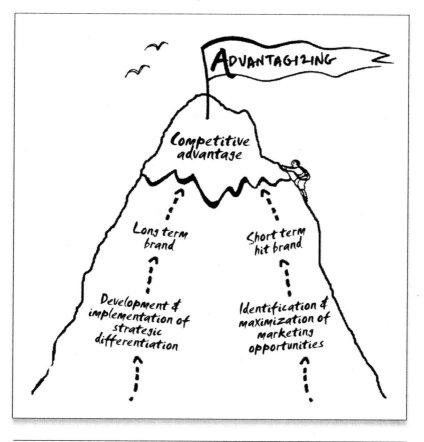

When you adopt the Advantagizing Approach, your thinking about how to achieve your competitive advantage proceeds on two parallel axes: long-term strategic differentiation (to the longest term conceivable) and early identification and fulfillment of market opportunities.

3

Some Surprising Insights about Strategy

Strategy—Very Scary Stuff

I have encouraging news for you: many of your competitors are afraid of strategy. You might call it *strategophobia*. Strategy has two terrifying characteristics. First, strategy is a choice. "We are going to go for target customers X, and not the rest," or "The major benefit we will offer consumers is Z and not all sorts of other things."

It seems that when you choose, you have to give something up. There are executives who are not willing to give up on a target group of customers, as if they "have them" or stand a realistic chance of getting them all. This is one of the sweetest but most dangerous illusions managers have. They aren't willing to define a particular benefit as the major benefit they have to offer their consumers, out of fear that the consumer might be tempted to try a different benefit elsewhere. Strategizing means choosing to focus and concentrate your energies in order to provide yourself with an advantage. You go about this by establishing your brand as the source of a certain benefit. If you don't, you probably won't be identified with any benefit and consumers will have no good reason to think of you and buy from you when they need or desire something.

When you adopt a strategy, you're "giving up" all sorts of things that you don't actually have in order to acquire something tangible, something you can sink your teeth into. That's how it works: *If you don't give up anything, you don't achieve anything.*

The second terrifying characteristic of strategy is differentiation from competitors. To be different—that's really a possibility that could cause nightmares. Why? Primarily because basic conservatism says that if that's what everyone does, there must be a good reason for it. And that's true. The component of "good management," which everyone strives for, is essential. It doesn't create an advantage over competitors, but it is essential. Beyond this, managers are always so busy dealing with competition that they are more worried about preventing their competitors from gaining an advantage than they are about creating an advantage for themselves. That's a classically fair game. And so those managers are busy trying to imitate their competitors rather than striving to be different. A good defensive game really does help you not lose. But in order to win, you need to score every now and then.

"I don't want to reinvent the wheel, I just want to implement *modi operandi* that have already proven to be successful," a senior manager in a large company once told me. His comment illustrates precisely the problem I'm talking about. He wants to avoid risk, but he might achieve just the opposite result—an even greater danger.

Imitating an "already successful" method is always dangerous, because no two business marketing situations are identical. What succeeded in one situation may fail in another. For example: those cheap products that brought you success during recession are not the ones that will boost your profits in a booming economy. I believe you have to monitor successes and failures around you all the time and accumulate a large arsenal of solutions, rather than merely imitate a specific solution for a specific situation. You have to constantly analyze and try to understand exactly what succeeded or failed. I am looking for principles and insights that I can implement in the future—not for ready-made solutions that I can copy. For every consulting project, I do try to "reinvent the wheel," to create something new and attempt to integrate knowledge, experience, insight, and tools, as well as the intuition I have developed. After I come up with something I believe in, I check my solution using all of the appropriate research tools. *The greatest danger in using successful methods is the fact that they have already succeeded. That is, your competitors are just as aware of these methods as you are, and using them won't give you a competitive advantage.*

One of the most powerful catalysts for the spread of *strategophobia* is the fact that hyper-competition is extremely tiresome and leads to burnout. At the same time, differentiation on the product level is becoming increasingly challenging. Product innovations, not to mention service innovations, are becoming easier and quicker to imitate. The great hope of the 1990s was the so-called "emotional brand." It subsequently became clear that there aren't an infinite number of emotions, and of course, everyone wants to arouse the same "good" emotions. Add to that the increasingly shorter job-lives of managers, the quarterly reports, and the general pressure for short-term results, which discourage bold, strategic, long-term thinking, and what do you get? Competitive squabbling at a tactical level and a form of competitive autism at the strategic level.

The most striking indicator of this squabbling and autism is the growing proportion of marketing budgets devoted to promotion. This can be a first-class competitive tool. But, in fact, the overuse of promotional campaigns (and I am referring to campaigns that are actually lotteries or disguised discounts) totally ignores two facts:

1. Your loyal buyers simply make their purchases a little earlier than they might have normally.

2. The next inevitable campaign by your competitor will cancel out any and all achievements of your current campaign. Promotion-oriented consumers will take advantage of your competitors' promotions just as they took advantage of yours. After promotional campaigns, sales tend to return to the same level as before.

Studies by the Marketing Science Institute in the U.S. in the 1980s and 1990s clearly demonstrated that the utility of these promotional campaigns is, at best, doubtful. On the other hand, the damage to the brand is certain and chips away at the consumer's loyalty. Concentrating on promotional sales is another way of putting off the development of a competitive strategy, which is what you really need to do.

Large strategy consulting companies usually encourage the dangerous tendency of their clients' executives to avoid developing a real strategy.

What is often called "strategic consulting" is very often anything but. It is usually mislabeled management consulting designed to foster good management practices. Of course, good management isn't strategy.

When I was VP of Marketing for a large group of insurance and financial services companies, I hired one of the largest and most prestigious strategic consulting firms and learned what it was, and especially what it was not, capable of providing. Even later, when I was called in as a consultant to correct the mistakes of such firms, I had the opportunity to read a large number of strategic consulting reports written by leading international consulting firms and to attend their presentations. All of them were characterized by sound logic and thorough methodology. The fact-finding and data collection were exemplary. The analyses were comprehensive. But what were the conclusions? The recommendations? The strategy? Totally banal! Textbook solutions with constant avoidance of any attempt to develop strategic differentiation that can achieve double-digit growth. Time after time, I asked myself, "For this they did all that glorious preparation?" Many executives are in awe of these international consulting companies (although, to be honest, some of them really see the firms only as a way to cover their own rear ends), but their proliferation, conservatism, and caution (since they have more to lose than to gain) lead their strategic thinking into stagnation.

Michael Porter, perhaps the most prominent expert in the field of competitive strategy, advises you not to try to run faster in a race in which everyone is a competitor because strategy is a choice to compete in your own race, the race in which you've trained yourself to win. Now what does that mean?

The 5 Percent That Makes All the Difference

Many marketers think that differentiation means that a company has to be different than its competitors from A to Z. Not true. The comforting secret is that you don't need to be different in everything in order to succeed, only in certain things. If you look at the managers of competing companies in the same market category, no matter what the field, you'll see that 95 percent of their concerns, decisions and day-to-day activities are very similar. It may be surprising, but in 95 percent of their actions, executives in competitive companies are doing nearly the same things. That's the "good management" that we talked about.

If you take cellular company CEOs, for example, and interview each of them separately, asking them what's important to them, you're likely to hear pretty much the same thing from all of them: "I want an infrastructure technology with a horizon for future developments;" "I want more exciting phones;" "I must have great client service, a flexible and efficient billing system, and great added value and content services." Everyone will say exactly the same thing, because that is what is expected of a good cellular company. But good management isn't a strategy.

If everyone does the same thing, and everyone is talented enough to do it well, would consumers differentiate between companies? Why should they prefer your company? Because you do it better? There's practically no chance that "better" is something consumers will notice, nor is it an advantage that you can maintain over time.

The secret is in the other 5 percent. The 5 percent you do differently is your *differentiation* which is your strategy. If 5 percent sounds too little for you, I suggest that you remember that human beings and chimpanzees are 98 percent identical in their genetic makeup. If 2 percent can make that big a difference, then 5 percent, planned wisely, can do even more. Other concepts you know, such as positioning (your situation, relative to your competitors', in the consumer's mind vis-à-vis his purchasing considerations), and "critical success factors" (what you must do in your field in order to succeed) relate to good management, not strategy. Note that positioning and differentiation are not at all synonymous! Positioning refers to the comparison between you and your competitors in all parameters that are significant to consumers, which they use to compare their options. Differentiation refers to what sets you apart. Since it's something that is true only about you, there's no comparison in this respect. Good management provides you with the entrance ticket to the competition. Strategy allows you to win the battle for the consumer.

I want to illustrate this for you with an admittedly unconventional, but very elucidating example. Mind you, I do not mean to glorify this company, just to make a point.

In Canada, there is a news company called Naked News, and it broadcasts upbeat news and current events programs to more than 170 nations daily on the Internet, as video on demand (VOD) on cable and satellite TV as well as over mobile phones and other handheld devices.

Most of what the managers and other staff in this news company do is exactly what their colleagues in any other news company in the world do. But Naked News does one thing a little differently, and that's the reason some viewers prefer it (despite the premium price). Tagged "the channel with nothing to hide," Naked News' attractive anchor persons (well, mainly young women) cover politics, business, sports, entertainment and the weather—while totally naked.

A Simultaneous Answer to Two Questions

Your competitive strategy is, essentially, a simultaneous answer to two questions.

Question 1: Which consumers are going to buy the products you plan to sell in the quantities you plan to sell them? What is it about them, their situation, or their current alternatives that makes them your potential buyers?

Question 2: What are you offering those consumers in order to turn the potential into actual sales?

That is what's behind the impressive term, *competitive strategy*. It might seem simple, but of course, it isn't that easy.

What you want to look for are answers that create one consistent marketing rationale. You need to go from one question to the other, again and again, until you have the simultaneous answer to both. Take an example: there are people (singles and workaholics, for instance, or busy two-career families) who don't have the time to shop for gifts during holidays and other events. Their difficulty is your opportunity. Creating a website for gift buying is one way to take advantage of the opportunity (that's the idea behind *www.redenvelope.com*). As you can see, the target group of consumers, together with the concept that enables them to improve their current options, provides a simultaneous answer to the two questions. There's really no set order in which these questions are asked. It is only when we have a concept for a solution to the problematic or uncomfortable situation of certain consumers that this situation turns into an opportunity for us.

Let's start with the first question: *Which consumers are going to buy the product and quantities that you are planning to sell?*

The question we must ask has nothing to do with demographic, socioeconomic, or psychological characteristics. The answer that you are looking for is not a list of characteristics classifying your target customers, such as "academic and career-oriented women ages 25 to 35 who are also mothers of kindergarten-age children." We'll save those concerns for later. The question is: what is the common factor that defines them as potentially promising for you? Obviously, you can improve these people's situations, broaden their range of options, or enrich their lives. What is it that all people in your target group share today that you can make better? In the example above, the group is people who don't have time to buy gifts. That is the defining factor that turns them into potential customers—even before we know anything else about them.

Following this insight, we'll ask a set of different questions: Who are these people? Are they already your clients? Would they buy larger quantities of the product? If so, why? Are they your competitors' clients who will switch to you? What would make them do that? Are they new consumers who haven't yet had a reason to come into the market? What will motivate them to enter? The basic question is: Who is likely to buy what you intend to sell, and how much of it will they buy? A corollary question: Are there enough of them? That is, do they have enough buying power that they can direct to you? Then, and only then, comes the time for asking if we can define them in demographic, socioeconomic, or psychographic (personality, motivation) terms.

The second competitive-marketing strategy question is: *What are you offering those consumers in order to fulfill the potential that they hold?* Will your offer maximize the opportunity? Your offer includes the product, a choice of versions and variations, personalization options, packaging, support services (guidance, installation, repair services, etc.), price, payment methods, terms of payment, marketing promotions, distribution channels and sales, points of sale, fulfillment of orders, and marketing communications. If this long list reminds you of the 4Ps of marketing, you are right.

Articulation of the competitive-marketing strategy must always include a one-statement answer to these two questions: "Our strategy is to offer X in order to maximize potential Y, which we have identified among consumers who share common factor Z."

A Goal is Not a Strategy

An aside, but an important one: your competitors often confuse goals and strategy. They say things like, "Our strategy is to obtain a large market share." Translation: "We are willing to forgo some of our profits in order to achieve a larger portion of the market."

Now, pay attention, because it's easy to get confused.

That statement can express a strategy, if what it really means is: "Since our goal is to solidify our position among the distribution channels, our strategy is to forgo a portion of our profit at this time to achieve a larger share of the market."

But in many cases, this statement actually refers to a goal, not strategy. This happens, for example, when what the statement really means is: "Since our goal is to reach a large portion of the market, our strategy is to lower our prices and relinquish some of our profit."

The guiding principle is: what you want to achieve is your goal. What you are doing to reach that goal is your strategy. From my experience, it's best to be very clear about the distinction between them.

The Strategy is the Brand

In order to realize the potential in your target group, you have to offer something that is currently unavailable or difficult for consumers to obtain, something that will improve their situation in some way, or make their lives somehow easier and richer, more pleasant and comfortable. At the very least, you have to offer them a new way of doing things. Otherwise, why should they buy from you? So I repeat: you need *differentiation*, strategic differentiation.

You'd be surprised to discover how few of your competitors ever ask themselves openly and rigorously these two competitive-strategy questions. In their everyday work, most of them relate to their marketing activities as some sort of voodoo ritual. If we perform a certain set of activities, if we make a wish about our sales, market share goals, or about our target customers, if we engage in all the "right" marketing activities, if we "brand," if we advertise, if we're active at the points of sale, if we run promotional campaigns and a customer reward club, the Market Gods will answer our prayers and will increase our sales or market share. The result: a considerable percentage of marketers have no strategy at all. They can't tell you exactly how their activities are supposed to produce the specific results that they want. They simply believe it will happen somehow.

But it doesn't often happen. The data, consistent throughout the world, reveal a failure rate of approximately 90 percent—failure to establish new businesses, failure to introduce new products, and failure of new brands—roughly an equal rate of failure for each. On the other hand, the research shows that the secret of the 10 percent who succeed is good strategy and uncompromising implementation. The decision is yours. What do you want? To cover your rear end: "We did everything we had to or that is customary to do," or to succeed? This book is written for those of you who opt for the latter, even if it's difficult, not generally accepted, or even impractical (after all, only 10 percent of the market behaves in this fashion).

Let's take this line of thinking one step further and connect the competitive strategy with the brand.

We've mentioned already that the brand strategy is the chosen promise of benefit to the consumer. But, as we've also said before, the competitive strategy is the differentiated benefit that we offer the consumers who we view as potential; its aim is to realize that potential. So what do you say? Can these possibly be two different things? Of course not. They are two sides of the same coin. Your differentiation, which is at the heart of your competitive strategy, is what you are promising the consumer in order to get the consumer to buy from you —and therefore it is also your brand strategy!

The strategy of your brand is none other than your competitive strategy, formulated as a promise to the consumer. Branding is the aspect of strategic thinking in which you consider the attractiveness of your differentiation to your target consumers.

Strategic Emotions

I can imagine that at least some of you are confused by now. Branding and brands—these are topics related to design and advertising, aren't they? What's their relation to competitive strategy? STOP! If you're thinking this way, then your brand is more an extraneous embellishment than a real brand. It is an empty shell brand. In days past, that was the mode of thinking. Once, branding was cosmetic. First you had a company or product, and then you would "brand it" through naming, design, and advertising, in order to make it more attractive to the consumers.

In order to understand the evolutionary process, let's go back a bit. Once upon a time, there was no branding. It was called "reputation." Companies, products, and professionals had reputations—good or bad. There were just two possibilities and they were completely unidimensional. It worked that way because everyone did the same thing; some just did it better than others. As competition increased, some competitors began doing things differently to create an advantage for themselves. At the same time, consumers began to form more complex impressions about companies, and they called it "image." Some companies were considered more "innovative" or "sporty" or "prestigious" or "humane"—all richer and more elaborate characterizations.

The idea that it is possible to shape consumers' perceptions and attitudes and thus create an "added value" beyond the value of the product or service itself was born later. The current meaning of the term "brand" evolved over time. The road to maximizing the potential inherent in the concept of brands is a long one, and I think we have only just started the journey. The problem is that many managers thought they could take a shortcut to creating a real advantage for their company or product by creating a "brand" (in the sense of visual identity and advertising) that would magically make it attractive to consumers and serve as a substitute for strategy. That idea was a total and painful disappointment. It simply didn't work! Branding gurus and pseudo-experts created the illusion that they knew how to do it. They misled managers time and again. We'll expand on this topic in Chapter 12.

Two types of branding, when misunderstood, contribute to the confusion. In one type, design is intended to create a supposedly advantageous customer experience. Design alone, however, will not do the trick. The specific and unique experience is strategically chosen and masterfully crafted to be the attraction factor. It usually goes beyond visual identity and advertising and is inherent to the product or service. The second type consists of brands whose strategically designated main benefit is not supplied by the function of the product itself but by the sophisticatedly created, psychological or social, intangible use of the product by the consumer. While executives often mistake "design" or artistically creative advertising as branding, it simply is not. Both types will be further clarified later.

Finally and fortunately, branding has taken on a more strategic role recently. Branding has become an important aspect of strategic thinking, that of ensuring that the consumer is attracted. The purpose of the brand dimension of strategic thinking is to guarantee that when we implement the strategy we have created, consumers will view it as a reason to buy from us. Later, in realizing the brand, the first task for marketing communications is to ensure that the target customers grasp the advantage we are offering them and recognize its attraction. In some cases, there's an additional task: the marketing communications also have a role in creating or delivering the benefit itself.

To understand how marketing communications can have a role in creating benefit (not just communicating it), consider this example. Take a brand like Calvin Klein, which promises that you'll always be *cool*—whether *cool*, at this moment, is sharp differences between masculine and feminine, unisex (such as ONE, the first perfume for both men and women), or even ambisex (ambiguous sexuality). No matter what's considered cool right now, you can be sure that Calvin Klein is there. Cool isn't in the underwear that Calvin Klein markets so successfully. It's the meaning of the brand, and marketing communications makes sure we are aware of it and accept it. Once everyone knows what the brand means, this meaning can be used by consumers to communicate. Consumers wearing Calvin Klein jeans send a message of being cool and shape how they are perceived by those around them.

This example brings us to a discussion of experiential brands and added-value brands, all those that are mistakenly called "emotional brands." Experiential brands offer an experience. This is how they deliver their benefit. Sometimes the experience is tangible, such as the taste of Nestlé ice cream. Sometimes it's both tangible (sensate) and intangible (emotional), as in the case of the PlayStation 3 *The Elder Scrolls IV* game. Added-value brands are brands whose primary benefit is psychological, interpersonal, or social. It is an intangible benefit that has little to do with the product's function. Attorneys, for instance, can use a Montblanc pen to project a message about themselves: they've succeeded, they can spend a lot of money on a pen, and, accordingly, they must be very good at what they do. This is an intangible use of a brand. Its usefulness depends on whether those who see the pen know how expensive it is. All these brands have been mislabeled "emotional" as opposed to "rational", because buying them is not a matter of reason and sometimes is not even justifiable, but rather, a matter of whim.

In Chapter 13, I will describe ten different methods for creating brands that offer benefits beyond those of the product. The point I want to raise here is that even though the primary benefit of the brand is intangible, a strategic decision is at play. In the cases of brands such as Montblanc, Calvin Klein, and certainly PlayStation, the competitive strategy is to create an intangible benefit for the consumer—to create differentiation and achieve an advantage by means of the intangible benefit. The intangible benefit, then, is not some embellishing "creative decision" in the realm of design and communication.

The Unique Success Formula

Essentially, we make three demands of competitive strategy. We want, simultaneously, to achieve a competitive advantage, to be profitable, and to be attractive to consumers.

With the Advantagizing Approach, these are three angles in a single triangle. None of the three can exist for long without the other two. Even two out of three can't exist without the third. Think about it: profitability and a competitive advantage without being attractive to consumers? A competitive advantage and attractiveness to the consumer without profitability? Attractiveness to the consumer and profitability without a competitive advantage? No such combination could succeed. Therefore, when designing your strategy, you have to integrate three points of view: a strategy for a competitive advantage, a business model, and a brand concept. The first will guarantee your edge, the second your profitability, and the third your attraction for the consumer.

I call this the Unique Success Formula (USF), which, taken as a whole, achieves differentiation. I believe in an integrative approach to strategy. I believe that a strategy's effectiveness goes down the drain when the numbers-and-graphs people formulate the business model, some other research-and-analysis people develop the competitive strategy, and yet other ideas-and-design people create the brand. There's no cohesive concept and no integration. Consequently, it doesn't work. In creating an effective strategy, it is crucial to cross back and forth between the business point-of-view, the competitive point-of-view, and the psychological point-of-view. You must do this until your strategy culminates in a unified concept.

A major weakness of MBA-clone thinking is a blurred understanding of strategy (believing that it is something other than differentiation). Another weakness is the distinction made between business-management thinking and psychologically oriented (people-smart, consumer-oriented) thinking, and the lack of understanding about how the two connect. Most of your competitors don't understand their customers very well. Here's your opportunity. Strategies are realized or not realized when consumers do or don't do as you planned (and the same is true of your workers, though they are not the focus of this book). That is why psychology is critical for strategic thinking.

4

The Three Myths about Competitive Advantage

The Biased Thinking of MBA Clones

W. Chan Kim and Rene Mauborgne of the INSEAD School of Business Management are well acquainted with MBA clones. After all, they are professors at one of the most prestigious MBA schools in the world. Over the last few years, they have also become prominent gurus of strategic thinking, and I highly recommend reading their book, *Blue Ocean Strategy*, (Harvard Business School Press, 2006). In the context of our discussion, I would like to share what they have to say about the thought-biases of executives who operate in the same market and the same product category. The points they bring up will teach you something about your competitors' way of thinking and give you an advantage over them.

1. All competitors agree, generally, about what is important to the consumer and what the consumer wants. In all categories and in every market, they tend to offer consumers the same benefits, tangible and intangible.

2. As a result, competitors try to one-up each other in doing the things "that are important in our market" (the Key Success Factors). On this basis, they define their relative advantages and disadvantages.

3. They adopt a similar segmentation of consumers, focus on the same attractive groups of consumers, and divide the market into

sectors in the same way (for example, "Luxury," "Value for Money," and "Economy").

4. They offer the same product or service components and think in either/or terms (for example, a trade-off between price and quality).

5. They focus on direct, immediate competitive threats and tend to overlook substitutes and other product categories in which competition could emerge.

Of course, the more managers in a particular category think and act in this way, the more it seems to be the "right" way to understand the market and compete in it. However, the result is that everyone's life becomes more difficult and less profitable.

Kim and Mauborgne make an effort to free their students from this rat race, and I value their efforts very much. In doing their research that included a five-year follow up of numerous large companies, it became apparent to them that successful companies that manage to maintain an impressive growth rate and high profitability can be differentiated from others by their attitude toward strategy.

For instance, out of 100 new business ventures, only 14 percent were innovative in terms of strategy. These 14 percent raked in 38 percent of the overall income and 61 percent of the profits of all the 100 businesses. Based on this insight, Kim and Mauborgne attempted to create a method that would enable managers to escape the "Red Sea" that is stained with the blood of cut-throat competition and enter the "Blue Ocean"—a new business model that has no competitors and is based on the "value innovation" (offering some new benefit to the consumer). Read about it. It's good stuff.

As you can imagine, I have studied their method in depth. My conclusion is that Kim and Mauborgne can teach you how to leap ahead of your competitors. If you succeed, they admit that at some point, someone will start to copy you. I'm not making light of this important time gap that can allow you to become very wealthy. Some of the methods we deal with in this book will help you reach precisely that goal. Even so, Kim and Mauborgne's method won't bring you an unfair advantage. The methods described in this book will.

A Competitive Advantage Isn't Objective

In this chapter, we'll note some of the soft points of the MBA clones. As I said at the end of the previous chapter, your competitors often don't understand much about consumers. Don't be impressed by psycho-babble. The psychology ("consumer behavior") that they study is superficial and often outdated. So, for instance, it's not unusual to hear them talking about Maslow's hierarchy of needs, a model created in the 1940s, as though it were the latest word in contemporary motivation psychology. Their typical curriculum contains a mishmash of approaches, models, concepts, and research that doesn't coalesce into a consistent, clear picture that offers insights into the consumer's psyche and behavior.

When they finally become executives, your competitors frequently employ market researchers, most of whom are statisticians who don't know enough about psychology; or social or behavioral science graduates whose understanding is superficial; or clinical psychologists who are unfamiliar with buying behavior. The models created by many market research firms (some of them world leaders) are appalling to experts in consumer psychology. It's hard to believe how few real experts there are in this field.

All of this may seem a bit exaggerated, arrogant, and full of chutzpah ("Is everyone else stupid and only you have the smarts?"), but wait patiently. Later on, especially in Chapters 8, 11, 14, and 15, you'll find exciting insights into consumers' motivations and behaviors. Afterward, I'm sure my statements here will seem more justified. Just as your competitors act on mistaken assumptions, so did economists for many years.

Economists assumed for years that consumers are motivated only by a desire to maximize their financial gain. That assumption persisted until Tversky, Kahneman, and others demonstrated that consumers don't act in that way. The first instinct was always to deride the consumers' irrational behavior. But proving that consumers are frequently "irrational" was not, obviously, what brought Tversky and Kahneman the Nobel Prize. It is worth reading Kahneman's explanations again. The significance of the findings in the field of Behavioral Economics is that consumers often prefer benefits such as comfort, stress-avoidance, disappointment, regret, or frustration-avoidance over an attempt to obtain maximum gain. Consumers are not stupid economists. They are consumers. Steven Levitt and Stephan Dubner, authors of the bestseller *Freakonomics* (HarperCollins, 2005), also speak about the fact that people often prefer psychological and social benefits over financial savings or even gain.

A competitive advantage isn't objective. You can score points and achieve an objective technological advantage over your competitors in a particular area (such as a somewhat better product formula), but your achievement will be meaningless. A true competitive advantage is only something perceived by consumers as such, because consumers make the purchasing decisions and thus bring you your business success. But as I have said, your competitors often fail to understand consumers, and as a result, they miss the target. They focus on competing instead of on attracting consumers. They are busy fighting dumb wars amongst themselves, over matters that are of no interest to consumers and, most often, go unnoticed by them.

MBA clones adhere to three myths about competitive advantage. None of them are true, but taken together, they are the reason your competitors misdirect their efforts. On the way to your competitive advantage, you have to free yourself of these myths so that you don't fall into the same trap. Once you've done that, we'll set off on the real road to a competitive advantage.

Myth No. 1: You have to be better than your competitors.

That's just it—you don't. If you're just as good as your competitors, it's good enough. Under no circumstances should you be worse. But the base for a winning strategy is to be different from (not better than) your competitors, in ways that I will explain later.

The TQM doctrine and Six Sigma method for producing perfect, flawless products that became mantras in the 1990s were two of the managerial fads that emerged from this myth. The ideology behind them is that the company should invest most of its efforts in creating total quality, throughout the organization and in all processes, through stringent quality control methods (famously used in Japanese firms). These fads swept through the business world and then disappeared, but not before they led to tremendous unnecessary expenses and endless frustration. In the end, it turned out that most of these projects failed. A Gallup survey for the American Organization of Quality Control showed that only 28 percent of the managers who applied "quality programs" said that they benefited from them to any significant degree. Why? Because it's impossible to achieve *total* quality and because effective management demands *priorities.*

Recently, a broad-based international study by Fred Crawford (from Ernst & Young) and Ryan Matthews (from FirstMatter) indicated that successful companies excel at one thing and are pretty much okay at all the rest. Think about Wal-Mart and IKEA. Think differentiation.

Companies that make an effort to outdo their competitors often use research to trace consumer satisfaction over time. Numerous companies perform regular periodic surveys to assess their consumers' satisfaction, and they judge their success according to the results. It's so logical! If the consumers are satisfied, why should they abandon you? Many companies have also installed customer relationship management (CRM) systems over the past few years, and many of them naively believed that these systems would produce a close relationship with their clients and a competitive advantage.

But as I've already told you, your competitors don't understand consumers. Here's the surprise: research on consumers who have switched their provider (for services such as banking and communications) reveals that most were fairly satisfied with the companies they abandoned, even on the day they decided to leave them. In fact, some 90 percent of them were satisfied or very satisfied. A series of studies by Forum, a British research institute, shows that more than

80 percent of consumers who abandoned one brand for another stated that they were satisfied with the brand they stopped buying (or were now buying less of). What does this mean? It means that satisfaction won't make the client stay with you. Don't get me wrong: this doesn't mean you should dismiss client satisfaction! It does mean that you can't count on it to get you an advantage. By the way, why did they leave? Because someone turned them on to something else.

That brings me precisely to the point I want to make. I think we should move from satisfying, subservient marketing—giving consumers what they want and expect—to what might be called *electrifying marketing*. Electrifying marketing surprises clients, in the positive sense, and consistently offers them something they didn't expect to get, something they wouldn't have thought of on their own. That something has to be exciting, even exhilarating. At best, it's something clients don't yet know they want, but the minute it's offered to them, they can't understand how they ever lived without it.

I can hear you sighing. "That's easy to say, but how do you do it?" In Chapter 8, I promise to give you rules and methods and even expand on the research methods you can use to identify consumers' future desires. Later on, you'll read Chapter 14, which is devoted precisely to this topic of electrifying marketing.

Brands that have gone through Electrifying Marketing sometimes even torture their clients a bit—in an enjoyable manner, of course. It's a form of S&M in which the "M" stands for Marketing. Take Harry Potter, for example. Before *Harry Potter and the Goblet of Fire* was released, the publisher announced the publication date (July 8, 2000) and then began a campaign unlike anything that had ever been conducted in publishing. It was foreplay intended to stretch consumers' enjoyment through mystery and anticipation. The name of the book, the number of pages, and even the price were kept a secret until two weeks before release. The publisher didn't send review copies to journalists and forbade the author to grant interviews and reveal any part of the story. The secrecy was strict, but rumors (one of the central characters will die; Harry will discover his sexuality, etc.) were somehow "leaked" to Internet forums. Then, suddenly and mysteriously, two copies of the book appeared: one in Ireland and one in West Virginia. Of course, journalists from all over the world made every effort to get hold of them. A few days before the release, copies of the book were brought to some stores in closed metal cages, as if to say, "Look, it's here, but you can't buy it . . . yet." According to all the principles of satisfying marketing, this is a no-no! You are abusing your clients and damaging their satisfaction. Conversely, according to the principles of electrifying marketing, it's a wonderful response to the hidden needs of the consumer—to be excited, to long for something, to feel part of a drama—needs that no CRM system could reveal. Electrifying marketing has accompanied all Harry Potter books since then. The enigma, the simultaneous release internationally at midnight Greenwich Mean Time, the celebrations—they all indicate that this isn't just one more book.

Here's another example. Remember the Soup Nazi from *Seinfeld*? His character is based on a real cook named Al Yagna, the owner of Soup Kitchen International in New York (*www.soupkitchenintl.com*). Al, who's now selling franchises throughout the world and marketing "heat and serve" soups in supermarkets, built his brand by antagonizing the clients who stood outside his original tiny outlet in Manhattan. The three famous rules of the Soup Nazi, which were intended to guarantee that the line moved flawlessly and without delay, demanded that clients reach the counter knowing what kind of soup they want, have the exact sum of money in their hands, and move to the left side of the counter immediately after ordering. If they didn't, they risked being handed the verdict, "No soup for you!"

Steve Job's Apple is another company that fully understands Electrifying Marketing. Take the iPod, for example, the company's very successful music player. You could listen to the MP3 before the iPod, but not in the same way. Not wow! in terms of design. Not wow! in terms of technology. Not with something like iTunes. The beauty of Apple as a brand is that Apple succeeded in bringing the consumer something new that is also wow! It garnered enthusiastic admirers around the world. Enthusiastic, but not *satisfied*. In fact, owning an

Apple computer can be quite annoying at times and require compromises and extra costs.

Pleasing the consumer is a Sisyphean task, and is pointless. Like Sisyphus in Greek mythology, whose punishment was to push a large stone uphill again and again, only to see it roll back down just as it approached the top, the marketers who pin their hopes on consumer satisfaction repeatedly discover that consumers are never totally satisfied. Any improvement is soon taken for granted, raises the threshold of expectations, and will never create a true advantage for you. You want to break out of this loop. That is possible only if you offer consumers something they don't yet know they want. And next, they will want something that isn't more of the same, but entirely different. You're right! Such an achievement is also temporal, and no achievement can guarantee the next achievement. That's true, but it's not pointless. It will give you an advantage for a while—maybe a long while—even if you have to keep innovating. Besides, it's fun for both the consumer and for you.

Myth No. 2: To succeed, you have to endear yourself to as many consumers as possible.

The second myth is that successful companies are the ones most consumers like, or whose products they like, preferably from the very beginning. Companies try to aim for this from the onset, and they do research that measures tastes, preferences, and so forth. The goal is to reach as high a score as possible among as many consumers as possible. But successful brands don't work that way.

Successful brands don't need to be liked by everyone. If everyone likes you immediately, then no one is really enthusiastic about you. Consensus doesn't excite. I know you're about to say, "Coca-Cola." Well, that brand belongs to the founding fathers of branding. That's a privileged group that enjoys a special status, and we'll deal with it, too, in a moment.

Successful brands begin with a small, truly enthusiastic group of customers. These enthusiastic consumers will later become the growth engine for the brand. They are the ones who "turn on" the consumers around them. Actually, even Coca-Cola began this way. A pharmacist, Dr. John S. Pemberton, invented the drink in 1886, and his accountant, Frank Robinson, suggested the name Coca-Cola (we'll get to the naming process in Chapter 12). It all began in Atlanta, Georgia. The drink was sold on tap in Joe's pharmacy. Sales weren't particularly spectacular. In the first year, they only made $50, which didn't even cover the cost of advertising, which came to almost $74. The brand wouldn't have survived if not for an enthusiastic fan named Assa Kendler who was sure he could excite every American about the drink. In 1891, Pemberton sold Kendler the company for $2,300, and it was Kendler who expanded it to its nationwide dimensions. During World War II, Robert Wordruff, then CEO of Coca-Cola, promised that every American soldier, wherever he was in the world, would have Coca-Cola within reach. The company made the effort and flew over cans (then a new form of packaging) to all regions where American forces were stationed. That's how Coca-Cola became a true global brand and an American symbol.

The concept is easier to illustrate with brands launched and marketed today. The worthwhile purpose of branding is not for consumers to prefer you over your competitors; it's to convince a particular group that there's simply no comparison. Do you remember our previous discussion about the opportunity to form a private monopoly with your brand? This is exactly what I mean. BMW fans don't want a Mercedes. It's a good car they will say, but it's not a BMW. Apple fans didn't think that IBM (before it sold the PC division to the Chinese Lenovo) manufactured bad computers, but in their eyes, there was simply no comparison.

You have to be irreplaceable for a particular group of consumers. The moment you've created this kind of a brand, you've essentially created a monopoly. It doesn't come from the authorities on high; it comes from the consumers below. Now tell me that a private monopoly isn't what you want. Yep, that's what I thought. But are you willing to do what it takes to get one? We'll see.

Myth No. 3: A competitive edge exists on a parameter that is considered to be important in the category.

According to this myth, successful companies need to have an advantage for their product on a parameter that is considered important in the category. That's simply not so. Competitive advantages don't come from great success in achieving parameters consumers rate as important in a product like yours. Again, I'm not saying that you should dismiss what consumers think is important. But if you try to achieve an advantage based on what is important to the consumer, your advantage will, at best, be brief. Why? Because you'll be imitated immediately. You have to continuously improve your product, according to the important parameters, as much as you can. That's what your competitors are doing too, and you don't want to fall behind them or become inferior. If you manufacture cars, you can't ignore the race for greater fuel efficiency. You have to strive for continuous improvement, but don't expect that it will bring you an advantage. It's cruel, but this great effort only buys you a ticket into the competition.

None of this should sound strange to you because we talked about it earlier when we dealt with your 5 percent differentiation. The parameters of a product that are important to consumers usually serve to screen out irrelevant options, but they have little to do with the choice of a brand. This is certainly true of sophisticated and competitive markets. How does it happen? At the beginning of the choice process, consumers quickly filter the market without even realizing they are doing so. Only those brands that address (at least at a minimal level) the parameters that are important to them make it into the choice process. But it only begins here! In the end, consumers choose from among the qualified brands according to perceived differences among them. This is a critical insight.

Their Mistakes are Your Advantage

Let's sum up. Every stock market investor knows that the big opportunities arise when you expertly buck the trends. A competitive strategy isn't any different. When your competitors are preoccupied with reaching goals that won't bring them any advantage, you have to move in another direction, one that will bring you great results. Okay. Now that we've cleared the table, we can turn to what's really important.

5

The Great Secret of Differentiation that No One Imitates

Successful Differentiation

Successful differentiation has two defining characteristics: (1) it is not imitated by your competitors, even though (2) it brings you unmistakable success with consumers. Impossible, you say? Not really. I am about to reveal to you the unexpectedly simple and wonderful secret of successful differentiation. Here it is: do not look for it among the core benefits of your product category; rather, think *off-core differentiation*.

"Core benefits" are the benefits that consumers already expect to receive from a product like yours. This is the list of "what's important to the consumer." Core benefits are more than essential product benefits. The core benefits of today's cellular phones go way beyond the possibility of conducting a conversation while you're in motion. Everything that the consumer has already come to expect from products in your category is included in the core benefits. These are the benefits that all of your competitors offer, because they compose the essence of the product and it is impossible to compete in the market without them.

That is precisely the explanation for what will happen if you really invest your efforts, are truly brilliant and innovative, and make a major break-through in improving core benefits: your competitors will imitate you at warp speed. You must understand that given your success, your competitors can't afford *not* to imitate you. You'd do exactly the same thing.

Many companies have learned this the hard way.

Tower Records created a differentiation for itself with a great core benefit. It enabled its music customers to listen to the music they were thinking about buying. "A great idea!" said Virgin Megastores and copied them without even blinking an eye. Today, you'll find this service in all music stores.

Starbucks thought its coffee shops would be cozier and look more like a neighborhood hangout if the seats weren't identical and if some easy chairs and sofas were scattered around. What a great idea! Today, you'll find this type of seating in many coffee shops around the world.

Colgate-Palmolive combined all of the known beneficial characteristics of toothpaste and created Total. The innovation caught on like wildfire. I would dare to say that there isn't a toothpaste brand in the world (first and foremost P&G's Crest) that hasn't imitated the idea.

Volvo created its brand around a central core benefit: safety. It did everything humanly possible. It invested a fortune. And it succeeded, particularly in convincing its competitors that it is very important to invest in safety. Today, no one (except for a few out-of-date marketers) will tell you that safety is Volvo's differentiation.

I could go on, but I think you've already got the message. So what should you do?

In order to create a differentiation that won't be imitated, you have to think beyond the core benefits that are already (or even potentially) considered important in your market. It works time after time. The companies that have succeeded in maintaining their differentiation over the years and weren't imitated, even though they were making tremendous profits, are those whose innovations went beyond the core benefits of their market.

I'm sure you remember Naked News. Its differentiation has no connection with the core benefits of any news company. What it is doing to make itself distinct seems strange, even shameful and degrading compared with its competitors. Therefore, there is very little chance anyone will imitate them.

Now, think about Apple. Its differentiation to begin with was the first operating system ever with a user-friendly interface. That is very important to customers! As computer users were increasingly regular folks and not just IT professionals, that user-friendliness became an important core benefit. Could Microsoft afford not to imitate them? Of course not! Over the past few years, Apple has changed its approach. Now, its differentiation is based on sophisticated design, an approach that views the computer as part of a well-designed office in which the iMacs and PowerBooks are show pieces. Is anyone in a rush to imitate them? Not really. In general, computers have become more attractively designed, but no significant competitor jumped on the bandwagon and allowed its product designers to go wild the way that Apple did.

Virginal Thinking

Virgin Atlantic is one of the examples I like the best. As airlines go, it's no better than any other. It doesn't have better planes or more comfortable seats. It doesn't have fewer delays, doesn't fly faster, doesn't serve better food or offer a better timetable than, say, British Airways. However, it's a company that almost always does something—something in that critical 5 percent—differently. But please note: none of these innovations are among the core benefits of the "airline company" category. That's not surprising. It's company policy of the entire Virgin group. Richard Branson, the billionaire who established the conglomerate and the brand known as Virgin, is a man who doesn't chant the market gurus' mantras. He sees the world in his own original way.

Branson turned his personality into a strategy. Marketing people often tell me that companies headed by charismatic entrepreneurs don't really have a strategy. "The man's character is his strategy" is the motto of an approach that belittles the overall importance of strategy. True, Branson is a real character, a far cry from your typical businessman. He is a driven man, flamboyant and uninhibited. He's an iconoclast who likes to live on the edge, a fun seeker and bon vivant, a marketing genius and master of publicity stunts. When he started out in the business, he acted on his personal instincts. He succeeded and he failed. But Branson turned his personal experience into a set of simple rules that are the essence of Virgin's strategy. I'll sum them up for you: Virgin penetrates markets and categories with established and satiated market leaders that then become targets for Virgin's attacks. Virgin breaks all the rules in ways that are fun for consumers.

That's it.

The first rule that Virgin broke was the basic rule of brand extension, which states that the way to extend a brand across product categories is to choose "neighboring categories," so that consumers can intuitively grasp that the brand's "credentials" in one category are valid in the new category as well. Virgin proved that this principle works only if the brand is initially created in a specific category and identified with it.

If the benefit that the brand provides for the consumer is not category-dependent (such as Virgin's "Let's forget the big fat cats and have some fun"), then there is practically no limit to the number of categories in which the brand can strive. The Virgin brand is a good example of a new technique for creating multi-category brands that replaces the old, limited method of brand extension.

I call the new approach Brand Abstraction. In short, the technique helps create brands that are not confined to any specific product category, or "pull" brands out of a product category where they are stuck, by defining their promise on a level that is more abstract than any category-dependent benefit. In the beginning, Virgin was in the music business. It was a rebel music label that contracted with scandalous bands like the Sex Pistols. But Branson's revolution came when he "pulled" that promise out of the limitations of any specific category.

Virgin is active today in over 300 unrelated categories, among them cellular communications, banking, flight, condoms, wine, hotels, and music. In every category, it offers that same 5 percent differentiation. It enters a well-established market or category that has a strong leader, makes a mess of things, and provides fun for the consumer. That is strategic off-core differentiation, unlikely to be imitated, and it can work in an unlimited number of product categories. And look what's happening. Every time Virgin moves into another category, consumers are immediately curious about what they're going to do.

But let's return to airline companies. As Branson and his crew figured it, people are on a plane for hours. How can we make the experience more fun for them? Their idea, already in effect for years, is to offer passengers massages, manicures, pedicures, organized social games, and more—all on-board. Some Virgin Atlantic flights offer "Upper Class" Suites (I hope you appreciate the subtle British humor), with the biggest flat bed in Business Class, Wi-Fi, a bar, and much more. Virgin Atlantic has VIP pre-flight lounges where you can try out the newest gadgets from Apple and Sony, and it also has revival lounges at your destination. There you can shower, have a makeup session, have your clothes ironed, eat and drink something light, and then your chauffeur will take you (yes, in a Virgin Atlantic car) to your destination.

Just visit the Virgin Atlantic website to see what I am talking about. They greet you with "Hello, gorgeous," a bit different than Lufthansa (which has a perfectly good website). On the Virgin site, you can reserve the flights and arrange for all the services you need for your trip, including travelers' checks.

Here is a method you can adopt (more details in Chapter 11): Richard Branson says that he and his crew made a list of everything that airline companies do (including the most trivial details) and then systematically thought, point by point, how they could do them differently, so the client has more fun. Ultimately, they used the best ideas they had. The result is that Virgin Atlantic turned a lonely, boring flight into something sociable and fun. But note that none of this belongs to the core benefits of the "airline" category.

What Are They Waiting For?

The most important thing: although Virgin Atlantic has been successful for over two decades and has taken a good share of the market, British Airways isn't imitating them. Why? Because Virgin Airlines seems ridiculous to them. They don't do things that are among the critical core benefits for the consumer! The serious people at British Airways say to themselves, "A massage on a flight? Who wants a massage on a flight?" By the way, if on-flight massages eventually turn into an industry standard some day, Virgin Atlantic will be the leader, but they will also have to innovate. Between you and me, however, what are the chances of that happening?

Google is the most successful search engine today, with almost no real competition. Google wasn't the first search engine. And in the not-so-distant future, all of its technological advantages may disappear. But one thing for sure was, is, and will be in the future: the winning technique is off-core differentiation. Thanks to this differentiation, the whole world is crazy about Google. I am talking about its simple, natural, and light-hearted interface. Instead of doing an elaborate search, you can decide to take a chance and use the "I'm feeling lucky" option that takes you directly to a single website that best matches your search criteria. With Google, you can search in exotic languages, such as "Bork, bork, bork" or "Pig Latin" or in semi-extinct languages such as Yiddish. Google calls its price comparison engine "Froogle." From time to time, its logo design changes to commemorate events in history or holidays. The "Guess-the-Google" game is another feature, presenting surfers with a collage of pictures that came up in Google searches and giving them 20 seconds to guess what the search word was. Consumers choose Google for searches that are non-threatening, friendly, and even bring a smile to their faces.

Do you need more examples?

Swatch decided to treat the watch face and band as a design area. What does this have to do with the core benefit of a watch? Exactly! As a result, no one has imitated them.

What about The Body Shop? There's no place for another cosmetics chain that actively fights against animal experiments, for the environment, and on behalf of needy people worldwide. No one even thinks about imitating it.

The Mob and The Mobile

Sometimes, off-core differentiation eventually can become a core benefit. Nokia is a case in point. It's something that happens when the differentiation is not really off-core, but is actually based on deep insights about the direction of the market and the consumers' future needs and desires. The Nokia brand has become so ingrained in our lives that we forget that it's only been a cellular brand since the mid-1990s. Nokia has been so successful, that it left Motorola, the inventor of the cellular market, behind in the dust. Motorola's Dr. Martin Cooper developed the first cellular phone and patented it in 1975. But Nokia took that market with a correct focus on GSM and with a classic off-core strategy. While Motorola was busy developing more technologically sophisticated cell phones until there was no product better than theirs, Nokia predicted that cell phones would become a mass-market product. People would walk around with them on the street, and they would become, in an individualistic era, a fashion statement. And thus, the idea that helped turn Nokia into the world leader was born: the idea of exchangeable panels that let you match the phone's color to your outfit. Not an obvious core benefit of the category, and totally irrelevant to the benefits that cell phones were supposed to be providing at the time.

However, when all companies reached virtually the same technological level, they began to compete on design. Samsung was able to hurt Nokia with Nokia's own weapon. Recently, Samsung joined with *Vogue* magazine and designer Diane von Furstenberg in an attempt to lead cellular fashion. Even Motorola stopped trailing behind. At the time of writing, Nokia's share of the market is still double that of Motorola's, while Samsung is dragging behind both of them. Nokia has lost its differentiation, but you must admire the lead it was able to gain for itself!

Today, Nokia is looking for new off-core differentiations. It's trying to lead the "cell phone as a personal multimedia and entertainment center" market. But this is becoming a core benefit of the category.

This idea is the natural outcome of 3G technological developments, and it is a core benefit of the category. In camera cell phone sales and third generation and above sales, the gap between Nokia and Motorola seems to be shrinking. What will happen next? Time will tell.

It's true that only a few companies have become leaders by means of off-core differentiation. In fact, most companies never become leaders, nor need they do so. However, if you are in a competitive market and trying to make a living, then an off-core strategy is the best chance you have of giving a group of consumers a good reason to devotedly prefer you and even create a private monopoly for you.

I'm not trying to argue that differentiation within the core benefits is a bad idea, if you can achieve it. It does open a window of opportunity for you, until your competitors start to imitate you. For a man like Michael Dell, that was enough to become a billionaire. Dell changed the way personal computers are sold. Michael Dell understood that the moment personal computers were standardized (thanks to the IBM clones and the foresight of Microsoft in the 1980s), people would buy them over the phone, and later over the Internet. Dell also understood that since PCs are assembled from standardized components anyway, you can put them together to suit each user's needs. That wasn't off-core differentiation. Dell simply saw the future. Today, everyone sells computers this way, but for the period of time when he had this shining differentiation, he became one of the richest guys on the planet.

6

Strategy Development: How Will You Know What's Next?

What's Your Vision?

How do you choose the future that determines how you're going to steer your company? How do you know what will bring you the success you hope for? In the not-so-distant past, company entrepreneurs and executives would weigh the attractiveness of various categories and markets against their capabilities and resources and then they would put together a strategy to achieve a competitive advantage in the relevant target market. Recently, all that has changed. For several years now, and especially since the publication of *Built to Last* by Jim Collins and Larry Porras (HarperBusiness 2004), companies have come to believe that they need a vision. "Vision" is an intoxicating word. Suddenly, we can transcend all the hassles of the business world, climb to exciting, dizzying heights, and begin to wax poetical. How noble and important it makes us feel!

A vision has two important components: 1) What kind of a company are we? What are our values? What is the mission we have taken upon ourselves? and 2) What is the future we want to create?

This is really an enjoyable exercise. Instead of rising to the challenges of strategic thinking, we move on to experiential workshops, social bonding, thrills, and dropping big words and heatedly debating them. We're far from the competition, far from the consumers, and far from the real problems. We're there by ourselves, dealing only with ourselves and our dreams and aspirations. "If we truly desire it and are passionate about it, anything is possible." Something wonderful happens during the process of developing a vision. All company employees, or at least a broad group of managers, become the designers of the company's future. The positive aspect of the process is the sense of common destiny, involvement, and commitment it generates. The negative aspect is that truly great strategists are rare, which is why the process creates mediocrity, albeit excited mediocrity.

Over the past decade, I have read dozens, if not hundreds, of corporate credos and vision statements drafted by companies the world over. What can I say? The documents are positive and filled with high-spirited optimism. But what banality: "to be leaders," "to be innovative," "to serve," "excellence," "the human advantage," and so on. There's so much self-importance in these documents and so little sense of competitiveness or winning strategies.

I have a suggestion. If you can, read the vision statements of some of your competitors. It might be a painful experience, but it's an eye opener. Most likely, your competitors' visions are remarkably similar to your own. Real visionaries like Martin Luther King are probably turning over in their graves as they see how banal the concept of vision has become in the business world. We've demeaned the true meaning of vision and replaced it with "the vision thing," and for what?

In my opinion, the approach companies use to develop a vision is tainted by the *strategophobia* and its resultant competitive autism that I mentioned earlier. I don't think you need a vision at all, but if you must have one, you should place two qualifications on the process to make it effective:

First, your vision must be differentiated, not only in your own eyes but most especially in the eyes of the consumer. If you conduct research on it, the result you want to see is that consumers believe you are different and special in a way declared in your vision statement.

Second, but no less important, your vision must offer consumers some important benefit that they can't get from competitors. In other words, your vision has to be a differentiation-based competitive strategy.

I really don't care what you call it, but I suggest that you articulate the two components of your vision in the following manner.

1. In which unique way do we (by means of our products and services) wish to be part of the lifestyle of our target customers, and what unique role do we wish to fill in their world? What type of business or organization do we have to be in order to do this?

2. What future that won't be possible without us do we want to make possible for our clients, as individuals and as a society? What future do we need to design for ourselves as an organization in order to accomplish that for our clients?

Like the trendy process of establishing a vision, most of the no-less-trendy processes for developing corporate identity or branding are also excellent examples of competitive autism. They, too, have become exercises in self-expression that articulate the values of company managers and consultants. It has become common to avoid developing a real brand strategy by "doing branding"—fleeing from the need for a clear focus and a competitive brand promise in favor of a fuzzy list of "brand values" that usually express little more than the normative values held by the people involved. Brand values are supposed to be positive and desirable, rather than differentiated and competitive. The excuse for this approach: that's what's important to the consumer. Notwithstanding, the consumer's choice between alternatives is based on perceived differences.

The Marketing Approach is Dead: Long Live the Competitive Approach

Another important insight on the path to developing a winning competitive strategy is the fact that the marketing approach on which we were educated is losing its relevance in today's world. The marketing approach articulated by Kotler and others was, in fact, a formula for business success. The formula goes something like this:

- Identify consumers' unsatisfied needs.

- Develop products and services that will satisfy these needs.

- Bring these solutions to the market and the consumer.

- And then laugh all the way to the bank.

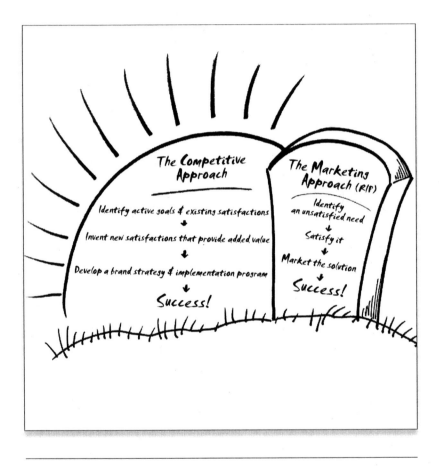

The marketing approach, based on identification of unsatisfied needs and how to satisfy them, is no longer a key to success for two reasons: first, there are few unsatisfied needs left. Second, in a competitive market it is undesirable that all marketers act in the same manner. The competitive approach, by contrast, is based on creating new ways to satisfy needs that are already satisfied.

That's what we were taught, and to our mind it is the most logical and natural thing in the world. But that's MBA-clone thinking.

In a competitive market, it doesn't work. Our markets are very competitive. I say this because if everyone is researching the same consumers, using the same standardized methods to look for "unsatisfied needs," the result will be that everyone identifies the same needs. And when everyone develops products and services that satisfy the same needs, the resulting products and services are similar. In a competitive market, that's a dead end. If everyone is trying to provide for the consumers' unsatisfied needs, they all end up doing the same thing, and that is non-competitive behavior.

And that's not all. In developed economies, we live in what the great economist John Kenneth Galbraith called the "affluent society." There are no more unsatisfied needs, unless we are referring to eternal youth or development of a cure for cancer. In most categories, our needs are pretty well satisfied. So what can we do to succeed today? Something new, something we might call "adopting the competitive approach." At its core, it is the *invention of new satisfactions for already-satisfied needs.*

The new rules of success are:

- Identify the needs, goals, and benefits that consumers are looking for, and understand the existing satisfactions and solutions.

- Invent new satisfactions and solutions that offer added value and will meet future or potential desires of consumers (in Chapter 8, I'll tell you how to identify them).

- Develop and implement a unique formula for success that includes a competitive strategy, business model, brand concept, and a realization plan.

There's no longer any need to go to the bank. Just raise your glass of L'Esprit de Courvoisier in a toast as you gaze at your bank account data on your Sony Vaio screen, just before you take off in your Gulfstream G550 to dine with Chef Guy Martin at Grand Vefour. *Bon Appetite!*

Opportunities Rather than Plans

In a competitive era, successful executives go to sleep at night and wake up in the morning asking the following question: "What could succeed now that my competitors aren't yet doing?" That is, before they discover the notion of an unfair competitive advantage. Then the phrasing of this question alters slightly: "What can I do that my competitors aren't yet doing, and won't imitate, in order to turn a lucrative and attractive group of consumers into my enthusiasts?"

To think and act competitively, you must overcome strategophobia. The answer to the above question can't result from competitive autism. The answer must result from examining the market, the consumers, and the competition using unorthodox methods—the kind you will learn in this book—based on fresh insights, creativity, cunning, and sophistication. This penetrating examination must be focused outward. We are moving from the age of *management by plans* into the new age of *management by opportunities*. Today, business and marketing success comes to those who know how to identify, invent, and quickly maximize market opportunities in ways that we will examine in the next chapter.

The methodical scan that follows examines two levels of opportunity simultaneously: strategic and tactical.

Strategic opportunities are chances to enter a new market or business category, use an innovative business model, appeal to new target customers, develop or expand the market, build a new and attractive brand, extend or even abstract an existing brand, build or improve a brand architecture, and so forth.

Tactical opportunities are chances to develop a product, service, "place" (a bar, for instance), or project that "rides" a developing trend or triggers the potential desire of consumers; to innovate service, distribution channels, promotion, and so forth; to refresh or renew an existing brand; or to take some other small, focused and specific step that will have maximum impact in areas where even a small change can deliver great returns.

Therefore, an opportunity scan has two managerial purposes. The first is to identify opportunities for adopting a new, outstanding strategy or for maintaining an up-to-date strategy that is navigated constantly in response to market developments over time. The second goal is to take advantage of short-term opportunities to develop marketing hits.

The Strategies of the Past

The classical process for strategy development, the one used by MBA clones, is pure logic. Its purpose was to provide a means of answering the question, "What do we have to do in order to achieve our goals?"

To simplify matters, the process has three stages:

1. Where are we now?

2. Where do we want to be?

3. How do we get there?

This process is based on a gap analysis of the distance between where we are now and where we want to be. The idea is that a competitor who performs this analysis intelligently, and then develops and implements a strategy skillfully and consistently, will have an advantage over all the others.

I contend that this process is out-dated, ill suited to today's competitive conditions, and useless in helping managers propel their organizations towards success, double-digit growth, and profitability. I call it "wishful strategizing." Often, it is the reason strategic plans fail. The result is that managers lose trust in strategic thinking altogether.

The flaws in the reasoning stem from three false assumptions implicit in classical strategy development:

Assumption No. 1: We know where we want to be.

How do we determine our goals according to the old process? At best, by estimating our growth potential, based on the current situation and what market research tells us consumers need and want. But the true potential, which we can't see through this approach, is based on what *could* be. The true potential is not "what's out there" but "what could be created and made to succeed." Our actions are constantly changing consumers' desires; products that no one considered lacking before they came on the market then became essential components of our lives that we simply couldn't do without. This is the source of famous historical errors in the evaluation of potential markets for airlines, cars, computers, and everything else. In the worst cases, the goals are based on the ambitions of executives and their degree of aggression, with no relationship to the surrounding reality.

Assumption No. 2: The world is stable.

We assume that if we define where we want to go, we can make our way there. The implicit image is one of traveling along an existing route or paving a new road that doesn't change as we move along it. But that isn't the way things are. Consumers have become obsessed with new options. Their expectations are constantly changing. Their desires are unstable. As I have already said, in many markets the distribution of market shares changes monthly, weekly, even daily. We can only talk about our average market share. We've already discussed the fact that there are no more sustainable competitive advantages and that our new mission is to achieve a repeatable competitive advantage. The old approach is one of control ("We are striving for market dominance"), while the approach that brings success today is more like dancing with the market and the consumers.

Assumption No. 3: We are the only ones engaged in this process, or we can do it better than others.

When we believe ourselves able to define our goals and simply move toward them, we assume our competitors are those we know and they will continue to do what they're doing today. They aren't. They won't.

Manufacturing in China, e-commerce, and consumers' infinite openness to innovation, among other things, have lowered the barriers to entering many categories. Executives don't last as long in their jobs. New executives come with fresh ideas, or at least fresh ambition. In the past, when the game was merely a race for the consumers' unsatisfied needs, you knew what your competitors were trying to do. However, more and more companies have come to understand the need for innovation and inventiveness in order to succeed at something their competitors aren't even doing yet.

The Strategy of the Future

So what am I suggesting? I'm suggesting that you move from plan-guided management to opportunity-guided management. I'm suggesting a new process of successful strategizing that has four stages:

1. What is happening now?

2. What's possible?

3. What's feasible and profitable?

4. What's next?

The question at the heart of the new process is: What's possible? True, the old process includes an analysis that you know as SWOT (strengths, weaknesses, opportunities, and threats), and part of it calls for identifying opportunities. But in practice, that is a fairly negligible part of the strategy development process. It's not systematic and doesn't provide the tools that enable you to implement it. It's as if this task were one point to be marked off on a checklist. In contrast, the process I'm suggesting is based on a systematic scanning and analysis of the opportunities available to the company at a given moment. From my experience, setting goals is much more inspired and far-reaching when it's done further on, after we've mapped the opportunities.

The Future Isn't Here Yet

My team and I have analyzed dozens of case studies in which companies found the next big thing and succeeded. We have concluded that the systematic search for opportunities must include five concentric circles that we will come to know better in the following chapters. They are part of the O-Scan methodology. The scan is relevant to two stages of the strategy creation process: "What's now?" and "What's possible?"

The new strategic process I am suggesting can be summed up as:

Open your "I's": Identify, Invent, and Implement.

Identify—by itself, this is not enough. Even if you use the best research, diagnostic, and analytic tools, they won't lead you all the way to strategy. Identifying existing opportunities pertains to the stage that we call, "What's Now?"

Unlike what proponents of the old approach told you, strategies aren't just "out there" waiting for you to discover them. In 99.9 percent of the cases, there aren't any neglected windows of opportunity sitting there on the once popular positioning map.

Strategic thinking is different. Based on a very deep understanding of what is happening, you have to invent your strategy—a new possibility that doesn't yet exist. That is the stage that we call, "What's possible?"

In the inherently static approach of the old process, strategizing rarely occurs since strategy isn't something you change every day. The approach I'm suggesting is based on *strategy in motion,* a constantly evolving strategy propelled by the constant tension between continuity and adaptation to changing conditions (in order to maximize opportunities). Therefore, the strategy development process is ongoing and nearly continuous, an essential part of never-ending managerial tasks.

Some Insights into Strategic Thinking

I want to raise a few more points for the benefit of those readers who want a more in-depth understanding of strategic thinking. If you don't have the patience or don't need the explanation, you can just move on to the next chapter.

Strategic thinking is conceptual thinking. A concept is an idea about a possibility that exists on the abstract level and the concrete level simultaneously. A "chair" is a concept. There is the abstract chair (which Plato called the "Idea") and there are chairs that exist in reality—all of which are different realizations of the abstract chair. At the heart of the concept is an intent, design, purpose, benefit, or meaning. The concept is the idea around which all sorts of things that exist in reality are organized, including material objects and human actions. McDonald's is a concept.

Innovation in business models is the invention of new money making concepts. Take the British company, Zopa (*www.zopa.com*), an Internet exchange for money lenders and borrowers. What brought about the very idea of such a business and the model it is based on are amazingly simple innovative concepts whose time had come once the Internet became sophisticated enough to handle money matters.

Conceptual strategic thinking has two parts. The first is *diagnostic*—the observation and detection of something in the surrounding reality, or in data about reality. That something could be a phenomenon, a process, or an opportunity. It never stands out. Your capability for insight, for perception—seeing something that's there, grabbing on to something that's happening there—demands that you ignore some of the facts that are merely irrelevant "noise." That's the challenge! You focus only on facts that you consider to be significant and integrate them under an organizing idea.

I sometimes encounter naïve expectations such as the belief that identification of strategic growth opportunities will come from consumers' direct answers to a direct question, such as, "What kind of new product would you like?" It doesn't happen that way, sorry. Most consumers (in fact, most people) cannot say they want something that doesn't exist in reality. The data that we can accumulate and analyze regarding a certain market situation never reveal opportunities or point to strategies. Analysts are not strategists. John Scully, the former Apple CEO, wrote in his autobiography, "I have never seen an effective marketing decision made based on the data." He isn't making light of data! His belief, just like mine, is that data are the crucial input for strategic thinking, but they are no more than input. Data help us understand reality, and that understanding helps us think about the response or initiative that creates a new reality—the strategy. To create a strategy, you must have strategic thinking and good tools.

Identifying an opportunity is only the first step. The second part of strategic thinking is the *creative or inventive* stage of designing a new concept—a concept that will enable us to shape a new reality in the marketplace and in consumers' lives.

Steve Jobs, the man and the legend behind Apple's success, has said, "Design is the soul of man-made creation." Strategy is about design. Strategy is not analytical thinking. It is a creative, even artistic, activity. A strategist designs a potential reality in his imagination, his vision, and then turns it into something real.

Tom Peters says, "The dumbest mistake is viewing design as something you do at the end of the process to tidy up the mess."

The strategic thought process has five characteristic steps, and they form the backdrop for our "What's Next?" process.

1. Understanding what's happening (the beginning part of the "What's now?" stage). In this stage, curiosity, empathy, and analysis help us understand what's already going on.

2. Insight (the part that completes the "What's now?" stage). In this stage, you can see something beyond the data—a phenomenon, process, or opportunity.

3. Ideation (the beginning of the "What's possible?" stage). In this stage, we arrive at ideas about a possible reality.

4. Generative thinking, concept creation, selection, and refinement (from the concluding part of our "What's possible?" through "What's feasible?" stages and on to the beginning of the last stage, "What's next?"). This is the stage in which ideas mature into concepts and design, on the road to prototyping and testing. Here, feasibility and attractiveness are also examined, and decisions are made about actualization.

5. Actualization (the culmination of the "What's next?" stage). In this stage, implementation is planned and realized.

Strategic thinking is a process that begins with current reality, passes through possible reality, and concludes with future reality. This is the process that designs future reality. I know this isn't what they told you about strategic thinking in your MBA studies. They should have, but they put something else at the heart of the integrative strategy course or project that culminated in the crowning glory of your degree. Not surprising, though. After all, most of what they taught you about "strategy" actually concerned good management, not strategy. When you really understand strategic thinking, you open up a considerable gap between you and the MBA clones.

The next chapters offer many tools to support and foster strategic thinking—the kind that can turn you into the very best strategist you can be.

part 2

The O-Scan: Identifying opportunities
for success and devising the strategies to
maximize them

7

An Overview of O-Scan: How to Identify, Invent, and Maximize Opportunities

What Are We Looking For?

In this chapter, I provide you with an overview of O-Scan methodology. Here are some of the questions we'll be asking: What are we looking for and where do we find it? Which tools does the methodology offer us? What kind of result will we obtain, and what will we do with it? This chapter presents many useful ideas, and the following three chapters go even further and deeper into the practice. I want to acquaint you with several O-Scan methods, some of which you will be able to apply immediately.

We use the O-Scan in two ways, first in the framework of a service we call, "the opportunities patrol." For clients whose marketing innovation is especially intense, we run the O-Scan regularly, one to three times a year, and we feed the opportunities to the marketing team. We also work with the team on developing a succession of "marketing hits," a topic you will read more about in Chapter 15. The second way we use O-Scan is in the process of creating a strategic differentiation in order to achieve an unfair competitive advantage.

On the **strategic** level, we are looking for opportunities to create and employ a new, winning strategy for double-digit growth. That is, we are looking for a group of consumers whose situation we will somehow be able to improve (and who will therefore hold potential for us), and of course, we're looking for a way to accomplish this. The combination of the two enables us to develop an innovative unique success formula

(USF) that includes a competitive strategy, a business model, and a brand perception. When I say, "a group of consumers," don't get me wrong. In many cases, they are not perceived as a group before we spot that common factor that enables us to improve their situation.

Canadian RIM's Blackberry, the surprising hit of the cellular business world in the past few years, identified the fact that managers and businessmen work more efficiently when they have access to e-mail in real time, at all times and in all places. All that Blackberry did better than the world's leading cellular phone manufacturers was push and feed e-mails in real time, without requiring the user to initiate a retrieving process. That's all.

On the **tactical** level, we are looking for opportunities for successful marketing innovations within the framework of our existing strategy: new products, new services, brand extensions, new distribution channels, fresh ideas for sales promotions, and so forth. These are opportunities for incremental growth or for meteoric and short-lived big successes. Early on, the O-Scan allows us to identify concepts that will grab consumers. It's important to emphasize this: the O-Scan is not an exercise in creative thinking or inventiveness. It's a set of tools that lead directly to the sorts of innovations that consumers will desire and that will become marketing successes.

Febreze observed that consumers are quick to adopt products that offer new sensory experiences and create a special atmosphere in the home. They latched onto a great idea for a new product that never ends (at least until the trend passes): an electric air freshener that operates with a CD-like device that lasts for two-and-a-half hours. There are disks that change the scent every 30 minutes and create an experiential process. The product is called Scent Stories.

Another example? Erin Cotter and Meredith McGann founded Passport, a company that specializes in beauty solutions for women-on-the-go. One of their latest hits is Lipsticket—a lipstick "card." Each card in the ten-card package includes three "kisses" (that is exactly what they look like on the card) that let you refresh your lipstick in seconds without a mirror—at work, in the gym, a minute before a date, or after a meal.

Four Satisfactions

The opportunity that we identify enables us to offer consumers something they'll desire enthusiastically. We have four broad options:

1. **To satisfy an unsatisfied need—in other words, to offer consumers a benefit that they are actively looking for and haven't been able to find (or could not afford).** That is the classic command of the old school marketing approach. Today, of course, it's hard to find unsatisfied needs. Even when you eventually find something at least close to it, the primary challenge is to create an innovation that's hard to imitate.

   A variation on this possibility prompted an enormous trend over the past 10 to 15 years: luxury for the masses. During this period, many companies throughout the world achieved success by offering the not-so-rich products and services that were formerly intended only for the rich. These new products were often somewhat lower quality or slightly less sophisticated. The very long list includes, among others, vacation resorts, spas, esthetic surgery, wine tasting, sophisticated furniture design, cell phones and PDAs, laptops, home theaters, and mineral water. High-fashion designer Stella McCartney, whose clients include Madonna and Gwyneth Paltrow, recently designed a collection for the European fashion chain Hennes & Mauritz (H&M), which has never been accused of being aristocratic. Karl Lagerfeld, the chief designer for Chanel, preceded her, with sweeping success.

2. **A new satisfaction for an already satisfied need, or a new way for consumers to obtain a benefit that is already available to them.** That is the most common situation today. Naturally, we need to offer some improvement over the product or service that is currently providing the benefit. Our innovation must be significantly more beneficial for the consumer, more appropriate for a group of consumers with special needs or particular preferences, customizable, cheaper or more accessible, more easily obtained, or more reliable in providing the benefit. It can

be simply newer in cases where newness is important, or less likely to cause collateral damage or risk (to health, for example), or less of a concession or compromise, or, and this is the most interesting quality, able to offer an additional benefit that is not a core benefit of the category, which allows for off-core differentiation and eventually becomes the primary benefit.

Joe Boxer is a brand that turned men's underwear into a source of fun. This brand is so great that we'll deal with it again in Chapter 14. In the meantime, we'll just note that the company markets boxer shorts, most of which are refreshingly white but some of which have hilarious designs. The real story has little to do with the product itself. Most of it concerns the cheekiness and entertaining approach of the company. As usually happens with off-core differentiation, the company is unashamedly succeeding, and no one is imitating it.

3. **Satisfaction of a regenerating motivation.** Regenerating motivations are the basis for short-term marketing hits and brands, and we will deal with them extensively in Chapters 14 and 15. In the meanwhile, a regenerating motivation is one that comes up repeatedly and demands a new fulfillment or gratification each time. The need to attract attention from those around you is one example. Only a week ago, you grabbed tons of attention when you came to the office wearing a new pair of pink alligator-skin Manolo Blahnik shoes that you bought in Manhattan (we won't tell where), and you even got change back from $2,500. How sweet it was—and how brief. That's it. It's over. To attract attention next time, you'll need something else. The opportunity to create a new satisfaction for a regenerating motivation allows companies to offer a trendy added value.

4. **Fantasy satisfaction of an unsatisfiable motivation.** Even needs that cannot possibly be satisfied can provide the basis for marketing hits and short-term brands, and we'll do them some justice in Chapters 14 and 15. An "unsatisfiable motivation" can best be exemplified by the desire for eternal youth. It can never be

achieved. So if you use a particular cosmetic product to smooth wrinkles for a few months and finally must admit that your skin still doesn't look like it did when you were 20, then you'll have to switch to a different brand to keep your fantasy alive and your hopes high. I'm not being cynical. I think that hope is extremely important.

The ultimate opportunity will enable us to achieve an unfair advantage. Short of that, we can settle for an opportunity that offers us an advantage for a certain window of time and will enable us to grow and maximize our profit.

Creating a Gap

To obtain a window of time large enough to allow you to become very wealthy, you must create a huge gap that stuns your competitors, creates doubt in their minds (are you brilliant or crazy?), and paralyzes them. They are too shocked to respond anytime soon, and that's your window of opportunity. Creating a gap means doing something extremely different from what your competitors do, although the differentiation in this case is on-core; that is, it relates to the core benefits of your category. This is a calculated, not an insane, risk. In general, I think that a single-step, bold, calculated risk is better than the "creeping risk" that you tend to disregard as circumstances slowly change not in your favor during the normal course of competition. Creating a gap won't bring you an unfair advantage. In the end, your competitors will come to their senses and imitate you, even improving upon your model. When that happens, you'll have to create a new gap or generate an unfair advantage.

When you create a gap, you must be willing to ignore your current business, your current assets, and your current abilities and to structure yourself to take full advantage of the opportunity you've identified. The example in the next paragraph illustrates this need. In many cases the creation of a gap is based on insight into what most consumers really want and boldness in focusing on this alone, abandoning the futile attempt to cater to all needs. This is the complete opposite of niche thinking.

Let's look at Kinepolis, which began in Belgium. Albert Bert and his sister-in-law, Rose Claeys-Vereecke, had each owned neighborhood movie theaters since the 1960s. Both went through the crisis in the movie industry and, like everyone else, moved from small neighborhood movie theaters to larger theatres, with five or more screens, in malls or city centers. Towards the end of the 1980s, the two decided to join forces and create a gap.

They did what I mentioned before: they concentrated on what most consumers were interested in. They provided:

- A wide choice of movies (for consumers who "go out to a movie" without having decided which one to see).

- Good accessibility and convenient, free parking.

- Round-the-clock screenings.

- Leg room so that you can get to your seat without stepping on other people's feet.

- Stadium seating so that no one's view is blocked.

- Large screens and sophisticated sound systems.

- The opportunity to hang out and spend time in a coffee shop, restaurant, pub, or bar before and after the movie.

In 1988, on the basis of these principles, on relatively cheap land on the outskirts of Brussels ("Not in the center of town?" their competitors asked. "Are they out of their minds? Who'll drive out there?"), they built a complex with 25 screens, a huge parking lot, comfortable and well-equipped theaters, and a wide range of options for entertainment. Before any competitor had time to form an opinion, they had become the dominant player in markets in Belgium, France, Switzerland, Spain, and Poland with more than 20 complexes.

Where Should We Look, and How?

One of the first decisions you face before you start o-scanning is the scope of the scan. You must decide if you're interested in the global, a regional, or a local market. You must decide how far you want to draw away from your category—beyond the necessary minimum that includes the markets of intermediate products and raw materials that you use, the markets of business clients for whom your product is an intermediate product or resource, and the markets of substitutes, alternatives, and complementary products. You could also take an interest, for example, in additional categories in which your consumers purchase goods and services that complement yours in suiting their lifestyles (an expansion of the term "complementary product"), as well as in categories similar to yours in one way or another.

The O-Scan search progresses through five concentric circles, from the external to the internal, which I call CCMCU. What's behind this?

C: Context
C: Consumers
M: Market
C: Competition
U: Us

"Us" is not the internal circle because of megalomania or egocentrism. The simple reason is that all of this is intended to examine ourselves, to identify opportunities open to us, and to create an advantage for us over our competitors.

We examine these five circles (we'll see what's inside each of them in a minute) in two motions. The inward movement, which we call

Zoom In, is intended to help us understand what's happening right now. That's the first stage, which is called "What's now?" The outward movement, which we call, Zoom Out, is part of the second stage, "What's possible?"

For the mission of searching for opportunities in each of the five circles, the O-Scan methodology provides tools for both the inward and the outward motions. The tools for Zoom In are research and analytic tools, because they should be able to inform us about "What's now?" The tools for Zoom Out are creative and inventive tools, because they are the means for discovering "What's possible?"

O-Scan offers many different tools, all very specific, and they were developed and perfected to do the work. You will be introduced to some of the most important tools in the following chapters. In the research and analytic stage, we use many methods, most of which are probably familiar to you:

- Interviews with executives and other staff members.

- Interviews with sales reps and people in the distribution channels.

- Surveys within the company and the distribution channels.

- "Mystery shopping" or "pretend consumer" surveys, with the use of hidden cameras and recordings.

- Analyses of sales data and financial reports.

- Analyses of market data.

- Information gathering from databases and the Internet (including blogs, forums, and talkbacks).

- Workshops for the development of scenarios regarding competitors' future behavior.

- Re-analysis and meta-analysis of past surveys.

- Consumer research, some of it according to our own original methods.

- Observations of consumers during purchase, consumption and use, and interviews during these stages.

- Visits to consumers' homes, with peeks into their closets and pantries.

The Topics We Scrutinize

Each of the five circles contains topics that interest us, topics that, if we examine them with our special tools, could identify opportunities for business, marketing growth, and success.

This isn't a textbook, so I'm not going into precisely what each term means and how we research and analyze each and every topic. I imagine that you are familiar with these by now. The list of topics is not what is different about what we are doing. After all, these are the topics that make up our reality. The difference is in our point-of-view and what it enables you to observe and do. First, go over the lists, despite the fact that they might make for a pretty boring read. Then, of course, you are welcome to use them as a checklist, exactly as we do. Some of the innovative methods will be presented, as I've promised, in the next three chapters, but these are the primary lists you have to relate to in the CCMCU circles:

Context—the broad context in which your market lives

- Trends and developments in the local and global business environment.

- International agreements and treaties, international relations.

- Political influences, laws, rules and regulations, norms.

- The security situation.

- Social and cultural trends.

- Economic trends.

- Technological developments (alternative technologies and innovations).

- Sources of inspiration (the same or similar fields, similar situations).

Consumers—the people who make us rich

- Who is the customer? Who isn't, but might be?

- Buying and consuming or usage situations and circumstances.

- Processes of purchasing, consuming, or using—all stages.

- Purchasing systems, such as a family, a group of friends, or an organization.

- Influences on the actual shopper or buyer.

- Motivations (actively sought benefits) and considerations applied.

- Core benefits that are expected or taken for granted.

- Compromises and concessions, collateral damages.

- Familiarity with brands, perceived differentiation, felt affiliation with brands.

- Long-term trends and passing fads.

- Various options of segmentation.

Market—the boundaries of the market and the way it operates

- The boundaries of the market (competitors, substitutes, and alternatives).

- Suppliers, on whom all competitors depend.

- Types of distribution channels and points of sale.

- Complementary products.

- Barriers to entry and exit.

Competition—our competitors and the nature of the competition

- Existing competitors and also potential competition, such as global players, our suppliers, our business clients, distribution channels, marketers of substitutes, marketers of complementary products, and marketers in other categories—especially not-so-distant categories—who appeal to our customers).

- The structure of the competition (how many players? what are their sizes?) and the current divisions of the market among competitors.

- Competition issues—over what, and in what way.

- Differentiations and advantages of the various competitors, and the covert coordinated division of the market.

- The competition's rules, especially the implicit ones that we comply with but don't notice.

- Prevailing "truths" about the market, the consumers, and "what works."

Us—where we fit in all of this

- Products and product lines.

- Infrastructure: buildings, plants, stores, vehicles, IT systems, etc.

- Capabilities: people, know-how, equipment, systems, methods, processes.

- Strategic alliances, licenses, franchises.

- Sources of revenue, business models, and how we make a profit.

- Status in the market and in the distribution channels (advantages, disadvantages, uniqueness).

- Resources, limitations, constraints, and "burdens" from the past.

- "Inevitable facts"—identified with us, for better or for worse.

- Brands, architecture, and level of brand development compared with potential.

How Do We Pose the Questions?

In the Zoom In process, we ask ourselves, "What's there? What's going on that we weren't paying attention to? What has changed, is changing, or is about to change (or merely could change)?" We ask ourselves these questions directly, but we also use other tools. Based on my experience, if you think about these topics deliberately or have a discussion about them and raise the kinds of questions that I've mentioned, then you will get to some of it but not everything. Structured workshops with our clients are one of the tools we use. One of the things we do are indirect, playful exercises in work groups that help us bring information to the fore and also have some laughs at the same time. I'd now like to introduce you to the process and very briefly describe a few of the dozens of exercises that we've developed for this stage (with more information coming in the following chapters).

Grumpy Old People—an exercise for spotting trends in consumer behavior:

The participants, divided into teams, are told to pretend they're old people who have gathered, nostalgically, to recall the good old days, complain about the deterioration in today's youth, and express their concern about where the world is headed. The teams compete over the number of original "sighing" complaints that they bring up.

The Big Consensus—an exercise for identifying accepted "truths" in the market:

This exercise also involves team competition. The purpose is to articulate, within a given amount of time, as many "truths" as you can about your market or category—things everyone agrees on. These are truths about who the clients are, what they want, how they behave, what products succeed, what sales promotions succeed—generally, what works and what doesn't. They can relate to any aspect of consumer psychology or marketing activity. Afterward, of course, we scrutinize these truths to help us gain our advantage.

God Have Mercy—an exercise to clarify your current differentiation:

The exercise is based on this story: God has been looking at your market, and He's decided there are too many companies in it. At the end of this quarter, He intends to wipe out at least half the companies in the market. But since God is all merciful, He is willing to review presentations in which each company argues why it deserves to be allowed to survive. The goal for each team participating in the exercise is to prepare the most effective presentation for God. It's important to emphasize that you can't fool God! You have to be very lucid and succinct in describing what's special about you and what the consumers would be lacking if you weren't there (because they wouldn't be able to get it anywhere else). You can't just sell Him B.S. about how good you are and how much your clients like you. Why should you be spared? That's the cruel issue at hand.

The Strategic Analysis Triangle: A Summary of "What's Now?"

We summarize the Zoom In by analyzing the points that emerge from the strategic triangle analysis. This triangle further simplifies the CCMCU to three points: us, the consumers, and the environment (which includes the broad context, the market, and the competition). The triangle image illustrates the fact that each of the points relates to the other points. That, in essence, is the heart of the analysis.

1. What is our situation, and how do we evaluate ourselves in relation to our environment (that is, the broad context, the market, and competition) on one hand, and consumers on the other?

2. How are our current and potential competitors doing vis-á-vis the consumers?

3. How do consumers relate to what is happening in the environment, to our competitors, and to us? How are they affected? How well are their needs and desires being served?

4. The information we gather, our insights regarding each of the five components of the CCMCU, and our answers to these three questions complete the "What's now?" stage.

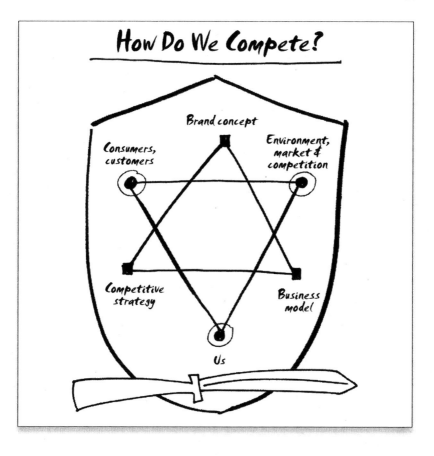

The strategic analysis (the triangle pointing down) is the one that examines and assesses your situation in relation to the environment, the market, and the competition, on the one hand, and in relation to the consumers on the other. These are the three points of one triangle.

The Unique Success Formula (the triangle pointing up) is also a triangle whose three points are the strategy for competitive advantage, the business model that guarantees profitability, and the perception of the brand that appeals to the consumer and creates alternatives. The Unique Success Formula is your response to the market situation and your means of competing and obtaining an advantage.

This is the "Shield of David" model of strategy creation. (The hexagon is an ancient Hindu symbol of being in harmony and protected, used in Buddhism, Islam, Christianity and most notably, Judaism.)

Identification of Opportunities

Studying "What's now?" and analyzing the findings at this point provide a good foundation for identifying opportunities. We examine what exists and estimate the potential for change, innovation, growth, and success in order to identify opportunities. We identify the seeds of what hasn't yet happened but is likely to happen or could conceivably happen if we do the right things.

In the next three chapters we'll deal mainly with the methods of the Zoom Out, in which we ask the "What's possible?" questions. As you'll discover, we go through a series of thinking exercises, which we can describe as creative, inventive or generative (personally, I prefer the latter). The process is often game-like. It's an exciting and enjoyable experience, but the result is the very serious identification of opportunities.

There are some useful types of generative thinking exercises and I'd like to mention them briefly here. You'll spot them in the exercises that appear later in the book. All are intended to help people who aren't particularly creative by nature attain surprising results.

These are the five main types of generative thinking exercises:

- **Directed, focused thinking**—The most basic method for encouraging generative thinking is to allocate time and define the task ("You have five minutes to think of ways to . . .")

- **Constrained thinking**—In these kinds of exercises, the participants are asked to describe something, solve a problem, or achieve something, but they are forbidden to do so in the way they are used to or according to widely accepted assumptions or commonly held beliefs.

- **Provocation that can create an impractical "stepping stone" that leads to a practical solution**—The participants might be asked to name the advantages of a situation quite different from one commonly accepted as desirable or "correct,"—such as insulting consumers who contact your information hotline.

- **Role playing**—The participants are requested to perform a problem-solving task, innovative task, or scenario-building task as someone else would have done it (i.e., a particular competitor, a well-known global company like Virgin, or a well-known personality like Donald Trump or Jack Welsh).

- **What if?**—The participants are asked to examine hypothetical situations, some realistic and some not, and to devise action options for them.

Mapping Opportunities

I have a few comments about the way we map and visually present the opportunities at the end of this stage.

First, we categorize the opportunities that we identified as strategic or tactical. Strategic growth opportunities require that we adopt a new strategy. The tactical opportunities require that we execute innovations in our marketing within the framework of the current strategy.

We draw the five CCMCU circles and, in each of them, list the opportunities we have identified. Each opportunity is characterized by its two main components: the group of consumers for whom we identified the opportunity, and the concept of the offer that will realize the opportunity. Phrased in one sentence, we recite or record something like, "By doing Y we can take advantage of the opportunity Z that exists in X."

Note that identifying opportunities can begin with spotting or defining a group of consumers whose situation we can improve (the next question is "how?"), and it may begin with something we can offer ("to whom?"). Whatever the case, we don't have an opportunity in our hands until we combine both of these components. They are the same for both strategic and tactical opportunities; only their meaning and scale are different.

What's Feasible?

The next stage in the "What's next?" process is "What's feasible?" That is, what can we implement profitably?

- Several principles guide the evaluation of the opportunities:

- The extent of the potential that the opportunity presents.

- Our ability to realize the opportunity within the framework of our constraints.

- Our ability to defend our achievement or the profitability of the time window.

- The commitment we are able to create within our company to take advantage of the opportunity.

In addition to considering these basic questions, we perform the evaluation according to accepted financial tools and procedures.

What's Next?

The last stage of our process is "What's next?"—planning to realize the opportunity or opportunities we have decided we want to realize. When we talk about adopting a new strategy, we move from the strategic analysis triangle to the Unique Success Formula (USF) that I described earlier, in all three of its components: the business model (How will we profit?), the competitive strategy (How will we create an advantage, preferably an unfair one?), and the concept of the brand (How will we shape our offer in the mind of the consumer?).

Everyday Guidance

Strategy is supposed to bring clarity and resolve to day-to-day management. It is supposed to help the firm's managers make their daily decisions. And so, I have a suggestion for you. Instead of framing posters of the mission statement, I recommend that you prepare a "strategy statement" for your management team and hang that on the wall instead. I recommend that you supply them with a wallet-sized, PDA, and cell phone version so they can receive the statement as an SMS every time they have a decision to make. The strategy statement sums up the strategy and translates it into a set of clear and simple principles. Here's what it should include:

> Our strategy is to fulfill the potential of target customers X [the definition will make it clear what factor turns them into potential for us] by offering them Y. What we do differently from our competitors is Z.

And so:

- The opportunities that interest us are opportunities for . . .

- Our top priority is . . . and after that . . .

- What makes our way of doing things special is . . .

- Our primary considerations and guidelines for decision-making are . . .

- Our primary measure of success is . . .

- We give up on or abandon an activity when . . .

- We will reexamine our strategy if the following conditions prevail . . .

Think about your managers when you articulate the strategy statement. Think about the situations they encounter in their work. Think about the conditions under which they operate. Ask yourself which guidelines will help them make decisions that are in accordance with the strategy. I view this strategy statement as an excellent way of ensuring that the strategy is implemented in real life and, just as important, that you are sure your strategy is clear to you.

8

Some O-Scan Methods: Obtaining Insight about Consumers and Their Future Desires

Start with These Two

I've chosen to share two methods from among the many O-Scan methods that enable you to obtain unbelievable insight into the behavior of consumers as individuals and as groups—what motivates them, what they will desire in the future, and so forth. As you will see, these methods are quite different from those based on MBA-clone thinking. By using the methods I recommend, you will understand things your competitors don't. You'll see things in a new way, one that can lead to an unfair advantage.

The two methods we'll discuss are:

1. **Contextual Segmentation** to segment the market in a new way

2. **ForeSearch** to identify future desires

Contextual Segmentation

When you segment the market in the usual way, you look for groups of consumers that are internally similar but different from each other. The variable that creates the similarity within each group and the differences between the groups is what we call the "segmentation variable" (hair color, for a simple example). After you've divided the consumers into groups, you'd probably like to do something with these divisions. Let's say you've defined a certain segment as your target group. You might want to carry out some selling activities within this segment or direct certain advertising messages at them. Sometimes, the segmentation variable is enough for you ("Redheads, listen up!"). But in most cases (for example, the segment of people who only drink beer outside their homes), you need to characterize the segment before performing these actions. In other words, you need to know something more about the characteristics of the consumers in the segment rather than just the segmentation variable. Who are they? What are they like? You also want to know about the ways they differ from consumers in other segments. Characterizing the segment is different from defining the segment.

If you are engaged in the old-fashioned type of segmentation and are honest with yourself, I am certain you've discovered by now that it really doesn't work well. What do I mean? According to commonly accepted segmentation theories, the people in each segment are supposed to be different in some way from the people in other segments. But they usually aren't. Let's say that in a certain segment, women are over represented—60 percent, compared with 50 percent in the total population. Even if this difference is statistically significant, does this make it a "female segment?" What about the 40 percent who are men? Or let's say, for example, that a segment of golfers contains a relatively high percentage of billionaires. Does this make it a billionaire segment? Of course not. In all probability, a high ratio does not mean that the majority of those in the segment are billionaires. And so, in each segment, despite certain disproportional representation, all population groups are more or less represented. What is the historical basis for the common theory of segmentation? In the quickly receding past (and in traditional and highly communal societies to this day), human behavior was determined to a greater extent by gender; national, tribal, or ethnic origin; religion, socio-economic status, profession, and stage in life. Appearance, behavior, and consumption patterns and preferences were more easily categorized. If you knew even one member of a group, it was fairly easy to make assumptions about the other members. But all that has changed. As we have become more individualistic, and as our opportunities have expanded, we don't fall easily into defined types.

In the 1970s we were taught that consumer segments can be internally homogenous in other ways in addition to the demographic and socioeconomic traits they have in common. We were told that we should examine the psychographic or lifestyle characteristics of segments. Approaches such as VALS (Values, Attitudes, and Lifestyles) divided the population into ten lifestyle groups that were subsequently collapsed into eight groups.

However, it is now clear that these classification systems don't reliably or consistently predict purchasing decisions or consumer preferences in any specific product category. Therefore, we've changed the way we use them. Marketing people have begun to use group classification as a psychological or personality variable, mainly as an indicator of a prevalent motivation. And again, just as with demographic and socioeconomic characteristics, we find in each and every segment, that there are "representatives" of all psychographic and lifestyle groups in each segment. There are no "pure" segments—not even close. It's pretty clear that we haven't progressed much at all.

If you've been doing segmentations for a while, you know that this situation just gets worse over time. Consumers pretty much refuse to be classified into any homogeneous group by demographic, socioeconomic, or even lifestyle characteristics. They often won't "act" their age, gender, or social status. They just won't behave or consume according to our stereotypical expectations.

Conversely, they pick up traits from here and there, which is why I call them "eclectic" consumers. They love old music and new technology; convenience items (like frozen food) and do-it-yourself and cooking projects that require real effort; expensive prestigious brands and cheap bulk discount stores; global brands and local grassroots products; sophisticated and simple; gourmet and fast food. We used to think that consumers of luxury brands didn't look for promotions and discounts, or for popular entertainment. Even if that were once true, it isn't any more. Many wealthy people don't want to be aristocratic.

La noblesse oblige is no more. Rich people feel that a certain amount of "slumming it" makes them more authentic, more interesting.

On the other hand, we also once thought that middle class consumers didn't buy luxury products. Now we meet more and more consumers who, at least in the one area that is dear to their hearts, make an effort and go beyond their usual level of consumption. We refer to such phenomena as Trading Down and Trading Up, and over the past few years they have been in the marketing spotlight. Eclectic consumers are addicted to having many options. They don't want to miss a thing. Eclectic consumers are motivated by the "fear of missing out," which I'll talk more about in Chapter 15. Eclectic consumers tune in with their diverse motivations at different times. Since these motivations don't necessarily go together, eclectic consumers go from stereotype to stereotype, from lifestyle to lifestyle. And so they consume plain, non-fat yogurt in the morning, put away a hamburger, fries, and a Coke (followed by a cigarette) in the afternoon, and meet up with friends for a Japanese dinner in the evening.

The marketing concept of lifestyles needs to be updated. To catch up with today's consumers, we should realize that a certain society and certain culture now produces a multitude of lifestyles which form a menu that people can choose from as well as combine or create variations. Consumers don't *belong* to any lifestyle. It is impossible to say that a given consumer belongs to a certain lifestyle group. The new model uses terms like "participation in lifestyles" (I am in debt to Harvey Hartman for some of these insights).

To demonstrate the point, we can consider many different types of lifestyles, such as new age, wellness, simplicity, back to nature, Western-style careerism, worldliness, fanatic nationalism, hedonism, techno-freakiness, connoisseur culture, and outdoors and off-road sports/activities lovers. Consumers, to varying degrees, take on characteristics of more than one type of lifestyle. Their needs change according to their level of participation in each type.

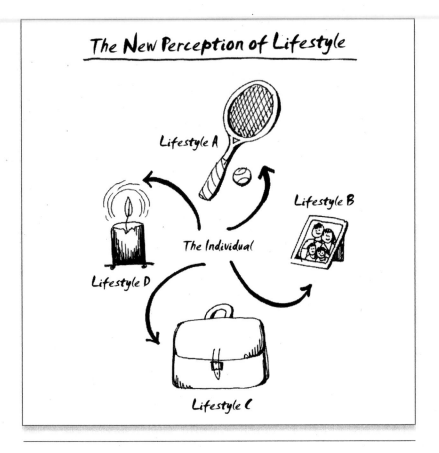

The New Perception of Lifestyle

Lifestyle A

Lifestyle B

The Individual

Lifestyle D

Lifestyle C

Today's consumer participates in several lifestyles, at different times and in different circumstances and moods. A sort of "menu" of lifestyle options is provided by the social and cultural surroundings. Within each of these lifestyles, consumers can participate at different levels. They might be deeply involved in the lifestyle or might prefer just a taste of it from time to time.

If they are deeply involved in some undertaking, they may need experts or specialized equipment, products, or services. Take off-road driving. People who are really into this lifestyle need fully equipped vehicles designed specifically for off-road driving (such as heavy-duty trucks and equipment, SUVs, ATVs, snowmobiles, motorcycles, or mountain bicycles) or vehicles that have extra ground clearance, sturdy tires, and in some cases, front and rear locking differential. Those who are less committed are looking for exciting experiences, but they need more guidance. They're not as knowledgeable. Their cars are less "professional." And then there are people who only want a taste of the lifestyle, with convenience and at a price that won't burden their wallets. They'll go on an organized off-road experience every so often. In parallel with consumers, brands that support certain lifestyles position themselves according to different levels of participation.

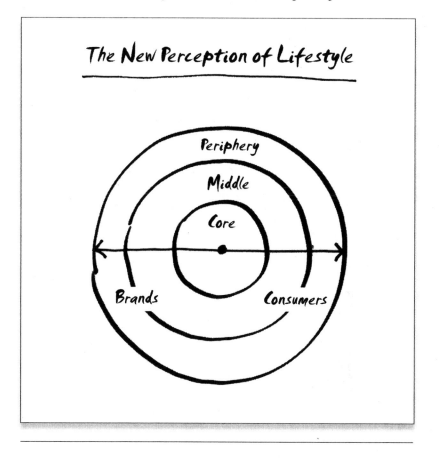

In accordance with all possible levels of consumer participation in a lifestyle, different brands support the lifestyle of those who are deeply involved and those who are less involved.

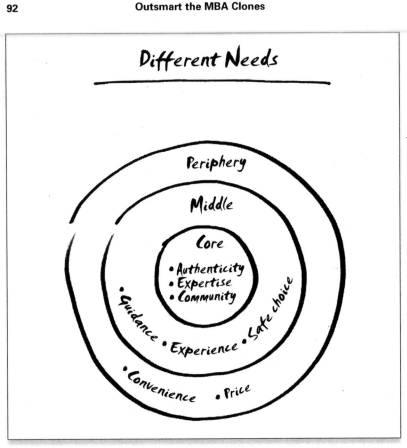

The needs of consumers who are deeply into a certain lifestyle are different from those of consumers who are on the periphery of the lifestyle. Those who are at the core need brands that provide authenticity and expertise, and they also want to be part of a community of like-minded people. The consumers in the middle need guidance so that they can be certain of their choices and experiences. Those who merely want a taste aren't willing to invest heavily or make a serious effort.

At the same time that we recognize the inadequacy of the old segmentation systems, we need to know that our consumers connect to brands differently than we used to assume.

Take the lingerie brand Victoria's Secret. In its current incarnation, it offers women an opportunity to flaunt their sexuality. Originally, as the name suggests, wearing this firm's lingerie allowed you to be respectable and serious at work or anywhere outside the house (in other words, not sexy or, heaven forbid, seductive or cheap), but still desirable and fun-loving in the privacy of your bedroom. Consumers have changed, attitudes about sexuality have changed, and in the mid 1990s the brand underwent a change. The benefit it provided for its clients took a dramatically different direction.

The brand changed its promise. It was no longer hidden sexuality; it was open, in-your-face sexuality. And the firm did it big time. Supermodels showed off sexy underwear at provocative fashion shows and in ads. The once-opaque store windows suddenly became transparent. The plain, unlabeled bags turned into hot pink, striped, and highly recognizable symbols. In one of its commercials, filmed in Venice, the firm even had a cameo from Bob Dylan singing "Lovesick." And all the while, the Victoria's Secret brand has undergone an "Abstraction" process (the alternative to brand extension: creating a brand promise that is entirely product category independent), and its new meaning is gradually emerging from the narrow category of underwear. The firm now succeeds in marketing nightwear, beach wear, jeans, fashion, perfumes, cosmetics, and toiletries. There's no limit, since many products are relevant when the brand's benefit is "a display of sexuality."

If, in the past, we said that certain women are Victoria's Secret women and others aren't, then today we would have to say that almost any woman can connect at one time or another to the mood and motivation to which Victoria's Secret caters.

The New Segmentation

So how do you perform market segmentation in an age when consumers refuse to aggregate into convenient segments across many product categories? In order to adjust to this consumer reality, our segments (and, as a result, our products and services, our brands, our advertising, and so on) cannot be about groups of people. The more apt approach in the new consumer reality is to view segments as composed of consumers that are in certain "consumption contexts." The name of this new method of segmentation, therefore, is Contextual Segmentation—segmentation according to context.

This is truly a revolution in the way we think about market segmentation. Let's remember the original reason for market segmentation—to divide the market into smaller units so that we can focus our marketing, branding, or advertising efforts and achieve differentiation and advantages that we can't achieve in the general market. It's clear that the search for groups of consumers just doesn't do this anymore. The search for consumption contexts provides new potential.

According to the old forms of segmentation, each of these segments can be characterized by a major need or preference or motivation. The new segmentation preserves this view. But given the new reality, a particular motivation is not characteristic of a defined group of consumers. Nearly the contrary is true. According to the new approach, all motivations are common to all consumers at one time or another. A "segment," then, is a group of purchases or consumptions, a certain context of purchasing or consumption. When performing segmentation using this approach, we analyze consumer behavior and identify the various contexts of product purchasing and consumption, as well as the driving motivations that characterize consumers in each context.

The new relevant segments might be emotional states (for example, the "I'll teach my husband a lesson!" segment), social situations (such as, "Wow! It's been a long time since we last met!"), or whatever is relevant to the product category. Note that in any consumption arena (i.e., a meal in a restaurant), different consumer motivations ("Tonight we're going out without the kids," as opposed to, "We're celebrating Grandpa's birthday") are considered different segments. Over time, any specific consumer might participate in one segment, in several segments, or in none. At the same time, just as with the old method, each segment represents a share of our sales that we can quantify and then weigh its contribution to our profitability.

Let's examine another example. If you are a shampoo manufacturer, the "I am going to look amazing at that party" segment contributes a certain percentage of your income, as does the "I need half an hour to myself" segment and the "These expenses are killing us; we have to cut back a bit" segment. At different times, the same consumer might be in each of these market segments.

When doing contextual segmentation, all levels of our marketing activity must be directed toward the purchasing, demand, or motivational contexts, rather than toward groups of consumers.

To be sure this is clear, let's examine one more example. One of the largest and most important segments of the fashion accessories market, especially in the lower price range, is the "Hey, is that new? Where'd you buy it?" segment. The main benefit that motivates this segment is psycho-social—the chance to get attention. According to contextual segmentation, you can launch a product or a brand in this way, but it won't be targeted at a consumer group. Consumers who are very different from each other—by gender, age, socioeconomic status, or lifestyle (family- or achievement-oriented)—might all buy the product or brand when they feel the need for some attention.

The ForeSearch Method

If you feel that today's consumer research methods haven't given you any truly amazing insights, you're not alone. And, in fact, time and again, *re*search (with the emphasis on the "re") sends you off on the same old routes. I want to talk to you about an alternative. This is a different approach with a different focus that I named ForeSearch. It will not only bring you to a completely different level of insight, but it will enable you to foresee and even engineer the future desires of your customers. You will be able to perform something we might call "mind surgery" that is both masterful and precise.

The inspiration for the ForeSearch method was a research method applied by Clotaire Rapaille for the design of Chrysler's PT Cruiser. Somewhere in the mid-1990s, Chrysler executives decided that a hit model was the only thing that could salvage their company's deteriorating image and provide it with the tail wind it needed for its marketing activities. It was clear they didn't stand a chance with the usual research methods they had tried so many times before, so they enlisted an entirely new team, composed of people from different disciplines.

It was the second half of the decade. Think back for a moment. Hi-tech was booming, globalization offered a promise of endless prosperity for all (it was just a matter of "time to market"), and "politically correct" was the behavior code—to the point that if you came to the office in a good mood and complimented your secretary, you might as well have started looking for a new job. That was the backdrop for Chrysler's research on a car design that would be launched in the year 2000 and become a tremendous hit.

The research findings were surprising. And no less surprising, they were made public. Research showed that in the year 2000, the American consumer was looking for a simpler world, a world in which a man was a man and a woman was a woman. A world in which the bad guys wore black and the good guys wore white. Consumers felt threatened by globalization and wanted to show some muscle to the world—to appear mighty and deterring. It's pretty amazing, you must admit, that this research predicted the social forces that put George W. Bush in the White House. It predicted the social-cultural attitudes that supported his foreign policy, even before the events of 9/11. Admit it—the research that you've been doing hasn't been providing you with those kinds of forecasts.

To back up their conclusions, researchers started looking for a time in history that was characterized by that same spirit, and they came up with the 1940s. And the vehicle that best expressed the spirit of that era was the famous gangster car from crime movies.

Chrysler's design team happily agreed to design a car inspired by the gangster car but with an up-to-date look. But every time they presented their sketches to research subjects, the researchers told them that it wasn't "similar enough" and sent them back to the drawing table. In the end, they came up with the PT Cruiser, which looks exactly—and I mean *exactly*—like a gangster car from the 1940s. On the outside, that is. On the inside, it is a comfort car with the most advanced amenities of the 21st century.

The PT Cruiser was launched into the American market in late 2000, early 2001, and it became the car of the year. It was definitely the hit that Chrysler had been counting on. And here's an interesting tidbit: in the U.S., buyers could purchase stickers that create the appearance of bullet holes, to add just the right touch.

The ForeSearch method has come a long way (one reason is that this method, unlike Rapaille's, has nothing to do with psychoanalysis) and is now quite a revolutionary tool in the field of consumer research. Its success stems from three key developments in the field over the past decade. Since it's fairly likely that you are not researchers, I'll mention them here, without going into great detail, and if you want to know more, I'm sure you'll know where to look.

1. The **Means-End** model, which in its most up-to-date version includes the connections among cognitive processes, emotions, and motivation.

2. **G. Zaltman's ZMET** method and its theoretical base. I recommend that you read his book, *How Customers Think*.

3. Research findings examining the efficacy of traditional types of focus groups and in-depth interviews.

ForeSearch is a qualitative method that permits diagnosis, exposure, and precise mapping of consumers' unconscious associations among:

- Facts about companies, products, and so forth which are focal points for consumers and determine their perceptions, without consumers being aware that this is happening.

- Automatic perceived consequences and meanings that consumers attach to these facts.

- Immediate favorable and unfavorable judgments that consumers make, usually unconsciously, as a result of these attached meanings.

- Beliefs that the consumer adopts regarding the benefit or harm in these products or companies.

- Emotional reactions and expectations that form the basis of the consumer's motivation to buy or not to buy.

I'm excited about this method and have been working with it and perfecting it for several years. The results are fantastic. First, the method pinpoints the facts that unconsciously determine consumers' perceptions. Sometimes, we know that these facts are hard to guess since they are utterly unimportant (for example, the sound a can makes when opened), and that is why we never paid any attention to them, even though, for whatever reason, consumers might.

Always, without exception, consumer beliefs about a product or a brand are rooted in facts that they know. Most consumer research methods ignore this, leading us to believe that consumer perceptions, beliefs, and attitudes come from outer space or result from some "irrational" emotional reaction. When I say, "based on facts," I don't mean a process of logical-deduction; rather, I am referring to intuitive, automatic, and unconscious interpretation. These *facts* aren't always characteristics or qualities. They can include the people who have already purchased the product, where it's being sold, and so on. Of course, when you know which facts shape consumer perceptions and how consumers interpret them to develop beliefs and, subsequently, emotions, you can influence this process, guiding it or changing the perceptions and references.

Here are two examples. In ForeSearch for a bank, as part of a project of designing a unique service for very wealthy clients, it became apparent that the most important fact influencing consumer perceptions and attitudes was not the special benefits offered to this group, the magnitude of the benefits, or similar factors. Rather, the willingness of bank managers to go beyond protocol and bend the rules for these client was the only behavior these consumers perceived as giving banks a superior status. That translated into a perception of importance and value, and it created a sense of loyalty to a particular bank. Make no mistake: not one of those clients said this directly. They rationalized about considerations that perhaps should have influenced their decisions, but they were fooling themselves and could have mislead the bank. The ForeSearch method made it possible to penetrate their true motivations and design an innovative and very successful service.

The second Foresearch example relates to cellular communications.

We were able to find out that the huge difference in the images of two providers originated in different interpretations that users attached to incidents of disconnected calls. In the case of one company, clients thought, "It just happens; it doesn't mean anything," while in the case of the other company clients thought, "This company is so screwed up; it can't get its act together." Following the ForeSearch process, the latter company made a focused effort to eliminate the specific problem of disconnected calls, rather than trying to change the perception. This particular improvement, to which we were able to direct the company, brought a dramatic change in overall beliefs about the brand ("What an amazing improvement!").

I'd like to sum up the primary benefits that ForeSearch provides:

- Understanding consumers' preferences, including spontaneous, instant preferences that they cannot really explain but only rationalize.

- Identifying the manner in which brand perceptions, beliefs, emotional reactions, and motivations are formed and how they interplay.

- Mapping graphically and understanding the internal structure of beliefs and the emotional reactions that follow them.

- In cases of success, understanding what exactly succeeded and how the success can be replicated.

- In cases of failure, identifying and removing the sources of failure.

- Doing a Pre-Test to anticipate consumers' future responses and know exactly what they are responding to and how.

- Designing and changing perceptions and emotional responses.

- Identifying the sources of differences in consumer responses to products, brands, and so forth (ours and our competitors').

- Identifying future or potential desires.

How to Conduct ForeSearch—In Brief

The Interview

ForeSearch employs face-to-face interviews that are unusually long—often 90 minutes to two hours. The interviews can be conducted individually or in "natural groups." Let me explain that. The method here is diametrically opposed to the focus group method you're familiar with. When you organize focus groups, you gather together people who have no known connection with each other. With ForeSearch, you interview a group of people who have a common relationship that is relevant to the research topic. A husband and wife are a natural group, as are a father and son or an entire family, or business partners, or friends who watch football games together. You form the group according to the topic you are researching.

Principles of the interview

ForeSearch requires skillful interviewers who are near-virtuosos in conducting a seemingly free-style conversation with a complex hidden agenda. The interview proceeds in cycles, each with two phases: bringing content to the surface and then exploring and scrutinizing it. Each cycle in the interview deals with a topic that concerns us, such as why the consumer takes a particular package off the shelf. The stage of bringing things to the surface "connects" the interviewee with a specific experience, one instance in which he or she performed a specific behavior. Generalizations about behavior are avoided because they are not reliable. The stage of exploring and scrutinizing resembles the stage in an archeological dig in which the archeologist uses a brush to remove the dust from the finding and expose it. At this stage, the interviewer exposes the unconscious structure in the consumer's mind and the internal connections between what the consumer is focusing on, the meaning attached to this focus, the perceptions it creates, beliefs regarding its benefit or damage, and emotional responses.

A basic rule is not to use any direct questions, unless the interviewer is interested in specific factual information. As I have mentioned, we never ask interviewees to make generalizations regarding their own behavior ("What do you usually do when . . . ?"), to explain the motivations for their behavior ("Why do you do this?"), to express an opinion ("Which is better?"), or to predict future behavior ("What will most convince you to . . . ?"), because research indicates decisively that interviewees' responses to questions like these are not reliable. During ForeSearch, the entire interview often revolves around a discussion of real-life episodes. It may seem more like gossip, with the interviewer acting like a chatty neighbor and feigning excited curiosity: "You're kidding! That's what he did?" The interviewer may also resemble Inspector Colombo from the classic TV series, with that "having-a-hard-time-understanding" style. "I don't quite understand. How exactly did he bend down to pick it up?"

Bringing Content Up to the Surface

To connect interviewees with their behavior patterns and with the motivations and beliefs underlying their spontaneous behavior, the interviewer uses several methods. Based on my experience, the first of the techniques that follow is the most important:

- Guided Imagery—probing for details about a specific incident in which an investigated behavior occurred, with the purpose of leading the interviewee to re-live it in his imagination.

- Individual Metaphor Creation—encouraging interviewees to create their own metaphors of a brand or an experience, e.g., a buying or using experience ("What's it like?" without the use of limiting cues such as, "if it were a person, car, or animal . . ." that distort the findings because they force the interviewee to think in terms that are not natural to him).

- Thought Listing—for two minutes, interviewees list everything that comes to mind about some topic and then rate these items as "good," "bad," or "neither good nor bad."

- **Free Associations**—similar to the above, but performed verbally and emphasizing the associative chain (what leads to what).

- **Intuitive Grouping and Comparison**—interviewees are requested to categorize some brands on the market according to similarities or differences they perceive (rather than according to any pre-set criterion). They are then requested to describe, in one word, what the items in each group have in common and how any two groups differ.

The role of these methods is to uncover at least one of the five components of a full unconscious mental construct which is a product- or brand-related belief. Each construct is composed of these five components: a fact, an interpretation or meaning attached to it, a perceived benefit or damage, an emotional reaction, and a behavior tendency (a fuller explanation of what happens can be found in Chapter 11). The main role of the interviewer at this stage is to listen carefully, detect one of the five components, and then go on to bring out the entire structure.

Methods for Exploring

After the interviewer has managed to bring one of the five edges of this structure to the surface and determine which of the five has been brought up (fact, interpretation or meaning, perceived benefit/damage, emotional reaction, or behavior tendency), he or she uses a special method of questioning in order to expose the structure of the four other components.

"It was clear to me that I would switch to them at the first opportunity," the interviewee said in the study of cellular brands that I mentioned before, following a story about a friend who had switched to another company and shown him his new phone. The interviewer noted to himself that he had identified a *behavioral tendency* and continued on.

"What is the turn-on about them?" he asked with interest.

"I'd be proud to be one of their customers," the interviewee said.

The interviewer had exposed the *emotional reaction*.

"What's special about them?" the interviewer asked skeptically.

"They're winners, they're a company of winners," the interviewee answered without hesitation.

The interviewer had exposed the *perceived benefit*.

"Why do you say that they're winners?" the interviewer insisted.

"Come on, they're out of this world," the interviewee answered, with an admiring expression. The interviewer had identified the *interpretation* that the interviewee attached to some fact but wasn't quite sure what it was.

"How so? How do you know they're great?" he continued to ask.

"Fact is, they were the last ones to come into the market and look how successful they are," the interviewee said. The interviewer had managed to identify the *fact* that was at the base of the entire structure. I have shortened this story a bit, but this was the process, more or less.

Personally, there's no chance that at the outset, I would have guessed the importance of that fact. The questions may seem naïve, but there's a sophisticated process at work here.

With a Bit of Luck

Here's an example of something that can be done with ForeSearch. In work we conducted several years ago for a national lottery, Fore-Search helped us identify eleven distinct motivations for participation in these games—benefits people expect to get from them—including three that were previously unknown. Furthermore, we were able to precisely identify the characteristics of the various games ("Instant Win," "Scratch-offs," and so forth), which are the triggers for each of the motivations. We came to understand how and why the motivational process occurs. Beyond this, with the aid of statistical research, we were able to determine the distribution of each motivation in the population and those people for whom each motivation is strongest. Essentially, we were able to categorize six basic types of players.

As a result, we created a method for developing new games for our client. The development people can now define which combination of benefits would be provided by a new game under development, know what its characteristics should be, and also estimate its revenue potential.

What is usually included in a ForeSearch project?

- Definition of the goals and an in-depth analysis of the task.

- Definition of the research population (individuals and natural groups) and creation of a sample.

- Personal or natural-group interviews, usually about 30.

- Mapping of the meaningful facts, their attached meanings, perceptions of benefit or damage, emotional reactions, and behavior tendencies that were revealed.

- Analysis and conclusions.

- Quantification using a survey, if necessary.

- Consulting and development of action plans.

9

Some More O-Scan Methods: Identifying Opportunities Using the Consumption Process Analysis

The Consumer: The Ultimate Executor of Your Strategy

Your strategy will work, or not, when consumers do, or do not do, what you intended. Every strategy should have consumer psychology at its heart. The branding aspect of the strategy creation process and the brand concept angle of the Unique Success Formula triangle are there to make sure this happens. Every opportunity you identify, whether strategic or tactical, can be fully taken advantage of only if you offer consumers something they will desire.

For this reason, understanding the customer is the most important factor for opportunity identification. In the previous chapter I described two of the ways to understand consumers and to predict their desires in the future. In this chapter I will show you the huge benefit that lies in the analysis of the consumption process, that is part of the "What's now?" and the "What's possible?" stages. As you will soon find out, the consumption process teaches us not only about the consumers, but also about ourselves and our competitors.

The 15 Stages

Understanding the consumption process constitutes the foundation for several important analyses and generative thinking exercises designed for discovering opportunities. In order to understand your customer's consumption process, you can use the 15 stages below.

First, ask in what way each of them applies to your product or service. Build a list of all the stages that you found to be relevant, and then find out precisely how, when, and where each one of them takes place in the case of your product or service. What are consumers doing, and what are they going through as they do it? Who is involved and how? Do not be tempted to make generalizations. Be concrete and pay attention to details. Understand what is going on, and do not just check things off the list. Have some empathy. Get over any inclination to mock your customer's stupidity. Get into his or her head and soul. Go through it like the customer would.

Here are the stages:

1. Arousal of need or desire or will

2. Heightened interest or active search for options, information observing, finding, and gathering (through the media, the internet, neighbors and friends, advertising, window shopping, call centers). Does habit affect future purchases? What can cause deviation from habit?

3. Discovering possibilities and developing familiarity with brands

4. Making the choice; and again, does habit affect choice? When does it not?

5. Purchase or order

6. Payment

7. Delivery

8. Installation

9. Instruction deciphering

10. Storage and maintenance by consumer

11. Preparation for use or consumption

12. Use or consumption—in what circumstances? When? Where?

13. How does the consumer derive and enjoy the benefit that your product provides? Which benefit is the crucial one? What does deriving it depend on?

14. Support, complaint management, fault management, repairs

15. Waste or dump handling

It could be that you discover a few variations of the consumption process. Great! Describe all the various consumption processes in detail and discover the source of variation: different market segments, in the usual sense of the term? Are there different purchasing or consumption contexts?

After having detailed your customer's consumption process, you can use it to perform various analyses for the "What's now?" stage, as well as a search for opportunities for the "What's possible?" stage. Following are three options. We perform some of these exercises with consumers during in-depth interviews. We also perform these exercises when we conduct interviews with employees at various levels of our client's organization, or during workshops. According to my experience, these exercises are worthwhile, especially when conducted with people who actually meet with the consumer at various stages of the consumption process, or who have the opportunity to affect the consumer's experience.

1. Identifying Opportunities to Eliminate Consumers' Pain Points

Our first exercise serves the two stages simultaneously: "What's now?" and "What's possible?" The types of opportunities pinpointed here will help you with your ongoing marketing innovation. Usually this exercise will not enable you to discover opportunities that will open a huge gap between you and your competition, and certainly not to create an unfair advantage. However, I recommend that you do not skip this exercise. You should go over the adapted consumption process, step by step. At each stage you must check to see if you can detect one or more of the following in your consumer experiences:

- Discomfort or inconvenience, difficulty, hold-up, cumbersomeness, unnecessary costs

- A need to make compromises or some sacrifice, a solution which is not full or optimal

- Some damage that must be tolerated in order to derive the benefit

- A need to acquire complementary products or services in order to derive the benefit

Once you have identified "pain points," you will have identified an opportunity. Then, of course, you ask questions such as, "Why is this happening?" and "What can be done in order to stop it?" The answers to such questions will lead you to find ways to capitalize on the opportunities you have identified.

2. Enriching Consumer Benefits

The second exercise is important because it can lead to the identification of strategic opportunities, maybe even to the creation of an unfair advantage. It serves the "What's possible?" stage.

Ted Levitt, one of the founding fathers of marketing, was a pioneer evangelist of differentiation as a foundation for a winning competitive strategy. One rule he created many years ago states that if you have a tangible product, differentiate it by fuelling it with intangible benefits. If you have a product that provides intangible benefits, fuel it with tangible benefits. This idea constitutes the basis for the following exercise, although we will take it much further.

First, you should go over every stage of the consumption process. At each stage, challenge yourself to offer your consumers additional benefits, preferably on top of your core benefits, which can differentiate you and create for your brand a sustainable advantage. When you think about "whether," you really should be thinking in terms of "how." The answer you should get will be integrated.

Now, thoroughly examine the possibilities to add one or more of the five types of benefits discussed below. (In Chapter 11 you will find a comprehensive elaboration on each of them). Keep in mind that we are not talking about core benefits, but rather about benefits added to the core that will help you differentiate your brand. I will accompany each type of benefit with one short example, but the purpose of this exercise is to find ways by which you can add each and every type of benefit to each stage in the consumption process of your product.

1. An experiential-sensory benefit

Can you please your customer's senses with beautiful sights, pleasant fragrances, sweet music, soft touches, and tasty flavors? Can you provide them with a relaxing physical feeling or an optimal temperature? Can this experience be multi-sensorial and harmonious? The Clorox Company, for instance, was the first to add pleasant fragrances to its detergents.

2. An experiential-emotional benefit

Can you offer your consumers an emotional experience? An emotional experience stems from a particular atmosphere or a certain stimulus, which enlivens a whole associative world in the consumer's mind (i.e., "European Towns," "Futuristic Technology," and so forth). Emotions are also called forth by suggestive words and even more by a narrative drama or a game. For example, think about Sicily by Dolce & Gabbana ("the Sicilian Mafia").

3. An interpersonal benefit

Can you offer your customer a way to add something new to existing relationships in his or her life, or a way to handle them better or advance them? Consider spouses, children, parents, siblings, friends, or any other type of relationship you can think of. Can you offer them a way to express or trigger feelings? Perhaps to increase their attractiveness in somebody's eyes? Or a way to tap into someone else's needs? To mark an occasion? McDonald's Kids Meals fit this category. They provide parents with an opportunity to treat their kids to a restaurant meal.

4. A social benefit

Can you offer consumers a way to send a message to their surroundings regarding their identity, personality, group affiliation and participation, status, or values? Can you provide them with an opportunity to do the right thing socially, ethically, or ideologically? Maybe you can help them mark some kind of ritual such as passing from one age group to another? Triumph, the famous underwear brand, created the concept of "my first bra," which symbolizes the passage from girlhood to womanhood.

5. A psychological benefit

Can you offer your customers a way to feel better, to release tension, to control their moods, to get away, to experience a fantasy, to feel vivacious, to exhibit competency and feel empowered, to see a purpose, to develop, to treat themselves? A brand like Nike empowers its customers with the feeling that anything desired is achievable.

3. Exposing the Competition's Hidden Rules of the Game

The third exercise partially serves the "What's now?" stage and partially the "What's possible?" stage. The importance of this exercise can't be overestimated. It may make you see things you can't believe you haven't noticed until now. It could dramatically change your ways of competing. It may even lead to the identification of a strategic opportunity and a chance to create a genuine unfair advantage.

The first step requires that you or some of your teams go over each of the stages of the consumption process. However you decide to do this, the questions that need to be dealt with at each and every step are: How does your category or your market normally behave at every step in the process? What do you all usually do? What are the areas of activity and how do all the players behave in each of these areas? This is part one of this exercise.

A special recommendation: do this first part of the exercise in personal and group interviews with customers also. Ask them about their personal experiences, about situations they had to tackle, but ask them to just tell their stories and not generalize. Then analyze, diagnose, or draw conclusions.

This is your opportunity to discover what everybody does within the framework of your category's conventions and what the covert rules of the game are. You can achieve even more. This is also your chance to observe the differences between the activities of your various competitors, to understand where they are coming from and what results they are getting. If anyone in your market has managed to build an advantage or differentiation, you will identify it and understand how it works. If any of your competitors have weaknesses, you will identify those as well.

While you are at it, I suggest that you examine how customers react to the industry's *modus operandi* as a whole, as well as to each of the players in the field. For this purpose, you can also integrate findings and conclusions from market research you have done in the past, especially during Foresearch, as well as other methods.

When you conclude the first part of this exercise, classify the various ways of operating in your industry according to the following scheme:

1. Characteristics and practices perceived by the consumers as mandatory, yet obvious (tied to core benefits)—they do not constitute an advantage, but a deficiency in these mandatory characteristics or actions will constitute a major drawback

2. Characteristics and practices perceived by consumers as blocking brand-switching or at least delaying it

3. Characteristics and practices to which consumers are indifferent

4. Characteristics and practices that consumers perceive as an exciting advantage

5. Characteristics and practices perceived by consumers as a brand-unique trait

6. Maddening problem areas or typical industry shortcomings that cause the consumer

   • Lack of comfort, unpleasantness, difficulties, delays, awkwardness, additional costs

   • A need to make compromises, sacrifices, non-optimal solutions

   • A damage to be endured in order to obtain the benefit that the product or service offers

   • Dependency on others

   • A need for complementary products or services in order to obtain the benefit

I recommend that you prepare a chart and compare the different competitors, including your own company, using the six perspectives above.

The second part of this exercise, which serves the "What's possible?" stage, consists of looking at the way your industry works at each stage of the consumption process, and of raising questions such as: "How can this be done differently? How can the rules of the game be broken in order to create differentiation?" Do it playfully, not tediously. Challenge yourselves. Compete. Have fun.

A methodical disruption of hidden rules has already yielded many business successes. Take for instance Konopizza pizza chain (*www.konopizza.it*). Renowned Italian chef Rosano Buscolo, founder of the Institute of Culinary Studies Boscolo Etoile, and author of many successful cookbooks, asked why pizza must be flat. The result? Pizza Cornetto—pizzas and Italian snacks served in ice cream-like cones. He developed a special furnace, which enables the cones to remain crisp even after the mozzarella and tomato sauce are bubbling inside it. The matching concept of restaurants, called Konopizza Kiosk, was designed by Marco Fiba. The new hit is already conquering Italy, England, Spain, Greece, New Zealand, Kuwait, and Russia, and the list of countries is growing.

An Intoxicating Story

Another inspiring story is that of Sidney Frank, who made $2 billion in seven years by methodical disruption of implicit competition rules, applying keen psychological insights regarding consumers, and implementing a creative idea, which he also realized with great perseverance. Moreover, this grand achievement started with a mere concept, without any manufacturing facility, product, package, or even a name. Two billion dollars! That's more than IBM got for selling its personal computer division to Lenovo. If all that does not impress you, Frank began this project when he was 77 years old.

It all began in 1996. The American economy was booming. The high-tech craze was generating new millionaires every week. Sophisticated cocktails were hot in the business of alcoholic drinks. Vodka was becoming increasingly popular in the U.S., especially after the collapse of the USSR. In a certain way, drinking frozen vodka constituted a mini-celebration of victory in the Cold War and a subtle expansion of superiority.

The vodka brand leading the premium market was Absolut. It sold for $17 a bottle, double the price of Smirnoff, the bestselling brand in the American market. Two other brands sold for similar prices. Launched in 1992, Skyy Vodka in the stunning blue bottle, relied on a unique brewing process of four refinement rounds and three filtering rounds in order to position itself around a relevant benefit as "The no hangover vodka." It sold for 50 percent more than the market leader. The second launched that year, Dutch Ketel One sold for 200 percent over the market leader's price, boasting a glorious 300-year tradition of "hand-made" spirits and a unique refinement process.

Frank showed interest in the developing vodka market and understood that opportunity lay in the super premium market. He was the first to see that there was a potential super premium category above

Absolut. Let us brush up on our terms: premium sells for 75 to 100 percent above the price of the most popular brand. Super premium is priced 100 to 200 percent above it. Frank understood that in the economic and social atmosphere of the 1990s there were more than a few who would be happy to pay more in order to feel that they had joined in on the "celebration of plenty." He had already walked a long path from his poor childhood in Connecticut and had a lifelong career as a successful marketer of spirits.

Frank knew that in order to lead the super premium market he needed a big story around which he could build his brand. This story needed to stimulate the imagination, to be unforgettable, to be viral, and to support the brand promise. He knew that the super premium category already existed in vodkas. Even though it was a major disruption of the rules of the game, and a pseudo risk, he based his reasoning on the assumption that vodka had already been disconnected from its eastern European roots in the eyes of consumers (as you may remember, Absolut is Swedish and Ketel One is Dutch). The next thing, Frank decided, would be super quality French vodka.

Why French? Well, France is associated more than any other place in the world with high-quality alcoholic beverages and connoisseur refinement in general. Plus, there had never been French vodka. A fantastic off-core differentiation! French vodka? Who would copy *that*? And indeed, nobody did.

How French? The vodka would be produced in the cognac region in France, from pure water from pristine French springs, filtered through champagne limestone and a unique blend of grains.

The concept led to the name Grey Goose. The association to the French *foie gras* was clear. Its bottle featured a flying wild goose and the French flag looked ravishing on the bar. It was priced at 250 percent above Smirnoff because luxury means spending much more than you have to. Outstandingly big 1.75-liter bottles arrived at the bars in impressive wooden chests. One must never underestimate the bartenders' role in creating buzz for an alcoholic beverage. The launching celebration was held at the prestigious Spago restaurant in Beverly Hills. It had its own headline in *The Wall Street Journal*.

You can count on Frank. The brand was marketed at the hottest places in town and spotted in the hands of the hottest celebrities, during the hottest of nights, perfectly frozen. In 1998 Grey Goose was named the best-tasting vodka in the world by the Beverage Testing Institute despite the "negligible" fact that vodka is by definition odorless and tasteless.

One thing led to another, and in one of the episodes of "Sex and the City," characters drank Grey Goose at their leisure. By 1999, Grey Goose was being served in limos carrying Oscar nominees to the big event. In summer 2004, Bacardi & Co. relieved Frank of Grey Goose for a whopping $2.3 billion. OK, so now it's your turn.

10

Still More O-Scan Methods: Identifying Opportunities through Self Analysis and Competition Analysis

Three Strategic Questions

There are three strategic questions that should be poised in the background of your search for opportunities. You do not have to answer them before beginning the O-Scan. You can postpone your final decision until after you can see the opportunities that open before you. But these questions should be in the back of your mind all the time.

1. Are you interested in continuing your existing strategy or are you looking for a new strategy to embrace? You may want to look for a new strategy because you have a problem with the current one or because you feel that you can take a quantum leap and achieve much more. Similarly, are you striving to protect what you already have, your status in the market, or are you going forth with an entrepreneurial approach? I assume you can do both, but which one is dominant?

2. Do you want to base your activities on a small scale or a big scale? Small scale means that you want to find a niche or a geographic area, and are not going after the market as a whole. Big scale means that you want to go for the whole market, i.e., as much as you can take from it. The market could be a local market, the global market, or anywhere in between.

Strategy Creation - Overview

Generative thinking in strategy

Consumer research & data analysis

Sighting inspiring/ benchmark models

Self analysis → Future / potential consumer desires ← Competition analysis

Strategy Creation

Marketing hit short term

Strategic differentiation (long term

Short term branding   Hit development   Long term branding   Forming a business model   Achieving a competitive advantage

I recommend that you develop your strategy while putting your customer at the focus of the whole process. Look at every step of the way from the consumer's point of view, including information gathering, analyses, and also the creative parts that involve brainstorming your strategic alternatives.

3. In your market, in your home court, do you want to lead, to follow, or go sideways? If you want to lead, that means that you want to open a gap between yourself and your competitors and drive the market ahead knowing that sometime, someone might attempt to copy your ways. Following means that you want to go on pre-paved roads, doing things already tried by your competitors, only doing them better, and taking all the market share that you can. Going sideways means that you want to differentiate your brand and offer your customers a unique benefit, and if possible also achieve an unfair advantage. By now, you know my own preferences, but I cannot make such a decision for you.

Three Levels of Searching

In Chapter 8 you encountered two of the methods you can use for reaching insights about consumers. In Chapter 9, you saw that the consumption process is a key for identifying opportunities of various types. In this chapter we will deal with some of the methods that take care of other CCMCU components (the five O-Scan circles: Context, Consumer, Market, Competition, Us).

We will focus on ways to look into our companies and into our markets and competitive environments in order to thoroughly understand "What's now?" and then dive into "What's possible?" Some of the tools I will introduce here relate simultaneously to the two stages. And, although we just moved on to a new chapter and new methods, note that the information and insights you have gathered, using the tools you became familiar with in the previous chapters, will continue to serve you in many of the tasks we will be focusing on here.

The methods described in this chapter appertain to three levels of searching for opportunities:

1. **Challenging the boundaries of your business and market** is done by investigating substitute and complementary categories, suppliers and intermediate customers (such as distribution channels),

all in order to examine your ability to change your category's accepted classifications or framings, and to offer certain consumers new benefits beyond the familiar core benefits they are accustomed to, thus creating an advantage for yourself.

2. **Spotting growth and success opportunities inside the market and within the competitive dynamics** by observing those things that are so obvious that they have become invisible, such as certain deeply entrenched beliefs or unquestioned assumptions. For example, these might pertain to how your market is organized, what it does, and the conventional rules of the game that are followed blindly by all. You may also find some other different insights that enable you to capitalize on changes occurring anyway, or to deliberately break down conventions in a profitable manner.

3. **Unearthing existent but latent opportunities at home (Us),** identifying unobserved assets which can constitute a foundation for future growth and successes, spotting potentials for activation of new business models, and inventing ways to transform weaknesses into strengths.

Challenging Market Boundaries

The purpose of this investigation is to identify potential opportunities in redefining or reframing your business, creating a new concept and applying a new business model, albeit without moving away from what you essentially do today (unless, of course, you are contemplating a new business altogether).

When taking advantage of such an opportunity you create a somewhat new category. This may sound intimidating, but actually it is not. Contrary to what most people think, new categories are formed all the time, and in most cases they do not represent big technological breakthroughs but rather are manifestations of new business concepts or models. Operational leasing is a relatively new category, and so are energy drinks and home gyms.

To identify opportunities of this kind you need to make observations in several directions:

- Substitute categories

- Complementary categories

- Suppliers

- Intermediate customers

- Additional benefits we can offer our customers.

Substitute Categories

First, you should be aware that your competition is made up not only of direct competitors, but may also include substitutes. Substitutes are products and services that deliver similar benefits to customers. For example, every agent offering customers solutions for leisure recreation (especially at home) can be considered as Blockbuster's competitors. Substitute competitors also can be very different from one another. For instance, a bowling alley and a movie theater are substitutes. Contrary to expectations, it is the examination of these not-so-closely related substitutes that usually yields interesting ideas.

An important point: substitutes are only substitutes in the eyes of the consumers. They are alternative choice options that customers come up with. In most cases you will require consumer research in order to be sure of your substitutes. You will discover that groups of substitute categories change from one market segment to another as well as from one consumption context to another.

Analysis of substitute categories is not meant to create a business model which can be placed midway between them. Opportunity identification is based on the following insight: the need to choose between substitutes places consumers in a dilemma, and usually means that some kind of compromise must be made with every possible choice option. Therefore, the opportunity lies in the creation of a new option, which eliminates the need to compromise, while focusing on the factor that has the power to win over the biggest number of consumers.

Take, for example, the dilemma between getting a new car and getting a used car. A new car is almost always in top shape, it comes with a manufacturer's guarantee, and . . . well . . . it's new. But it is also expensive. Buying a used car enables you to buy a better brand and model for the same money. However, you cannot be certain about the car's condition, it has no manufacturer's guarantee, and . . . well . . . you know . . . it's used. Huge used car sale centers such as CarChoice, Autonation, and CarMax created a new category. The customer buys a used car but it has been checked, fixed, renewed and treated, cleaned, its new seat covers wrapped with nylon and . . . it has a guarantee. True, it is more expensive than what used cars cost the traditional way, but with many advantages similar to those you get when you buy a new car. This is the idea.

Sometimes there are simpler solutions. Supermarket chains canceled out the customers' need to decide between conveniently getting a not-so-oven-hot loaf of bread while shopping in the supermarket and making an effort to buy a fresh baked loaf at the bakery. They did this by placing small bakeries inside their stores.

We perform this search using a methodical process for developing business models, which can separate consumer dilemmas of this sort into benefits versus "costs" in reference to each and every alternative. Then it assists the creation of new business models that offer a maximum number of advantages while at the same time minimizing the number of compromises and sacrifices needed.

Complementary Categories

Products and services which complement your own may be in an array of categories beginning with the vital (your product cannot be used or consumed without them, such as batteries for electronic devices) and ending with products and services that are designed to improve, enhance, or enrich the use or consumption (vanilla milk for your coffee, for instance). In this case, as in others, you have to investigate your customers and their behavior. Sometimes you will discover that a completely unexpected product will be perceived by some of your consumers, some of the time, as complementary to yours. For instance, a bed and a condom. Imagine a simple installation to be fastened under the bed, which enables an easy retrieval of condoms when needed.

The obvious inclination that needs to be treated respectfully, but also needs to be surpassed, is the creation of sets or kits, i.e., packaging complementary products together. A business model which creates a new category is usually not a simple "this and that, too," nor is it a case of "horizontal integration" as it is sometimes labeled. Here too the consumer holds the key. Ask yourself whether there are factors of discomfort, inconvenience, delay, potential damage, or other unpleasant implications embodied in your customers' need to use complementary products when they are using yours. What are their resulting dilemmas? This new concept, which makes up your opportunity, will be designed to ultimately eliminate that unnecessary negative implication. In some cases, the new concept will cancel out the need to use a complementary product, just as MP3s did to the Discman/CD combo.

In 2001 Whirlpool created a sensation in the American market. Chief designer Chuck Jones designed a matching duo of washing machine and dryer in a stylish appearance, with a door shaped like a porthole, and available in several attractive colors. They named it Duet. "It's like having a Ferrari in your laundry room," Jones told journalists. Are these two complementary products, designed as twins, worth more than the sum of the two of them separately? Let the facts speak for themselves. The price of the Duet set starts at $2,000. That's very expensive for laundry equipment in the United States. And what happened? Whirlpool went all the way from 0 percent market share to 20 percent market share. That then-outmoded company, founded in 1911, which looked not even a day younger than its age, turned itself into a smashing success within just a few weeks.

Suppliers and Intermediate Customers

Here, I am not referring to simple vertical integrations (i.e., doing yourself what your supplier or intermediate customer does for you today), but rather I am talking about spotting opportunities for creating new categories, that somehow alter the chain. Let us look at two interesting examples.

A company in Wisconsin, called Super Fast Pizza, found a way to deliver phone orders in 15 minutes or less (and to think that in 1993 Domino's Pizza called off its 30-minutes-or-less delivery promise to customers after a terrible accident in which one of its pizza delivery messengers was involved). The key? Vans equipped with high-tech ovens enabling on-the-road baking of pizzas.

Another example: a new category is quickly expanding in the American market and already showing signs of expansion worldwide. Dream Dinners already has more than 50 stores in 14 states in America. Dinner Helpers and Let's Dish are not far behind. These are well-equipped and sophisticated kitchens where customers can prepare a supply of meals for their families. The service includes grocery shopping according to customers' orders and cleaning up afterwards. Customers go there only to cook.

This new category eliminates several steps in the value chain (the marketing of food products, and some consumption stages as well). However, it also eliminates a customers' dilemma between substitute options (eating home-cooked meals, with all the mess involved, or going out to a restaurant).

You may say that my examples fall into more than one category. That's true. What does it mean? It means that you could reach the concept in more than one way. Not bad!

Please understand: these are not theoretical classifications of strategy innovations, but rather practical ways for finding opportunities. If there are opportunities out there that are reachable in more than one way, then why not?

Additional Benefits We Can Offer

Remember that within the framework of our thorough treatment of the consumption process in the previous chapter, we dealt with thinking of benefits that are, as yet, uncommon in your category and which you can add to your product to make it more attractive. But let's rethink this issue one more time, from a different perspective. Additional benefits are, of course, off-core, added to the core benefits of the category in which you operate (which are essential but not differentiating).

Such benefits may be functional, meaning that you offer a supplementary benefit that will make your customers rejoice, on top of the benefits they usually get by consuming your product. They are not accustomed to getting the additional benefit; therefore, they do not expect it from your product. This is what made all the energy drinks and especially Red Bull, the category opener, so popular. People did not expect to get an energy boost from a refreshing drink. Essentially, this fits the case of all functional food categories (i.e., foods designed to offer a unique contribution of health and other factors, rather than simply being delicious and wholesome).

Let's look at Red Bull more closely. While traveling to the Far East, Austrian Dietrich Mateschitz encountered a caffeine-rich drink used by Thai workmen for energy. It was called Krating Daeng (Red Bull). Mateschitz envisioned a different and much wealthier target of Western, workaholic, career-intoxicated, and overworked drinkers. It didn't really catch on. Later he discovered another target group of young clubbers who love their cocktail of liberating vodka, enhanced with a boost of energy, which enables them to perform better during their sweet lapse of uninhibited exuberance. At this point Red Bull evolved into a mixer that does something more than just make the alcohol tastier—it also wakes you up and gives you energy. Thus Red Bull became a hit.

Another example. Xplory is the first stroller by Stokke, a Norwegian furniture company. Someone had the insight that strollers had not been reengineered for a long time. Furthermore, they are uncomfortable and hard to handle in today's urban areas. Cooperating with K8, a design firm from Oslo, they developed a stroller with a completely new outlook (*www.stokkeusa.com/xplory*).The baby sits aloft, closer to the parent than to car exhausts, a situation that responds to current parenting trends and attitudes towards babies (and also favors the back of the not-so-young parent when lifting the baby up). The carriage takes up less space and does not create a problem in crowded elevators. The back wheels are collapsible, which makes stair climbing easier. The baby can sit either facing the parent or watching the view. When having coffee at a cafe, the chair is at the table's level without the carriage becoming a public nuisance.

Beautiful! You always have to ask if the time has not come to let go of all conventions and redesign your product to bring it up-to-date. However, this high-tech carriage costs $749 while the conventional one costs only $100. Do not look for the reason in the cost of material, nor in the sophisticated engineering and production. The Xplory was made especially for those happy fathers (yes, they make up the majority client group) as a toy and also as a way to signal to their surroundings. "Hey, my baby deserves the best and, yes, I have no problem funding it." Let's do the arithmetic. The buyer pays, say, $249 for the sophisticated carriage, an additional $200 for the amazing eye-pleasing design, $200 more for the gadget satisfaction factor, and an extra $100 for the show and pretension. Not a bad deal after all. I recommend that you use this logic every time you consider pricing issues.

The Xplory is a great success. During the first 9 weeks, the company sold more than it had planned to sell in 6 months. You can get the Xplory in 23 chain stores in America. The company insisted that all salespeople undergo special training. They know that a customer who spends $749 on a stroller needs to have a lot of explanations, both for himself and inquisitive friends.

Spotting Opportunities Within the Market

The O-Scan methodology is comprised of many methods that help you understand what really happens in your market and in the competitive dynamics of which you are a part. It also helps you find the resulting opportunities long before your competitors spot them. Some of these are opportunities to achieve an unfair advantage.

I want to brief you on ten searching angles we use to perform our methodical research, and then to describe two workshop exercises we often use in this stage.

10 Searching Angles

1. List the 5 to 7 major considerations or choice criteria (whether conscious or not) that guide buying decisions of consumers in your category. If you don't know them yet, use consumer research to find them out. Then draw a table and analyze how the various brands in your market are positioned vis-à-vis each of them (to what extent is every brand perceived as capable of satisfying each criteria). You will find out that in most cases each brand has its stronger points, or promises. By doing this analysis you will understand how your market is constructed in terms of various brand positions. Now look for deficiencies in the market. Surprisingly, sometimes it works. For instance, does your market have a high end, a low end, and a middle ground, quality and price-wise? Sometimes interesting opportunities lie therein. If one end is missing, you can find your opportunity by creating it. By the way, in pointing out the various ends, I am not referring only to price, quality, or prestige. I am referring to each and every one of the relevant positioning axes which exist in your market and which (and you will read more about it in the next chapter) guide the buying decisions. The axes are no other then the consumers' choice criteria, explicit or implicit. So, for instance, if "sportiveness" is a consideration (in cars, watches, fashion , and so forth), then there is a full axis of sportiveness which includes high and low ends and a middle ground.

2. If you have used traditional customer segmentations or classifications of products, I suggest that you look into alternatives. For example, the contextual segmentation method may help in this case. Or you may be able to use alternative classifications to create an advantage. If you are marketers of a shampoo brand, and everybody classifies shampoos by degree of oiliness of the hair or by its level of curliness, maybe you should consider alternative options such as hair scenting, strength of scent, or type of scent (as a major benefit), or a product for use before or after a sports activity.

3. **Think about your prospects**—those who are not buyers in your category today, but could be one day if . . . *something*. Even if at first glance it seems like this something cannot be achieved, do not just give up. Maybe something similar or a substitute can be done. Microsoft markets a simpler and cheaper version of *Office* in areas around the world where the standard *Office* is far too expensive. It could also develop an age-adapted version for older users who are much less computer-literate and more internet-phobic than younger users.

4. **Look for customers who do not interest your competitors because they are not profitable enough.** In many cases, implementation of a different business model will render them attractive after all. People who are not so rich, who never invested in the stock market before, did not generate profits for brokers until Charles Schwab showed up and created a system for handling and servicing the small investor.

   ICICI Bank, India's second-largest bank and its largest private bank, recognized that poor people are bankable, and that microfinance is a new, profitable opportunity. The bank approves loans as small as $100 at places such as bank branches and ATMs located every six miles across India, including areas where most of the households lack access to essential banking services. ICICI earns a healthy profit from rural lending and says the default rate on those loans is less than a half percent.

5. **Look for missed opportunities to sell.** Survey various contexts of consumer lifestyles (actual, not stereotypical) and ask whether there are additional places or situations in which consumers will benefit by buying or consuming your product. On the primary level, opportunities like these will enable you to improve your distribution and sales; however, down the road you could discover new opportunities to develop different product versions or benefit bundling and capitalize on them.

6. **Continuing this same line of thought, try to find customers who are "underconsumers,"** meaning that they could benefit from

increased consumption of your product. In the insurance category, for instance, the term "under-insured" is common. Do not
choose the automatic solution and try to give extra incentives.
Instead, put your finger on the reasons for under-consumption,
and provide a real solution to the problem.

7. **Up market.** If your category accommodates a low-end brand for
the mass market, which has no premium version, try to develop
a premium one that offers additional benefits.

8. **If your category accommodates a premium brand but has no
low-end, look into offering such a brand.** This way of thinking
revolutionized the cosmetic surgery market, among others.

9. **Maybe you can offer solutions for consumers trading up or
trading down.** Trading up means buying more expensively than
their usual standard. There are many customers who trade up
in certain categories, circumstances, situations, or events. Since
they can't trade up on a regular basis, they need classic products
rather than fashionable ones that are hot today but out-dated
tomorrow. Polo Ralph Lauren is an example: not a changing
fashion but a classic appearance. Trading down means buying
under their usual standard. These could be wealthy customers
who want to or good bargains without feeling degraded, or they
could be looking for an "exotic" experience. Are there any of
those in your market? See what you can do for them.

10. **Most importantly, make sure that what you sell is what they
buy or want to buy.** In many cases you will discover that your
consumers' perceptions of your product differ from yours. You
might find that the unit you and your competitors sell is convenient for you, but the customer really needs something else.
Cemex, a Mexican manufacturer and distributor of cement,
found that while everybody was selling cement by the ton and
competing on price, what construction firms really needed was
precision in delivery times. Cement is a perishable product. If it

does not arrive "fresh" and ready to use exactly when needed, it might be cheap but useless. Construction projects do not always stand up to pre-planned schedules; therefore flexibility to supply on need is worth a higher price. Following this insight, Cemex built a sophisticated system that enabled it to provide what the client really needed. Today it is the third biggest company in the world in its category.

Asking the right questions means advancing towards a solution. However, I believe that before asking questions and plunging into deliberations and discussions, it is preferable to engage in some exercises which open the mind to creative options that are unlikely to surface otherwise.

Following are two of the exercises by which we proceed in this stage.

Exercise 1: Create an imaginary killer competitor

This exercise is great practice in workshops conducted with senior management as well as sales people. The mission is to establish a competing company or create a competing product or service designed specifically to bust your business. Participants need to consider each and every aspect when creating this adversarial company or product. How will it be organized, who are the customers at its focus, what will it offer them, what are the pricing aspects, how will it sell, how will it advertise, and so on? It is essential that participants in this exercise free themselves of their feelings of loyalty, which may interrupt this task. It helps to set up groups to compete against each other in creating the perfect killer competitor. A moderator who thinks like a competitor may also prove beneficial (one of the big advantages of an external consultant).

Benefits from this exercise can be astounding. Within a few hours you can identify all your weaknesses as well as some opportunities existing in the market that you have never acknowledged before.

After lunch and a break, this exercise continues. Now your people need to go back to who they are and plan their defense against that killer competitor they invented in the morning.

Exercise 2: Create a new player, with no inhibitions and no history

This exercise is fit for higher-rank positions in the marketing scheme. In most cases, we are referring to headquarters personnel. The mission is to think like a new competitor who is planning on entering your market and grabbing major volume. That new player, relieved of history, gentlemanly agreements, and market conventions, has no inhibitions. It is ready to do whatever it takes, nothing excluded, in order to penetrate and succeed. Participants in this exercise, in competing teams, should plan every single aspect of their activity. What will it do? How? When? Where?

Benefits from this exercise are different than those of the previous one. Here the focus is not on competing but rather on fresh thinking about your market.

Spotting Latent Opportunities In-House

The third level of searching for opportunities focuses internally. In this level you find opportunities in your own infrastructure, such as your existing assets and capabilities. Some of the questions we usually ask at this stage are:

- Can we use our existing infrastructure and capabilities as leverage for creating a new business using a new business model?

- How do we take "things we know how to make or do (such as technology) but do not know what they're good for" and turn them into sources of profits?

- How do we take "inevitable facts"—things you cannot possibly change or things your customers know about you (actual or mythical) that determine their perception and vision about you—and turn them into advantages? How do we take a perceived minus and turn it into a perceived plus?

- How do we take temporary advantages and transform them into long-term perceived advantages?

- Do we make compromises in order to sell to certain customers? If we gave them up could we sell to many more or to potentially more profitable prospects?

- What are the areas where a minimal effort or a minute alteration can bring about the highest output? What are those minimal efforts or minute alterations necessary for that?

Workshop exercises such as the three that follow make up some of the tools we use in order to answer these questions.

Exercise 1: A new business using the same foundations

Some of our workshop exercises have "warm-up" drills designed to invigorate, stimulate, and activate the kind of thinking necessary for conducting the later exercises successfully. Even this effective exercise needs its own warm-up. This is the story: you have a blooming and profitable business in the red-light district in Amsterdam. One day, the Dutch government is replaced, and the new government is conservative. They decide to make prostitution illegal in Holland. You're stuck. You have great talented employees who have signed long-term contracts. Your shops are equipped, and now you need to use all these and transform your business. Getting rid of them is not an option. What will your new business be?

After you have some good fun with this warm-up, you will move on to the real thing. The story is as follows: for some obscure reason you must stop all actions in your current line of business. Your mission is to create a business model in a new area, which will be able to take advantage of as much of the existing infrastructure, resources, and capabilities as it possibly can.

Exercise 2: A new angle on your problems and weaknesses

This insightful exercise is simple yet it leads you to fascinating realizations. It begins with a routine serious discussion. On the agenda is one of the following questions:

1. What are the central problems we face today?

2. What are our major weaknesses?

At the first stage, the moderator collects various views, opens a discussion, and leads the group to the creation of a short list that includes 2 or 3 problems or weaknesses. At stage 2, the "skeptical" moderator asks, referring to each item on the list, "How do we know that this is in fact a problem or a weakness? How, when, and where do we tackle it as such? What are the symptoms? How does the problem or weakness manifest in reality?"

Finally, in stage 3, the moderator writes on a board all the phenomena found in the second stage as the indicators of the problems or weaknesses (they are dealt with one after the other). Then the moderator challenges the participants with a suggestion: "Let us say that your explanations for these evident phenomena are not the problems or weaknesses you assumed at the beginning of this exercise. What other explanations could there be?"

Exercise 3: Freeing ourselves from our typical train of thought

This exercise is simple too. In order to be free of the limitations caused by the common prevalent perceptions in the organization, as well as to liberate thinking from typical restraining paradigms, the participants are asked to think about problems needing solutions, about initiatives, about ideas for marketing innovations, and so forth as if they were someone else who could be regarded as a worthy model. The possibilities abound—business people like Richard Branson; managers like Jack Welch; imaginary characters like Jack Bower (24); firms like Apple, Disney, Nordstrom; organizations like the Mafia, the Samurais, and so forth. The goal is to think like someone who might know how to solve the problem, or find the right idea, or inspire the right spirit.

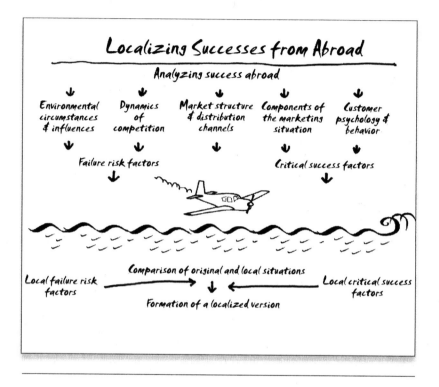

If you ever see successful models in other places around the world and you would like to implement them with your own company and products, do not forget to localize them appropriately. The localization process begins with understanding exactly what went right in the original case, and what could have caused model failure. Then check whether or not these factors exist in your local market, and also whether there are any additional local factors you need to consider. On the basis of all of the above, create your localized version.

part 3

More tools for managers compelled to
"think outside the box": innovative approaches
and methods in marketing and branding

11

Insider Information from the Consumer's Mind

The Consumer Test

As I have already told you, the ultimate test of your strategy is the consumer test. Will he or she do (or not do) what you intend? The consequence is clear: success or failure. Your strategy is realized (or not) through your consumers' behavior. You identified an opportunity, created your competitive strategy in order to realize this opportunity and actually achieve your competitive advantage, and you articulated a profitable business model. These cover two out of three angles of the Unique Success Formula triangle.

The third angle of the unique success formula triangle is the branding aspect, i.e., the attractiveness that all this holds for your target customers. Your brand constitutes the contact point where your strategy meets your consumer. Essentially, your brand is your strategy facing your consumer. Without attractiveness you will not get motivation. There is no behavior where there is no motivation. Without that behavior, your strategy is worthless. Hence you can see how important it is that you understand what motivates and what throttles the behavior you are seeking.

In this chapter I will lay some foundations for a shared understanding of the consumer. This chapter is not a simple read, but there are some important key insights in it. In the chapters that follow I will add more insights and illuminations. This type of understanding is very different than the ones MBA clones operate by. First, it is more updated, absolutely contemporary (usually new and innovative psycho-logical insights take years to be integrated into the MBA curriculum). Furthermore, it is an integrated and workable model. Meanwhile, your competitors will still be trying to somehow find coherence in the huge jumble of models and theories they've had to memorize in school.

The Gut and the Head

A consumer will experience a gut response to well-built brands almost instantaneously. In all cases, consumers are not even aware of the swift cognitive processes, lasting less than a second, in which their brains decipher the brand promise, distill the benefit therein, and form a belief which credits the brand as the source of this benefit. The spontane-ous emotional response to a brand, experienced consciously by the consumer, is but the end of a whole cognitive process, which is way too fast for the consumer to be aware of it. Awareness pertains only to the resulting emotional response. A consumer can "be hot" for a brand without even knowing why.

In most cases this process can take place gradually. The consumer is exposed to a promise of a benefit made by a certain brand under various circumstances. Between TV commercials, street posters, the web, word-of-mouth, newspaper items, testing the product at a friend's house, or going through catalogs, "suddenly" he or she kindles a liking for the product, without having the slightest awareness of all those previous instances in which his or her brain processed the brand's promise.

You are probably familiar with branding "experts" who make this mistake: if the consumer responds immediately, spontaneously, and emotionally then it means that the purpose of branding is simply to arouse feelings. The fact that consumers are unaware of their inner processing is inevitable, but experts cannot be so naïve. An expert who proclaims an ability to influence the consumer's response must understand the underlying processes thoroughly. The expert must be sophisticated enough to know what the consumer does and why.

Therefore, we must consult with the discipline of psychology. Soon enough you are bound to understand that branding is a methodical influence on the creation of beliefs in the consumer's mind. These beliefs pertain to a brand's "instrumentality," meaning the degree to which it enables consumers to achieve, do, or be what they want. Consumers create beliefs about brands to help them decide what to buy. We generously aid their decision-making by way of supporting the creation of those beliefs in order to help them choose our product.

Unsatisfied but Driven

One of the most important thinkers about motivation, Abraham Maslow, once said that "man is a perpetually wanting animal." In his eyes, this is the main characteristic that typifies our lives as human beings. We want to accumulate stuff, to create certain circumstances in our lives, to reach achievements, or to avoid damages and unpleasant situations. We always want something, usually more than one thing. We expect that if we get it, if we achieve it, if we reach it, if we succeed, then something good will happen to us. This good something is always accompanied by positive emotions or pleasant sensations, which are also good. In the context of marketing we often refer to these positive outcomes as "benefits;" in current psychology they are frequently termed "goals" and in popular psychology, "motivations." In this book I generally use these terms interchangeably. However it might be more precise to say that as long as they are unattained, these good things are goals or motivations and once they are attained they are benefits.

The basic things we want out of life are partially dictated by our physiology. Our body demands satisfaction of thirst or hunger, and it's never too soon; our body likes to avoid pain (or stop it), not to feel suffocation, and to live in optimal temperature, pressure, and stimulation conditions. Our body wants pleasant sensations: sights, scents, flavors, sounds, touch. Our body wants erotic pleasures. At a less basic level we look for security, love, and a sense of importance. Other things we want are influenced by the society and culture to which we are born, in which we are educated and raised, and with which we interact, led by our own private personalities.

What Are We Trying to Do?

Behind every product and brand we desire, behind every desire we feel, hides a benefit towards which we are striving. Take Guy. He is a brilliant, 26-year-old lawyer, specializing in business law, taking his first steps in the legal profession, but marked for greatness by the elite law firm for which he works. He fantasizes about the not-so-distant moment in which he will be able to buy himself a shining silver Smart Roadster Brabus Xclusive, which costs a little over 26,000 euro in Western Europe. Why? Because he is at the beginning of a get-rich-young trip, because it is *the* one car that matches the picture he envisions in his mind. It is classy, sophisticated, sexy, totally not "square" (this is so critical), and swift like the devil himself. Plus, it will look amazing in the parking lot under the office building in which he works every day as well as parked at the club next to his friends' vehicles. It will deliver the right feeling for him, a confirmation that he is okay, moving towards the right place at the right pace. It will be wonderfully integrated into his lifestyle. It will convey the right message to the world around him. Okay, it is not a Mercedes-Benz Brabus SLR McLaren that costs 435,000 euro, but hey, he's still young.

All our lives we strive to realize our goals and in this way, we try to attain benefits. That results in positive emotions and pleasant sensations. Striving for benefits is something that we do perpetually. What allows us to do it are "instruments" for attaining benefits. The "instrumentality" of brands means their ability to serve as instruments (or means) for reaching benefits.

We can divide all benefits that humans seek into five major types:

- experiential-sensual

- experiential-emotional

- psychological

- interpersonal

- social

As marketers, what type of "instruments" can we offer our consumers?

Experiential benefits (sensual and emotional) lead us directly to pleasant physical sensations (experiential-sensual) and positive emotions (experiential-emotional). When we strive to reach such experiences, what do we do? We pleasure our senses (for instance by listening to our favorite music) and our senses go on to please the pleasure zones in our brain. Or we manipulate our emotions with, for instance, a comedy or a soap.

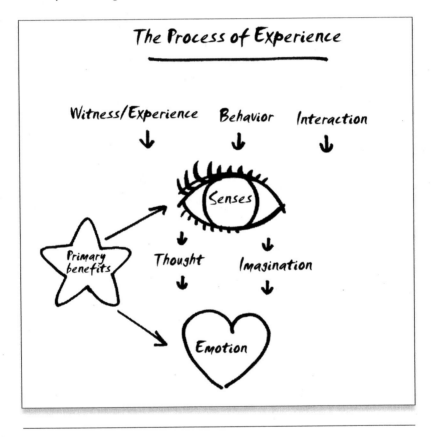

The things that happen to us, the things we witness or experience, our behavior and its outcome, and our interaction with others are all sensory inputs reaching our mental system. Two major processing mechanisms in our mental system govern data management. Imagination handles the processing of the tangible data (like sensory input or sensory-like information, internally sourced), and thought handles the processing of abstract items, ideas, symbols, numbers, and so forth. If personal relevance exists, emotional arousal follows processing. What happens ultimately is that we "extract" benefits either on the sensual level (pleasant feelings), or on the emotional level (positive emotions).

Psychological benefits are reached within the context of self-to-self relationships. They are about the way we feel about ourselves, the way we manage ourselves amidst circumstances and contexts of this world. Psychological benefits eventually lead us to positive feelings. The following are a few examples to help you understand exactly what consumers (and yes, you too) do when seeking psychological benefits. Our customers are trying to:

- Understand the world around them, find their way in it

- Assign personal significance to events, places, dates, and so forth

- Be in control, free, autonomous and independent

- Exhibit capability, resourcefulness, and proficiency, to attain achievements

- Influence, to leave a mark

- Defeat or to win

- Get even

- Relax, unwind from stress

- Change mood

- Refresh or restore themselves

- Feel alive and active

- Encourage themselves, arouse optimism

- Find motivation to perform challenging or difficult tasks

- Protect themselves and exhibit durability and vigor

- Strengthen their individuality and uniqueness

- Create and establish a self-image and a sense of identity
- Design a consistent and stable world image
- Uphold certain interpretations about reality
- Reward themselves, strengthen their sense of value and importance
- Achieve and sustain a sense of purpose and meaning
- Take care of themselves or pamper themselves
- Develop themselves
- Compensate themselves
- Build up self confidence, to win self legitimacy
- Build, create, experience ownership
- Escape reality, get away, take a break
- Live fantasy experiences unavailable in their reality

Interpersonal benefits are attained within the context of relationships, not on the abstract social level, but rather one-on-one, in one's personal and private life. We are referring here to relationships of all kinds. Interpersonal benefits lead to pleasant emotions and sensual gratification. Consumers are attempting to do things like:

- Create attractiveness, to attract or to seduce
- Make someone feel special, bestow a special value and attribute status to them
- Express feelings (love, respect, thankfulness)
- Experience intimacy
- Create an atmosphere, arouse emotions, manage closeness
- Create mutual experiences, meanings, rituals
- Create alliances, partnerships, togetherness, commitments
- Sponsor, care for one another
- Influence, control, educate, or change

- Pay back (good or bad)

- Celebrate, to mark special occasions and events

Social benefits exist in the wider realm of surrounding social contexts, such as cultural and group-oriented ones. Social benefits place us within our social fabric. They are positive results of our way of functioning and acting within our social realm.

- Social benefits also lead to pleasant emotions. Consumers are trying to attain, sustain, or exhibit:

- Personal traits (conscientiousness, bitchiness, etc.)

- Affiliation to certain identities (yuppiness)

- Affiliation to ethnic or other socially defined groups

- A social role (parenthood) or an organizational role (CEO)

- Membership in a social-economic class.

- Sophistication, refinement, "connoisseurship," style

- Tastes and personal preferences

- Values, stances, ideologies

- Continuity, consistency

- Being up-to-date, involved, participating

- Mark shared meanings such as symbols, significant dates, and ceremonies

- Mark passages between different life phases (rites of passage)

- "Do the right thing," obey convention

Very often people do all these things by means of buying products and services, and choosing certain brands. As marketers we design our products, services and brands to be effective instruments for consumers to use in attaining their goals and benefits. This is our *raison d'être*. We must never forget this. Sometimes the instrument we offer our customers is in the function of our product or service, but as we will see in Chapter 13, sometimes the major benefit offered by our brand goes beyond that function. I know you have heard this before. However, I suspect no one has ever explained to you exactly how this works and how is can be achieved. I assure you that after Chapter 13 you will be much more knowledgeable in this respect.

Brands Deliver Benefits

Purchasing products, using, or owning them serves consumers in several ways.

There are purchases of *"infrastructural" products and services* that *promise a steady, long-term delivery of benefits* to the consumer. Purchases that have to do with shaping consumers' environments: a house, a car, an office, or a yacht, fit into this category. If you bought a home entertainment center lately, what you really bought was a steady delivery of benefits. Purchases relevant to identity definition, time management and lifestyle (regular activities, areas of interest, and occupation) are also of this nature. If you began playing golf, you just got certain steady benefits. Purchases linked to creative activities and establishment and management of relationships of various types also belong here. Married? Well, now hopefully you've got benefits for good!

Purchases of a *"strategic" nature* are *purposed to create a point of change or a turn of events.* Did you get an academic degree to advance your career or accomplish a career change? You just changed your life and opened a way to new benefits. Did you enlarge your breasts or have a hair transplant? You've just achieved a kind of turn, which will eventually bring about a wave of new benefits.

Most purchases, however, are of a more *immediate and ephemeral* nature. They provide *local and timely benefits.*

I find it difficult to think of many human benefits that are "uni-satisfied," meaning that once you've achieved your goal, you will be satisfied forever, exempt from having to achieve it again. Most human benefits—lucky for us as marketers—are "multi–satisfied," regenerating goals, meaning that we feel the need to attain more of the same benefit, again and again, often in new ways.

There are also unsatisfiable benefits, like eternal youth. Don't believe for a second that benefits of this nature are void of business value. Human beings are not ready to give up on benefits just because of the very minor fact that they are unattainable or unsatisfiable. Consumers are ready and willing to furnish themselves with benefits in fantasy too. We will discuss this again, in Chapters 14 and 15.

Abstract Goals, Specific Satisfactions

The major things we want in life, whether they are called benefits or goals, are general or abstract. Their satisfactions, on the other hand, are very specific. Our body wants to get rid of that headache. It doesn't care how. Our need for love comes before our need of specific love partners. We name these basic conditions not desires or wants but impulses, needs, benefits, motivations, and goals. Personally I prefer to use the latter three. The terms "desires" and "wants" are reserved for solutions, realizations, and specific satisfactions—namely products or services and their brands.

Out of our myriad goals, or the benefits we seek in life, only a few are active at any given time. They become active in several ways. Perhaps we've reached a stage in life in which certain goals become pertinent or come naturally. Perhaps certain circumstances awoke them, a film we saw, a friend's story, or even a commercial. On the other hand, it could be that we encountered an opportunity to realize a certain goal. For instance, maybe the smell of steak sizzling on a grill in a nearby restaurant aroused a need and we fulfilled it with an impulsive buy.

But how do we know what we should desire? How do we know what will deliver our craved benefits and realize our goals? How do we know what will serve us as a good instrument? Here is where we put our beliefs to use, including those pertaining to brands. When a consumer seeks a certain benefit (getting attention, arousing interest), and believes that a certain brand (a futuristic cell phone by Nokia) can be a good instrument to attain this benefit, then he or she can actually imagine having that benefit, sometimes even subconsciously, or semi-consciously, and thus an expectation is formed. This expectation creates a will to buy the product. This want, or desire, ignites the inclination to act. Notice that it is the very same expectation experienced by our customer and directed at a certain source which constitutes the essence of a brand. *A brand is an expectation or anticipation consumers feel for a specific benefit that will be derived from a company, product, or service.*

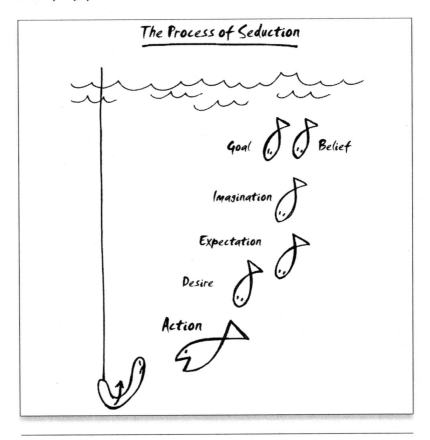

Our desire to behave in a certain manner (for example, to purchase a certain brand) begins with our awareness of a goal or benefit that we seek, and which will be realized through the action. A belief is needed in order to persuade us that this certain action will allow us to attain the benefit. The combination of these two will enable us to envision what it will be like when we attain the benefit. Our imagination will ignite us with expectation, which, in its turn, awakens our desire, the leader of our behavior.

How Are Beliefs Formed?

There are only two ways in which beliefs are formed. The first way is by collecting personal experiences. You have experienced benefits generated from a certain brand, and as a result you have formed a belief. For example, imagine your back is in a lot of pain. You go to a Chinese acupuncturist and he performs his magic on you. Lo and behold, your pain instantly disappears. You form a belief that this specific healer (or perhaps Chinese healers in general), knows how to ease a backache. Not a big surprise. Both founded beliefs and superstitions are formed in similar ways.

The second way you form beliefs is through imagination. It seems that the human mind attributes almost the same experiential value to actual experiences and to imaginary ones. It may sound unlikely, but I assure you that it is absolutely true. There are numerous implications to this, in various life contexts. If you are able to imagine yourself performing a certain behavior or deed (what we call a mental rehearsal), then you can also do it in reality. Psychotherapists who cure phobias, blocks, and inhibitions of various types know this. Coaches know this. If it happens in your imagination, it is already half way towards happening in reality. This way we embrace beliefs about products and brands. We see how they provide us with benefits in our imagination and we believe that benefit will come our way in reality, at least until experience teaches us differently.

How do we see the product or brand deliver benefits in our imagination? There are several ways. Perhaps we identify with someone we know who has already benefited, or we see a TV or web commercial (whether a testimonial or story plot). It could be by following a real life story we encountered about someone who tried it, by an example we saw or by a metaphor which demonstrates how the benefit is achieved, by understanding or internalizing a certain explanation we just heard about the product, or by following a feeling of trust we have in someone (like an authority figure or a friend) who confirms that it works.

If you think that I have not dedicated enough space for processes such as studying facts or understanding explanations, let me reassure you. I have dedicated more than enough. Our mental activity, our understanding, our way of thinking, all constitute merely an introduction to the ways by which we can see any benefit in our imagination. When we feel a need to overcome doubt and maybe even fear, our mental conviction provides us with all we need in order to envision these benefits in our minds and embrace the relevant belief.

And Now, Give it More FEEEEELING

How do emotions fit into this description? And moreover, how do consumers develop an emotional attitude towards brands?

As soon as the benefit is envisioned, emotions awaken. These are not yet actual emotions towards a brand, yet they are feelings that have weight in the process of creating beliefs regarding a specific brand. Once we desire the brand, we've already developed emotions towards it. In order to understand what exactly stimulates them, we must first understand more about the nature of our emotions.

Our emotions can be either positive or negative—never neutral. Our positive emotions include, love, joy, happiness, excitement, pride, satisfaction, and more. Note that there is something that all positive emotions have in common. Positive emotions awaken in response to anything (real, potential, or even fantasized) that brings us closer to reaching our goals in life. They are always about just that.

Now make a sharp turn and think about negative emotions, like anger, frustration, disappointment, disgust, and hatred. These emotions awaken in response to anything that takes us farther away from reaching our goals in life.

That is the secret. Our emotions are not as haphazard as it may seem sometimes. They also do not constitute an independent system that is detached from our cognitive system. Our emotions are inner signals which blink whenever something or someone appears to bring us closer to, or take us farther from, what we need or want.

Since positive emotions are pleasant, and negative emotions are not, our emotions are simple motivators of our actions. Positive and pleasant emotions encourage us to act in a way which will ensure the "steady delivery" of more of the same, from the same source, while negative, unpleasant feelings encourage us to get away from their perceived source. In reality this picture is more complex, but for our purposes here, this is the basis for understanding emotions, including emotions towards brands. An emotion towards a brand awakens following a belief that the brand is an instrument by which we can obtain its benefit—it brings us closer to something we want. A feeling does not just "glue" itself to a brand because we watch an "emotional" ad.

When Steve Jobs, CEO of Apple, wants to sustain and inflame strong positive emotions consumers feel towards his brand, he knows what to do. He develops and markets products which are a celebration of beauty, a wow! for the soul, and a true offer of performance levels which are no less than spectacular, in ways which "do it" for his consumers. The iPod holds up to 20,000 songs, up to 25,000 photos, and up to 100 hours of video—or any combination of those! As I write these words, it is still one heck of an amazing feat. Apple products "do it" for consumers, not for the research and development staff, as happens too often at Microsoft. The benefits Apple chooses to offer its customers, and its way of offering them (which embody the Apple brand strategy as well as the firm's competitive strategy), are managed by Apple in such a way that the firm knocks out competitors completely, rather than just gaining a few extra points of advantage.

There are two things consumers respond to strongly in brands: when they offer a way to achieve a meaningful and not-so-simple-to-acquire benefit, and when they have a formidable achievement. It can be in any area. In products such as Apple's or in service levels such as Nordstrom's; in tangible benefits, or intangible ones (experiential-emotional, psychological, interpersonal, or social). This is how any brand can compel its consumers to develop strong emotions towards it.

From Belief to Choice

Beliefs that we form about brands help us make brand choices. How does it work? Let us assume that you've gotten a promotion and now you are a senior manager. The CEO's secretary hints to you in her typical subtle and witty manner, "I hope now you'll start to dress better." Suddenly you have an active goal, a benefit you are seeking. It is important for you to feel that you belong to that group of senior managers, to be accepted and also to prove to yourself and the rest of the world that you've achieved something in your life. How do you do that? She gave you a hint. So, you go out and shop for a senior manager's suit.

Your newly active goal dictates your considerations in the buying process. You'll choose a shop where you can buy clothes fit for a senior manager. Consumers' active goals, those sought-after benefits of the moment, create the context for all the rest, though not always consciously. They dictate the relevant considerations and choice criteria. Consumers use several considerations each time they buy something. Considerations such as, "How sporty is this watch?" stem from the active goal of "sex appeal" and from pre-set beliefs about ways to attain the goals or benefits (sporty = masculine = sex appeal). The considerations direct a search for facts signaling possible satisfactions of the choice criteria.

But how will you know which shopping center to go to, which shops to enter, what suits to choose? Here your beliefs lead the way. You go to a shopping center where you know there is a big enough selection of men's clothing shops. You enter only those shops that connect, in your mind, to this style of clothing. You choose according to your beliefs regarding the features of a business suit, a business tie, and so on. Your beliefs, in many cases, are connected to specific brands.

Now perhaps you already understand better why I say that building a brand equals shaping a consumer's belief. It is a belief that is supposed to serve the customers during their process of buying. It is supposed to arouse within them an emotional reaction towards that brand since it takes them closer to winning a wanted benefit, or to attaining a wanted goal. This is an anticipation-creating belief, and that anticipation is the brand.

Impulsive Beliefs

I guess you can see with no difficulty how beliefs work in a planned purchase. But what happens when the purchase is not planned, but rather spontaneous or impulsive? In such cases, is there still that strong significance to pre-existing beliefs about brands? You may be surprised, but in these cases, the significance of such beliefs about brands is even more crucial, even though there are cases where these beliefs are formed at the point of purchase and not before.

Let us say that you bought the business suit we were discussing earlier, plus a few ties, shirts, some socks, and a pair of shoes or two. In short, you really got carried away. You made some impulsive purchases. You had not planned to get those shoes, but you passed a shop that carried a brand of shoes you've noticed before and you already have in mind that unmistakable achievers wear them. You want to be one too! And you're swimming deep in that notion. You can almost envision yourself in one of those ads! It's part of your new look, an exact fit. No doubt about it. So you took it all.

Then, heavy with bags, you walk through that mall fantasizing happily about your new future when suddenly you detect the fine teasing scent of good coffee, coming from an espresso bar. You already know that coffee chain. You remember the taste of that coffee, the familiar sensation of sitting up on the high stools. You go straight after your nose, buying impulsively again but guided by your pre-existing brand beliefs that arouse your anticipation.

It is important to remember that always, when it comes to impulsive buying, there is an underlying pre-formed belief activated by some trigger in the surrounding environment. That belief might be based on some kind of prior experience or exposure to a commercial, but it is always there. Moreover, the impulsive buy is much less unpredictable than what is normally thought and not at all random. Then why do we call it "impulsive?" The reason is that the cognitive process is so quick and subconscious that we are misled into feeling that our sudden lust just popped into our brains out of nowhere.

A planned buy begins with a newly awakened goal (benefit) which becomes active. An impulsive buy begins when a stimulus you encounter in your surroundings draws out your belief from the bottom drawers of your consciousness or memory, and that belief is what activates your goal (or the search for a benefit).

Beliefs Are Structured

When we discussed the ForeSearch method in Chapter 8, I mentioned that a product-or-brand-related belief is an unconscious mental construct. I also said that each construct is composed of five components:

1. A brand-related fact

2. An interpretation or meaning attached to that fact (which is wider than the mere fact)

3. A perceived benefit–that follows the interpretation or meaning

4. An emotional reaction to the perceived benefit

5. A behavior tendency motivated by the emotional reaction

The purpose of a ForeSearch interview is to expose all the components of such structures in the consumer's mind, thus unlocking the secrets of how perception finally guides behavior.

Looking more closely, the root structure of our consumer's belief that brings about a desire for a certain brand is: Fact > Meaning > Benefit. The emotional reaction and subsequent behavior tendency result whenever this belief is activated. Here's a somewhat simplified example. Cool athletes wear Oakley sunglasses (fact). Whoever wears Oakley is cool (an assigned meaning). "I will be cool if I get Oakley sunglasses "(a perceived benefit). The belief creates the anticipation that the consumer feels. This way people connect to brands and render them personally relevant. A belief is what makes a brand appear as a means, or an instrument, for getting benefits. It is exactly the manner by which an expectation of benefit is formed, and that anticipation is the brand. The result is a positive emotional reaction. The positive emotion encourages us to behave in a way that will extend the presence of that positive emotion, meaning to purchase that brand. We call this process "the fact-to-feeling chain reaction." Once it is already established, we call it "the-fact-to-feeling mental structure."

Strategy Means Belief Structure

The smartest way to formulate a brand strategy, namely its promise of benefit, is in parallel with the structure of the consumer's beliefs that guide his brand choice: Fact > Meaning > Benefit. The purpose of your brand's promise is to tap into desired consumer goals (coveted benefits) and present your product or service as a means of attaining the said benefits. Therefore, we want to choose a certain fact to put forward and emphasize (of a kind already used by consumers as they make their choices, or a new type of fact that we put forward). Correspondingly, the way we interpret this fact, the meaning we attribute to it, is linked to existing buying considerations and choice criteria or to new ones that we are teaching our consumers.

Seen in this manner, the brand promise is in fact a belief we are suggesting that the consumer adopts.

I want to say something about "positioning" which is probably different from what you have heard in the past. Consumer considerations or choice criteria activated during the buying process are the only positioning axes you have available. To continue my earlier example, if we decide to make tailored conservative suits in shades that already signify "businesslike" to our prospective customers, this is what we call "positioning"—using the manner in which the consumer compares his alternatives in order to present our brand as one of his options. These five to seven considerations or choice criteria are the only ones that exist and there are no others. It is only upon these axes that your consumers compare you against other brands. Every attempt to position on the basis of a quality or a value that does not constitute a consumer consideration is not positioning but a waste of money.

This point is well worth elaborating on. Let us look at a typical example. Marketers of a large communications company say, "Let us position ourselves as the market leader." The fact is that in many markets the consumers do not use this type of consideration at all during their decision-making process. Simply put, they do not care who the leader is and it means nothing to them. Nevertheless, this firm invests heavily in promoting and advertising "the leadership positioning." Then their research company phones a sample of consumers, and asks them what they think of the brand. Consumers, who for several months couldn't turn on their TV without hearing that X company "is the market leader in communications" recite its "positioning" easily, and everyone is elated. The positioning process is declared a great success. But will it affect sales in any way? No, of course not.

There is one exception. That exception is not positioning but rather differentiation.

We can also teach our target customers new tricks, such as (going back again to the suit purchase example) offering them tailored, sophisticated suits in shades that are close but not exactly conventional, and showing them that by wearing those suits they are communicating individuality. Let's say that "exhibiting individuality" is a new benefit in the formal wear market. It is not a benefit currently sought after by consumers and we are now offering it for the first time. We are the only ones because our competitors all assume that when buying formal wear people want to conform, not exhibit individuality. This is what we call differentiation. We educate consumers and teach them to adopt and use previously unfamiliar considerations, or even seek new benefits that they did not realize could be attained from this product or service. That's how we differentiate ourselves.

Your bathtub can give you the greatest massage. That is what we learned from the Jacuzzi brand. When should we teach our consumers new considerations or benefits? Only when we offer them benefits not previously available in our category and the benefits constitute a good reason to prefer us. This is what differentiation is all about. I hope the difference is clear: positioning only marks your spot within an existing big competitive picture. A strategic differentiation opens a gap between you and all the rest. At best, the big potential exists in *off-core differentiation,* which your competitors do not tend to copy.

The price you have to pay at the gateway to differentiation is educating your consumers and teaching them about a previously unfamiliar benefit. You teach your consumers about a new consideration once you offer them a new possibility, a new benefit, or a new way to attain a benefit. When it is not a core benefit, your competitors are not inclined to imitate you. If you've succeeded in achieving that, then you have freed yourself from competition. Your customers rightly feel that you are like no other. You have established a privately owned monopoly. This is an achievement which cannot be overestimated in our hyper-competitive markets. This is what an unfair advantage is all about.

Three Layers of Strategy

Think of your competitive strategy as having three layers, the first one being the choice of product category. If we continue the previous example, first you have to classify yourself in a category described by consumers as "men's fashion." The second layer is your positioning, which helps consumers figure out where you are situated within your chosen product category. You answer the question: which of all possible benefits, attainable by buying men's fashion, do we promise to deliver? Are we offering leisure apparel? Or are we offering tailored suits? Is it high end and distinguished, including price, or does it do the job without wringing your pockets dry?

Finally, and this is the third layer, you better try to differentiate your brand. Differentiation means attributing a unique quality to your brand, which no other brand has, and which makes you relatively more attractive in an exclusive manner. Bagir, a men's tailoring company, developed technologically sophisticated suits for the traveling business man. Their elasticity helps increase the owner's ease of movement, the material allows ventilation, and the pants come with an elastic belt which fits comfortably in any situation, even after a big meal. They wrinkle less than regular suits and they are machine washable and dryable. A recent joint venture between Bagir and ElekTex, maker of touch-sensitive smart fabrics, resulted in the iPod suit for men. The jacket integrates Eleksen's ElekTex smart fabric touchpad technology, which transforms the lapel into a 5-button electronic control panel. The iPod suit is machine-washable and wrinkle-resistant.

As you already know, my opinion is that the best differentiation is an off-core differentiation, which is able to provide you with that winning unfair advantage.

12

The Real Reasons for Brands' Success

About Orange and about Naïveté

Brands inflame our imagination. It seems that when they succeed, they are responsible for soaring market shares and profits. The excitement and hope they provoke are enormous. But most of the time they do not succeed. To be more specific, 95 percent of the new brands in America, and 90 percent in Europe fail. Brands are also elusive. In some cases they are like meteors. They hit the skies with great momentum, but then they vanish. At other times they look like the beginning of a great success only to burn out later. In many cases it is not even clear what went right or wrong. Was it the product? The marketing offer? Maybe the brand itself? Actually, if we think about it, according to common MBA-clone wisdom, there is no clarity on what exactly is *the brand*.

Let us look at Orange, for example, a strong international cellular brand that sprouted in the British market and is often marked as a crushing example of branding success. To what does it owe its fame?

A little bit of history will illuminate this story with a fundamentally new light. Ever since the 1980s and up until 1993, there were two companies controlling the British cellular market: Vodafone and BT Cellnet. They controlled the small business market. Private cellular markets, at that time, were still nonexistent. Both companies operated analog technologies; apparatuses were big and awkward; usage costs were huge. However, in the early 1990s, a new and revolutionary technology broke through—the GSM. By the end of 1992, GSM-based networks were launched in Denmark, Finland, France, Germany, Italy, Portugal, and Sweden. In September 1993, Mercury One on One launched the first GSM network in Britain. However, the company was weak on marketing. BT Cellnet also began converting its infrastructure. The GSM technology and its widespread standards brought along small, light, and finely designed phones by Nokia and also introduced natural roaming with the phones around the world. But most important of all, it caused a major decline in prices and costs for the phones as well as the service, rendering cellular telephony, as mass telephony, a fact.

At the beginning of 1994, GSM had already taken its first step in England, but still had not gathered momentum. Hutchison, the Hong Kong-based communication mogul, on the lookout for a good opportunity, founded Microtel. It had already experienced a major flop with a limited cellular technology before, and this time it was determined to do it right. It decided not to use Microtel as the brand name. On March 28, 1994, approaching market penetration, they chose the brand name Orange. There were other names on the table as well: Pecan, Gemini, Amber, Ami, Indy, Egg, and Miro.

As it turned out, Orange was the main brand that opened the British market for the masses. It heralded the drastic decline of prices that was a general trend. Orange managers took to the mass-market strategy, understanding global evolution of cellular telephony. They decided not to focus on existing business markets but rather to expand their market to new realms. At the time, they took a risk. Although there was good reason to believe that the masses would choose cellular telephony when it became affordable for them, it was definitely not a sure bet.

Microtel had to be really revolutionary in its customer orientation in order to take advantage of this opportunity to its maximum capacity. The Orange brand pioneered in areas such as package simplification, fair pricing in seconds, 24-hour customer service, and many other customer-friendly innovations. In light of the GSM vision of a wireless world for all, Orange was launched as a wireless brand and not as a telephone brand. In order to render its strategy attractive in the eyes of its consumers, it enlisted the Wolff Olins branding company.

Wolff Olins company did a wonderful job. It gave this brand its unconventional name among British telecommunication firms. Eighteen years before, in April 1976, Steve Wozniak and Steve Jobs named their first computer Apple. The idea was that computers used by regular people and not computer whizzes had to have a mundane name, closer to the users' immediate worlds. Apple was also the biblical fruit of the tree of knowledge that opened human eyes. Since Orange was planned to be the first cellular mass brand in Britain, Wolff Olins acted on the same logic, albeit with an added touch of sophistication (an orange square emblem instead of the obvious orange fruit).

The idea was to dress this brand with a feeling of warmth, friendliness, energy, and optimism about the future. The colors orange, black, and white were chosen for the brand's visual identity. To the British mind, oranges are associated with the Mediterranean, and the Mediterranean is identified with vacation, joy, freedom, warmth, and blue skies. The whole language was designed to be simple, unambiguous, and clear cut, just like the fair pricing policy and the company's dedicated customer service.

According to the legend, the teams of Wolff Olins and WCRS advertising were forced to shut themselves inside a conference room until they reached unanimous agreement regarding one concept that was to be manifested in both the corporate identity and the advertising campaign. The WCRS advertising agency came up with the classic slogan, "The future's bright, the future's Orange," and the brand's exquisite advertising style.

The Orange brand in England took upon itself a Prometheic role. In Greek mythology Prometheus stole fire from the gods and gave it to humans. Orange brought to "normal" people possibilities that were, until then, only for the rich to enjoy. The financial accessibility and the wireless mobility took on a symbolic meaning on top of the down-to-earth benefits. The brand became an emblem of equality, open possibilities, and freedom due to technological advancements. Therefore any customer who wished to could find psychological benefit in that feeling of equality, freedom, and open possibilities. The branding created for Orange a psychological instrumentality, which served as an added value (or an added benefit). It was the emotional benefit that a customer could achieve by joining Orange. This benefit carried a special value in the British status-plagued society.

There were many reasons for Orange's success. Thinking back, I can say that their timing was perfect. Finally technology made it possible for there to be small, light, attractively designed, and user-friendly phones at low prices. The company's management chose a strategy of opening the market for the masses (instead of competing on existing mobile phones' clientele). It introduced appropriate pricing and service policies. Corporate identity design was effective, and so was the advertising. Everything worked together in perfect harmony.

I downloaded the Orange case analysis from Wolff Olins' website. I read it and was pretty astounded. They claim, point blank, that they are solely responsible for Orange's success. I would have to say that this is quite an infuriating *chutzpa* on their part! Their description says nothing about the historical opportunity; there is no mention of the company's strategy, low prices, or innovations in the area of pricing policy and customer service policy. There is even complete disregard of the advertising agency. According to them, Orange's success is theirs and only theirs.

I leave you to decide what was Orange's most decisive success factor, if you must assume that there was only one. But I have to ask this: do you really think that any sane person would believe that Orange England succeeded *mainly* because of Wolff Olins' conceived name, logo, and corporate identity, as great as they were? Personally, I believe that Orange would have been just as successful had it been named Pecan or Gemini, and launched with a slightly less astounding "corporate identity." The only difference would have been, maybe, fewer branding and advertising awards.

How Important is the Brand Identity as Such?

You can learn an important lesson by studying the differences between Orange Israel and Orange England. In both countries they have the same name and logo, the same colors, and even a very similar advertising style. And yet, the Israeli Orange and the British Orange offer consumers psychological benefits that are different in each country. In England, Orange was, as mentioned, the first brand to open the market, offering first-time cellular telephony for the masses. In Israel, however, this brand is conceived as somewhat elitist.

In Israel, Orange was the third brand to enter the market. The mass market opener, in early 2005, was Cellcom. In order to anchor its orientation as a broad and popular brand, Cellcom turned itself into an emblem of local existence, the Israeli experience. It became *the* Israeli cellular brand. The flaws, voice distortions, reception disruptions, and line break-ups of the early days were all overlooked since they were conceived by consumers as befitting its low pricing and local image, unsophisticated and crude, yet authentic, and "homemade."

Unlike Cellcom, Orange penetrated the market as a professional and slick brand, enjoying global presence as well as high quality standards to match it. Orange was the first GSM in Israel. Therefore it was the first to offer natural roaming abilities, allowing customers to travel anywhere with their personal phone. Orange's temporary technological advantage had been turned into a long-term perceived advantage by converting it to a psychological benefit. Orange was presented as a brand appropriate to customers who were "people of the world." The Israeli Orange's brand promise was based on the insight that a large sector of the Israeli public likes to view itself as connected to the world, and as being a part of the global community. The feelings of detachment and claustrophobia that many Israelis feel makes the connection to the rest of the world a vital psychological need for them. This same claustrophobic crowd is also full of fervent travelers.

Notice the extent to which the name, symbol, and color do not dictate brand conception at all! If I may be somewhat extreme, it is possible to give any meaning you want to any name and any symbol in this world.

Another example: After a vast re-branding process (with its name's original meaning of a woman appearing pious on the outside, yet hot and sexy in the privacy of her own bedroom) Victoria's Secret turned itself into a brand that is all about a proud and bold sexual declaration! The name didn't change at all. Only the meaning changed. The meaning is all that matters!

"Branding" Does Not Create Brands

In the beginning of the 1990s, many hurried to mourn brands. It turned out that most of the new brands developed in advertising agencies did not catch on. At the same time, it became evident that many brands, like Coca-Cola and Marlboro, were no longer able to charge a fat premium because of their "brand," as they had done in the past. It seemed that the brand did not protect firms like IBM or McDonald's from changes in markets, competition, and consumer preferences. Private brands have eaten into leading brands and some of them even turned into strong ones, rendering all branding rules meaningless.

But then a new breed of firms mushroomed, claiming a new area of expertise: branding. Their proclamation fueled a flame of hope in managers, who looked forward with anticipation to someone who could finally improve their brand's success rates.

The first wave of frenzy was about brand *names*. Firms paid huge sums for the development of the right name for their firm and its products. The hottest brains were searching for names with specific branding virtues. Naming research labs flourished. After a few years this trend came to a halt. In time it became clear that a top-quality name is useful and even recommended. However, you can also get by pretty well with a name like Abercrombie & Fitch.

It also became clear that naming processes do not have a monopoly on the creation of good names. Look who came up with some of the best, coolest, and most catchy names ever. IKEA is an acronym for "Ingvar Kamprad Elmtaryd Agunnaryd." The first two words are the founder's name, and the second two are the name of the town where he grew up. Steve Jobs gave Apple its name in memory of the best vacation he ever had picking apples in Oregon. The name Yahoo! was coined by its founders, two doctorates in electronic engineering, named David Filo and Jerry Yang, and it is an acronym of "Yet

Another Hierarchical Officious Oracle." That's one part of the story. The other part is that Yahoo! founders selected this name because they jokingly considered themselves "yahoos" as described by Jonathan Swift in his 1726 masterpiece, *Gulliver's Travels*. Yahoos were a race of ugly human-like creatures, portrayed as being bestial, uncultivated, and violent.

Amazon.com was nothing but an offhanded mistake made by Jeff Bezos, a finance man (who thought in error that the Amazonas was the longest river in the world). By the way, the first name offered by Bezos was Cadabra, but he gave it up after his lawyer asked him in a poorly connected cellular conversation, why on earth he wanted to give a good business the name Cadaver. Would Amazon have failed had it been called Cadabra? I think not.

But the world of marketing does not learn from past mistakes. By the mid 1990s, the market was swarming with yesterday's designers who became today's branding companies. They demanded and received five figures for designing logos and corporate or visual identities. Almost all branding companies were founded on the basis of graphic designers, who reinforced themselves with "strategic experts" in order to justify their newly adjusted tariffs, which were much higher than previously accepted. They offered a whole range of services, from strategic consultations to naming and logo design, as well as other aspects of brand identity.

Like the naming firms in their time, these companies offered a completely groundless working process, albeit seemingly sophisticated. Within a few years conventions were rooted regarding methods and working processes of branding companies, who quickly aligned with each other's ways, imitating one another fervently (in the hope that others knew what they were doing).

According to the emerging model, "brand values" constitute the brand's basis. These brand values are transmitted to consumers by the brand's communications while the brand attempts to realize them in its organizational conduct. They stand for values praised by consumers, or they constitute benefits sought after by consumers. An integrated process of inter-company discussions around the question, "Who do we want to be?" as well as qualitative consumer research to identify consumer moods and needs creates the list. The formation of brand values and the brand's promise to consumers is essentially the strategic consultation offered by branding companies.

The creative facet follows, beginning with a process of personification of brand values to form the "brand personality." Branding companies then use certain processes to transform words and symbols taken from a brand's aspired associative world, expressing the brand's values and personality, by extraction and refinement, to syllables, sounds, shapes and colors, out of which they create the name, the logo, and other brand identity factors. These are supposed to identify the brand as well as communicate its meaning.

When the process became rather standardized, branding companies won the trust of managers, who as a matter of fact did not really understand all this stuff. After all, if these are branding companies, then it is pretty safe to assume that their specialty is creating brands. Brilliant. From this point on, the way to success was freed. Every branding company quickly feathered itself with its clients' successes, sometimes completely ignoring other factors besides name and logo that contributed to success.

This method is totally void of validity. There is no reason to believe that the original meaning of words and symbols taken from a "brand's aspired associative world" (in itself a questionable worth) is preserved in a logo and derived through this process of extraction. I don't wish to dwell on this, but I do want to emphasize that there is a massive over-exaggeration of the impact and significance related to logo, symbol, colors, shapes, and so forth.

Perhaps the blue in IKEA's logo does indeed inspire trust, and the yellow, happiness, optimism, and imagination—at least according to the color-theory approach. However, the logo's influence on IKEA's general conception in consumers' minds is partial, and is at best marginal. The logo's weight is surely almost insignificant in comparison with the weight of this brand's competitive strategy: a high level of design and functionality in easily affordable furniture. One needs to be quite naïve to attribute IKEA's success to the quality of its logo, and this is true with every brand. The anticipation that the competitive strategy evokes in consumers' minds is what gives the logo its significance and thereby its emotional appeal. The logo has little inherent power.

Take most retail banks. Most consumers do not really expect to see a significant difference in the experience of being a customer of bank X versus bank Y. Consumers are aware that banks all have different names, logos, and colors. Still, they do not feel anticipation for a revelation every time they switch banks. This is the point: logo, color, fonts, symbols, and slogans do not constitute differentiation. They are also not a brand.

A good and catchy name, which communicates a promise effectively, is better than a bad name. A skillfully designed logo is better than a poorly designed one. A well-designed visual identity creates a general wow! and also contributes to a well-planned impact on consumers, which brand managers wish to create. All these aspects are simultaneous ways to communicate the brand's promise, and also (sometimes) contribute to its fulfillment. For instance, if a credit card brand like American Express' Centurion promises high prestige, its black color helps create this impression. I agree totally that advertising is sometimes not just communication but also an element of the brand experience, i.e., the fulfillment of the promise. For example, funny advertising helps make a brand fun and not just promise that it is.

Nevertheless, and I say this unequivocally, all of those are completely worthless when they are not planned to affect consumers as a part of an integrative concept that also includes its competitive strategy and its business model.

Managers should never believe that positive brand values, a good name, and a logo will suffice for winning competitive advantage, and that any effort required in order to create real differentiation or to develop a valid competitive edge could be spared.

The focus of attention must always be the real success factors behind a brand. There is no real need for a fanatic zeal for nonsense (relatively) such as the placement of the logo in ads and catalogues (a major issue in brand books where branding companies customarily summarize a brand's dos and don'ts).

Brands' powerful potential of delivering a benefit to consumers which exceeds their actual product, a unique benefit which consumers are happily willing to pay for, has hardly began to be exploited. In spite of ten decades of branding, I believe that only now has its time come. In the near future, we will begin to see what branding can really achieve.

No Relationship, Sorry!

In the branding world, people sometimes freely utter crazy terms, which in other contexts would have resulted in forced hospitalization. The idea of brands having relationships with consumers, similar to their relationships with their spouses and families, fits in this category. I do not agree with the claim that these are only metaphors. I think that marketers often deceive themselves into using terms that are irrelevant to consumers and brands, such as loyalty, commitment, love, and relationships. I personally think that anyone who cannot see the difference between his or her lover and his or her brand of soft drink has a serious problem indeed.

Marketers probably never felt bound to reciprocity and mutuality in what they call a "relationship with the consumer." Furthermore, do marketers, for their part, express any loyalty to their consumers? The contrary is true. A prospect almost always gets better treatment than a client. But even looking at it from a consumer's point of view there is no relationship. Not many sane customers send flowers on a brand's birthday, or help their favorite brand in need by contributing money or work. Yes, consumers may be excited by brands. They can also say they love a specific brand. But this is only a manner of speech, and there is no reason to understand these expressions literally. It's like saying, "I love ice cream." Does that mean the same as, "I love my mom?" I think not.

I am enthralled with Amazon.com, and I love buying my books there, even if I have to pay a slightly higher price than I can find on other websites. Nevertheless, if tomorrow a better competitor rises, cooler and fresher, and graciously offers me an even more pleasant buying experience, I simply can't see myself thinking, "Well, sorry, already married to Amazon.com." But then again, maybe it's only me.

On Brands and Anticipations

I suggest here a new understanding of a brand. It is not a name, a logo, a tagline or another identifying element such as an emblem, color, font, sound, or fragrance. It is also not a "package" of emotions or perceptions, nor is it a list of values. It is not any of the terms that commonly come up in brand discussions. Why do we need a new understanding? Because the existing definitions do not help us understand what the consumer sees in our brand, how this brand works, and how you make money out of it. So, how can I help?

Let us assume that you are about to see a new film directed by Quentin Tarantino (director of *From Dusk Till Dawn, Death Proof, True Romance, Reservoir Dogs, Pulp Fiction, Jackie Brown,* and *Kill Bill* among others). Could you imagine the experience you are about to go through, even when you haven't seen the film yet? If you have had a chance to see any of this director's work, or even discussed it with someone, I guess the answer would be yes. If I invited you to try out the new Ferrari, you would visualize an experience that would most certainly be different than it would have been had I talked about an Audi. And a Paris vacation is not much like a New York one, is it?

What I'm saying is that whenever a strong brand comes to mind, there is an expectation of deriving a very specific benefit that you feel every time you see a name or a logo or any other brand identifier. That anticipation *is* the brand, and nothing else. Of course, that anticipation needs to be positive, or else the brand will not inspire consumer desire. And if this anticipation is distinct and pertains to something much desired by consumers, which is unlike expectations spurred by other brands, then you have a strong brand. Anticipation for a unique experience with a Harry Potter or 007 film is exactly what brings you to the theatre. Hence the brand's significance: a specific consumer anticipation for something good will take consumers out shopping. Not the name, not the logo, but a genuine expectation connected with it.

Now, hand on heart, tell me this: considering this new perception, do you really have a brand? Say yes only if your existing customers and targets feel towards your brand an anticipation of the type described above, which would be different than any expectation felt by them for other brands.

Consumer expectations have their origins in the company's competitive strategy. Through that strategy a choice is made regarding which benefit to deliver to which consumers, and how, in order to create an advantage. Its implication within the framework of the company's business model will enable profiting from delivering the benefits. A brand strategy determines how to present to your consumers the attractiveness of what you are offering them, and how to design the meeting point between consumers and products from the consumers' view point. When this happens, your customers have something to look forward to.

Brands as Instruments

The major reason for excitement about brands is their capability of delivering to consumers an additional benefit on top of what the product or service or firm can deliver by itself. Up until now, this is a commonly accepted notion. However, from this point on, vagueness rules. The first question is: What exactly is this additional benefit? The second question is: How do we "charge" our brand with this added benefit? I promise you clear and useful answers to these two questions later on.

The key term is "specific usage," or even "instrumentality." If you wish to understand brands as well as create strong ones, forget terms such as "brand values" or "brand personality" and the like. Instead, think for a minute about your brand as a tool with which your consumers can do something they want to do. Does this spell "product" in your mind? Maybe you think I am confusing products with brands? Well, no. Surprisingly, the basic logic of developing brands that carry extra benefits for consumers is similar to the logic of developing products. In both cases we create a tool or a means for consumers by which they can achieve or accomplish something desired.

It is important to understand my meaning of "achieve or accomplish." I refer, among other things, to psychological usage such as mood-management, strengthening of self-image, and supporting fantasies, as well as social usage, such as signaling group affiliation to others, creating an atmosphere, and managing the impressions that others form of us.

Consumers attempt to reach benefits that are experiential, emotional, psychological, interpersonal, and social, just as much as they attempt to achieve more tangible benefits. In fact, tangible benefits are only intermediaries to intangible ones. We find Samsonite's promise—that our stuff will not become a mess while traveling—appealing, because we want peace of mind and because we want to avoid distress. Brands with an added benefit always constitute the means by which consumers can achieve such goals. A brand without a compelling scenario, specifying how consumers will use it and how they will derive its benefits, is not really a brand. It may look like one, it may have an identifiable name and logo, but consumers will not desire it. All rules for successful innovation in products and services apply to brands as well. A brand will succeed if, and only if, it enables consumers to do something desired but not possible or difficult without it. In Chapter 13 you will discover exactly how it's done.

To sum up, the instrumentality approach says that it is a bad idea to talk about brands as if they are independent entities with personalities and values, existing outside consumers' worlds and lives. Why is it a bad idea? Because it misleads marketers and they forget that they must create and manage a means by which consumers may attain their desired benefits. The result is that these marketers create a brand that may be rich with personality and values (at least the visual identity and campaigns reflect personality and values), but they are not designed to be a means by which consumers can achieve a desired benefit. Can you guess what the result would be? Consumers are not interested. Period.

In order to escape this trap, the instrumentality approach suggests that you should think about brands only as instruments by which a consumer can achieve or accomplish something desired. This means that you must think about how a brand becomes entangled in consumers' internal and emotional worlds, experiential worlds, lifestyles, relationships, and most importantly, the role it plays there. What purpose does it serve? What does the brand enable consumers to do, which is indispensable? What is the unique value it brings into their lives? It is for these reasons only that consumers will continue to want brands.

The ABCDE of Brand Success

The instrumentality approach brings forth five measures of brand success. We use these measures in consumer research to enable us to identify the extent of success enjoyed by a brand, both relative to its own prospects and to other brands, as well as to track a brand's development over time.

The five indices are:

Attribution of benefit—Do your target consumers attribute your promised benefit to your brand? Do they perceive your brand as a source of this benefit?

Believability—To what extent do your target consumers believe that your brand will indeed deliver the promised benefit? To what extent are they certain of it?

Craving—How much do your target consumers want your brand in comparison with their desire for competing brands? I recommend that you consider also the strength of desire consumers exhibit for your category in general, and the importance they attribute to it, which is sometimes referred to as their level of involvement with the product.

Differentiation—Can your consumers see the difference between your brand and competing brands? How much do they view your brand as the sole source of its promised benefit?

Ease of acting upon desire—Do your consumers feel that they can easily realize their desire for your brand? Or do they experience hardships such as conflicts, fear of damage, or even prosaic matters such as overpricing or lack of availability?

These five indices enable us to determine whether our strategy is the one that delivers our planned brand attractiveness. Furthermore, they also enable us to check whether our strategy is being implemented effectively, and if it works as well as it should.

13

How Do You Create a Brand that Is More than the Product?

Some Definitions

I owe you answers on two questions from the previous chapter:

What is the benefit that could be added to a product when creating a brand?

How can we "charge" our brand with this added benefit?

In this chapter you will find answers to both questions, but before that, I would like to hone our definitions, as they will be used in the rest of the book.

Brand Concept—the integrative idea of your brand's attractiveness in consumer eyes, based on its competitive strategy (How can an advantage be achieved?) and its business model (How can money be made?). Today, brand building no longer constitutes a mere manipulation of the consumer's perceptions and desires, but it is a creation of a system that on the one-hand makes promises and arouses anticipation, while on the other hand delivers and realizes the promises that it makes.

Brand Strategy—your specific promise of benefit to your consumers; translating your competitive strategy and your business model into a language that conveys a benefit to the consumer.

Branding—arousing the anticipation for benefit felt by consumers.

Brand—the anticipation felt by consumers for specific benefits from your company or product.

Two Purposes to Branding

When we set out to build a brand, we want to achieve at least the first, if not both, of the following two goals.

The most fundamental goal is the creation of a perceived advantage in your consumers' eyes. This purpose is achieved when consumers identify your product as a preferred way to attain a specific desired benefit. In the best cases, this preference results from the fact that the benefit offered is exclusive. However, preference could result from very simple reasons as well, such as a consumer being just a little more certain of your brand than he is of a competitor's. This can most easily be seen in extreme situations. Xerox makes document copies. This is so clear (they opened this category) that it became a verb in spoken English. You can ask, "Can you Xerox this for me, please?" and be quite certain that your request is understood. Every American will understand the request, "Please FedEx me the package," and many worldwide say, "I'll just Google this." If you happen to be in this situation, you have earned an advantage, at least temporarily (look under "Frigidaire," once a synonym for kitchen refrigerators and still existent).

The second goal is to supply a benefit that extends beyond your product. By this I mean a benefit to the customer. Brands can surpass the benefits supplied by the product itself. A brand can become an instrument by which consumers are able to attain intangible benefits on top of the benefits provided by the product per se. Such brands can offer what I like to call *intangible instrumentality.* In cases such as these, that extra intangible benefit is the differentiating benefit that is at the heart of your competitive strategy, and this is the benefit for which consumers will prefer your product to any other.

An important insight is that *you can base your competitive strategy on the creation of an instrument for your customers, by which they will be able to achieve intangible benefits beyond the benefits of the product.* Potentially, these benefits can be unique and external to the core benefits of your category, and then they will be an off-core differentiation. Therefore you have a good basis for achieving an unfair advantage. It's up to you. This chapter deals with attaining this second goal. I will reveal to you the psychology of consumers that enables branding of this type to be done, what your possibilities are, and how you can realize them.

Who Wants to Live in Reality Anyway?

The possibility of intangible instrumentality originates in the widespread yet often concealed sentiment that reality is no big deal. Even people who live in an acceptable reality always encounter limits and suffer pain of various types. I do not mean to depress you here, but losing dear and close people, illnesses, psychological distresses, old age, and death are all inevitable adversities awaiting us. Even without going this far, this world consistently refuses to grant all our wishes or arrange itself according to them. What do we do? We enrich our reality on a regular basis. We live in a mixture of reality and non-reality, which is so fully integrated that it is a wonder, sometimes, that we manage to go through our daily responsibilities and function effectively.

Need proof? Think of the last time you left your house in the morning, got into your car, and drove to your office. Around you, you see many drivers who you would think are going to their offices too, but is that what they are doing? It really does not look that way. You see them racing and cutting each other off wildly, showing off and flaunting pseudo-virtuoso road acrobatics. Look at them; this is not reasonable behavior for someone on the road from home to the office.

Usually when you want to come up with an explanation for a certain behavior that seems unreasonable, ask yourself in which situation this behavior would be reasonable and fitting. Suddenly it all becomes clear. Inside their minds, these drivers are not driving a Peugeot, a Toyota, or a Hyundai, but they are racing with their very own Lamborghini Murcielago Roadster. They are not bored to death on an everyday urban highway, no sir! They are entertaining a crowd on a racing course, if not playing Rambo off in some distant war zone. This is not unusual. While performing our everyday routine activities, we all fantasize. We are all living in our own movies.

None of us lives our reality "as is." This is completely human. There are four levels of enriched realities, and all of us, without exception, live in all four levels alternately and in parallel, whether or not we step up bravely and admit it and this includes the most grounded people you know.

The four levels of enriched realities are as follows:

Our shared and coordinated reality

It begins with our culture and religion. The mere fact that we run our lives according to cultures and religions is the first evidence of our need for enriched realities. We have sacred sites such as the Muslim's Kaaba, the holy black stone in Mecca; we have sacred people, such as the Dalai Lama; we have sacred music, and sacred texts. We have flags and sanctified symbols; we have people like us who are kings and queens to whom we ascribe greatness; we have professions once considered contemptible that today credit their holders with celebrity status such as football players, models, and actors. We have substances such as gold or platinum or diamonds, for which we are willing to pay absurd sums of money; and we have behavior patterns that are considered the "right" way as well as abnormalities. We have current fashions and trends, and we act as if this is reality. But is it? No. It is an enriched reality, one that is shared and coordinated.

We have groups based on nationalities, ethnic origins, political parties, or our families. Just like all the other people who make these groups, we too believe that some things or values are important or sacred or right, and we tend to understand what happens in reality and also respond to it, in a manner which would be similar to the other group members. We relate to our enemies or our rivals as though they are far from being human, and attribute monstrous mutations to them. From time to time we have certain "lifestyle fashions" that everybody sees as the right way to do things, such as the current spirituality trend. We act as if this is reality, but is it? No. It is an enriched reality, which is shared and coordinated.

With our spouses or partners, with our friends and acquaintances, we create mutual ways of seeing the world around us, embrace mutual ways of thinking that render certain things important and others humorous; we believe that certain people mean certain things, and that certain events have certain implications. We behave as if this is reality. It is *our* reality—enriched, shared and coordinated.

Our personal interpretation of reality

On a personal level, we make interpretations of realities, not to mention superstitions. Here's a short illustration:

June is making herself a cup of coffee in her office kitchenette and John finally collects himself enough to utter, "I like you very much, June." Can you imagine what goes through her mind? There are at least five possibilities, compatible with various interpretations she might make of her reality:

1 – "Hey! Great!"

2 –"Now I'm in a real mess."

3 – "He probably wants to get laid."

4 – "Had he really known me, he would not have said that."

5 – "Why do I always attract men whom I find unattractive?"

We all do this every day, and create for ourselves an internal, fun world at best, and an internal inferno at worst. It is easier for us to notice this in others, but a little honesty and a spoonful of courage will enable you to see it in yourself as well.

We fall in love. She is the best and most fabulous person in the world. We have never met anyone like her before. Only our sour-faced friends look at us, completely shocked. They don't understand what we see in her.

You see what I mean? We do not live in an objective reality. What we see happening around us, we translate into perceptions. We view other people through our heads and not through our eyes. We are convinced we know where our life is leading us, and yet we are often surprised ("I got sacked, but that's the best thing that could have happened to me"). All sorts of things are happening, in our heads and not in our realities.

Our reality distortions and self-deceptions

We distort reality constantly. There are people who look in the mirror and see what they want to see or ignore what they don't want to see, but this has nothing to do with what somebody else would see there. I'm sure you know these people who brag about how successful they are, and all you can do is pray for them to wake up. But you may also encounter a very thin woman who tells you in tears that she has grown really fat lately. You may feel like asking her, "Where?" You look in the mirror and your eyes focus on your good angle. You look at your sculptured torso but your eyes ignore the belly inflating underneath.

Kurt Cobain, the lead singer of the rock band, Nirvana, was talented, good looking, and successful, but he took his own life at the age of 27. Many people could not understand why.

We lie to ourselves. We tell ourselves that if we accept this or that job, or buy this dress or that makeup, then things will be fine. Fine? Talk about perpetual. There is always the next thing waiting.

If we can achieve all that so easily, then "rewriting" our past should be a cinch! We can remember things differently than how they really happened and even remember things that never happened at all.

Do not let my informal style mislead you. What I say here is research based, with references to the absolute latest psychological research at the time of writing this book. This research says that people who have a tendency to see reality with a slightly rosier shade generally function better and are more successful than more realistic folk. "Realistic?" Did I really say that? What I meant was, people who color their life gray.

Our fantasies

We fantasize. Don't be so shocked! We fantasize about the future to get encouraged by the good that awaits us, and also in order to get ready. We fantasize about what would have happened had we made different choices in our lives. If we behave in a way we hadn't expected of ourselves—for instance, in a way that embarrassed or degraded us—then we can spend hours running different scenes in our heads over and over, in which we behave completely differently, as we should have. It calms us a little.

We also fantasize about rare possibilities (but who knows, they might just surprise us) such as winning the big lottery, fateful encounters, love at first sight, life-changing events, life transformations (like Cinderella) and personal metamorphoses (such as the shy introvert who will wake up one morning assertive and outspoken, or the overweight snack-food addict who will turn into a health freak). These are long shots, but still possible. We also fantasize about things that will most likely never happen because we are not ready to do what it takes, to be brave enough, or to put in the effort and pay the price. This includes fantasies about success and glory, enormous wealth, adventure and turbulent lifestyles, different and exciting sex, and so forth. We fantasize about events that better not happen as well, such as murder or the natural death of someone whose death would solve a problem for us.

Some of our fantasies are controlled and others spontaneous. Some occur repeatedly, and others come and go instantly.

Why do humans find that their reality is not enough? Why do we need an enriched reality? There are many good reasons for this. Here are only a few:

- Getting over fears and anxieties, becoming stronger

- Keeping a positive self image and staying optimistic

- Getting ready for forthcoming events

- Reaching beyond limits and constraints

- Living the impossible

- Experiencing a world more like we wish it would be

- Finding or creating legitimacy and significance

- Creating a sense of "togetherness" with others

People need hope. Hope is the yearning we feel towards the realization of a goal, or the achievement of a benefit, which is uncertain yet feasible. Uncertainty is the story of all of our lives. As far as "possible" is concerned, we are all willing to be flexible and optimistic. Something very rare could still exist within the realm of "the possible." As the old saying goes, "Hope is the only liar who never loses credibility." Hope takes life's adversities and renders them bearable. It gives us a reason to progress when things get rough. If this entails having to forge an enriched reality, then so be it. It's a compromise worth making.

There also exists a reciprocal relationship between our "real" reality and our "enriched" reality. Sometimes we fantasize about a better future and that gives us motivation and energizes us. I will even go as far as saying that everything we create in our lives, we create in our imagination first. Even changes in our personality and our behavior happen this way. I can tell you from my own experience with hypnosis that hypnotized individuals who perform a certain behavior in their imagination, one that they were not able to engage in beforehand in real life, are often capable of performing this behavior after. This method is used both for treating phobias and anxieties and for changing behavioral patterns and habits, as well as influencing other personality and behavioral changes.

Sometimes we distort reality and ignore risks, and that gives us the courage to initiate endeavors that succeed in the end. Both our perception of reality (the distorted one) and our self image impact our belief in our chances to succeed, our inclination to take action, and the range of possibilities we can see. "Whether you believe you can do something or you believe you can't, you're probably right," said Henry Ford, and he was absolutely right. People around us respond to us in accordance with our perception of self and our perception of reality.

The culture in which we live encourages realism, maybe less today than in the past. Is enriched realism a bad thing? Must we do our best to live our lives in pure reality? We do need to acknowledge a certain level of reality, no doubt about that. Beyond that, I am persuaded that enriched reality is all right, on the condition that we do not screw up our lives on account of it. But even then, we are referring to an exchange of one enriched reality with another. An enriched reality is a human being's natural way of living. Even if you try to live in pure reality, eventually you are bound to discover that you are only deceiving yourself. Anyone who does not understand that cannot understand the human psyche, and therefore should not and could not be a marketer.

Just Do It

When we decide to adopt a competitive strategy based on an intangible added benefit, we essentially decide to develop for consumers an instrument they can use in order to create and sustain some enriched reality. Brands with intangible added benefits, by definition, support consumers' enriched realities.

Take Nike, who famously tells its customers "Do what you dream and do what you want! Don't let anybody or anything stop you! Go for it, and win!" This inspires customers to believe that everything is possible. What does Nike do other than develop high-quality, innovative, and well-designed products?

- They awarded this brand the name of the winged goddess of victory from the Greek mythology, attendant of Zeus, father of all gods, and Athena's best friend. There aren't many Nike customers who are aware of that.

- They chose an easy symbol to recognize, the Swoosh, which communicates vigor and dynamics, and resembles the "V" sign we all use to indicate something that has been finished successfully. (By the way, this symbol was purchased by Nike in 1971, for $35.)

- Later, in 1988, they added their inspiring slogan, Just Do It!, which encourages a "can do" and determined attitude, counting on gut instincts. This slogan was formulated during a conversation between the advertising guru Dan Wieden and Nike employees, in which he complimented them by saying, "You do not hesitate, you just do it." So it seems that Nike's organizational culture authentically supports its "can do" brand concept.

- They got together with sports stars, among which the most outstanding was basketball superstar Michael Jordan. Together they created satellite brands such as Air Jordan. Michael Jordan, by the way, was not born a star, and did not even make it to the basketball team of his high school. He built himself from scratch, and he worked hard doing it. Cyclist Lance Armstrong, with whom the company has cooperated in the past few years, almost died of cancer, but he came back and added to the championships of the Tour de France that he began in 1996—altogether winning an amazing series of seven tours.

- They give out sponsorships and carry out advertising activities which never stop, and which are always consistent in their message.

How is a psychological, added benefit created in this case? How did Nike become a brand (an instrument) with which people can motivate themselves to make extraordinary efforts because they believe that anything is possible? Across all activities, Nike demonstrates to its consumers, using well-known examples from real life and first-rate storytelling, that nothing is beyond desire, and that everything is possible. Nike gives its customers a chance to experience this notion imaginatively, and to tell themselves, "Just do it!" during their inner conversations. They tell themselves and remind themselves of this by wearing Nike.

In addition, with its unique way of conducting business-marketing activities, Nike demonstrates (with only a few flops) the win-win spirit that is focused entirely on initiative and action. Nike innovates constantly, embracing almost every new idea that arises in marketing and branding. They widened the scope of their brand to include sport fashion and accessories for sports activities. They erected shopping palaces under the name Niketown. Their design and development center in Beaverton, Oregon continually emits new products. The goal is to produce new products with more diverse users. Nike makes fashions out of those innovations, using principles of short-term branding, to which you will be introduced in Chapter 15. Recently they launched the NIKEiD, an Internet customization service for shoes and other products. Bottom line: Nike built an instrument consumers can use to attain psychological benefits.

Giant companies such as Nike can do many things involving giant budgets. I want to reassure you that you can also conduct focused activities, which are more workable and less expensive, in order to turn brands into instruments for attaining intangible benefits.

Instruments for Attaining Intangible Benefits

There are ten different methods to create brands that are instruments for attaining intangible benefits. These are essentially ten different extents of branding. They gradually grow more complex with each higher level, and each one includes many options of all the previous ones. As they progress, they go further away from the tangible product, and are more engulfed in enriched reality. Let me elaborate on these ten methods.

1. Creating a perceived connection to a tangible benefit

The most basic branding method is the creation of a perceived connection between a tangible benefit, which is a direct outcome of the product itself or of any other component of its branding mix, and a brand name and other brand identity factors. In other words, the task of branding means making consumers identify specific tangible benefits with your brand. A tangible benefit is a practical benefit or a sensuous-experiential benefit. Do not underestimate this basic method. Successful brands like Pantene shampoo, which promises to treat the six symptoms of unhealthy looking hair, can attribute their success to this method. The added benefit here is minimal, albeit crucial: helping consumers choose by offering certainty of benefit attainment.

As I have already mentioned, this benefit can also be an experience. In the 1950s, for example, Club Med introduced to the world the "everything-included-high-spirited-active-family-vacation" concept, carried out in specialized resort villages. The Club Med experience is still specific in the minds of millions of consumers around the world, although today the company is struggling to make a comeback after a near collapse in the 1990s. They were cruelly copied, with improved models and lower prices, but they did not fire back and stayed inactive for years.

2. Building mental context—an organizing concept

The next method is based on a brand creating a "mental context," an organizing concept that clusters together otherwise seemingly unrelated facts and creates a non-obvious connection between them. This gluing idea connects together various facts about the product or marketing activities supporting it, which suddenly fall into some pattern or reflect a hidden purpose behind them. This over-arching significance may be some kind of company policy behind the facts, or a marketing idea that is manifested in them or any other shared quality. The mental context delivers a benefit, which constitutes an intangible added value. The important thing is that the brand's major benefit is not a direct result of the brand's tangible facts, but rather of their inferred meaning. Are you confused? The next example will make everything clearer.

If you are in a boutique hotel such as the Hudson or the Royalton in the heart of Manhattan (both belong to Morgans Hotel Group) without knowing what a "boutique hotel" is or being aware that you are in one, you still enjoy them tremendously because these hotels have many beautiful and entertaining elements. However, being aware that you are in a boutique hotel, your experience is different. A boutique hotel is a concept that is the opposite of the traditional idea of hotel chains such as the Hilton. Hotels belonging to a boutique hotel chain differ from one another. Even the rooms inside differ from one another. This concept of boutique hotel and the mental context it shapes suddenly connects various elements in a new way in your mind, and sends you off on a "find-the-differences" quest.

Branding of this type helps turn a temporary tangible benefit into a conceptual long-term benefit. Remember the Israeli Orange? This brand was a GSM pioneer, and for a short time was the only one offering world-wide roaming with your personal phone. This brand was designed to offer the benefit of a self-image boost as a person who is "citizen of the world." When building the brand, the temporary technological advantage of free roaming was leveraged for creating a long-term psychological benefit by interpreting it as being just one manifestation of a cosmopolitan lifestyle.

3. Directing experience using expectation

The third branding method actually creates a hypnotic effect. Here, the branding mission is to create an expectation that alters the sensuous experience. The branding creates an instrument for consumers to gain a richer experience than they would have gained from the product alone.

You are probably familiar with this method from the upscale wine industry for gourmet consumers. When a brand of wine is presented compellingly as meritorious, people who drink it tend to experience it as such. If someone tells you, "Notice how the bottom layer tastes like almonds," I can bet that some of you will taste almonds there. Likewise, I believe that an expectation related to an energy drink like Red Bull will cause a consumer to feel a boost of energy unrelated to the actual physical effect of that drink. This brings us to an important insight: brands built with this method may have a placebo effect. If you never encountered this term before, a placebo medication refers to the phenomenon where a fake medication achieves the same physical effect as the real one, due to patients' expectations. This phenomenon occurs pretty consistently. We can use it for far-reaching purposes indeed.

4. Creating a means for communicating a message of identity

In the fourth method, branding creates a symbol of a specific identity, to the point where its significance is familiar to all within a consumers' group. This way, anyone can use it to communicate a message of the certain identity. A "symbol of identity" can signify any type of identity. For example, it can attest to personal characteristics such as "gourmet" or "up-to-dateness" (knowing what is considered fashionable or cool); belonging to a certain social group (e.g., enlightened spiritualists); affiliation with a certain stereotype (for instance, intellectual); or a certain socioeconomic status. After branding familiarizes the symbol's meaning, it becomes an instrument by which consumers can characterize themselves. It can help them conduct internal conversations with themselves (in order to strengthen a positive self image) or to convey a message to specific others (in order to create a certain impression) or to an entire social groups (in order to communicate affiliation or status).

Absolut vodka, which I mentioned earlier, turned itself into an instrument for yuppies so they could signal their "yuppiness" to each other and thereby turned the brand into a smashing success. In some cases, you can create a community around brands of this type and facilitate mutual interactions.

5. Creating a means for conveying specific messages

Similarly, in the fifth method, branding also creates a symbol that carries a meaning familiar to all. Therefore, it too can be used as an instrument for conveying specific messages. In this case, however, the symbol is not about identity. With this method, the symbol enables consumers to communicate a specific message or convey specific emotions to those around them.

In 1948, African diamond mogul Cecil Rhodes created one of the most powerful instruments ever for conveying an interpersonal message. That year, his company De Beers, together with its advertising agency, N. W. Ayer, which had been representing them for over a decade, came up with the idea that a diamond is a symbol of commitment, and above all, marriage. The physical fact that diamonds cannot be destroyed became a symbol of indestructible relationships. Therefore, said De Beers, when you give your loved one diamond jewelry, you declare your eternal love for her. The slogan was, "A diamond is forever."

After generations of men bought diamonds for their chosen ones, and after women became more independent economically, De Beers identified a new potential. In September 2003, De Beers began creating a new instrument for conveying a message. This time it was for women. The idea: the left hand is reserved for the ring given to you by your lover, and it symbolizes your attachment status. Now, wear a ring on your right hand as a symbol of independence. The Right Hand Ring is a tremendous success story. The company invited jewelry designers to design specialized right hand patterns, and they responded. The advertising campaign cried out for women to raise their right hand. Ads read, "Your left hand says 'we', your right hand says 'me'." In the U.S., right hand rings became a way for women to signal that they are available. Brilliant!

6. Establishing a source of social-cultural authority

The sixth branding method consists of the creation and establishment of an authoritative voice that can be used by consumers as a road map, helping them understand what is going on in their surroundings while informing them which behaviors are normal, how they should shape their lifestyle, what will make them happy, and so forth.

In the 1980s Apple turned itself into such a source. Remember the mythical commercial "1984"? It is only one example! Apple introduced the personal computer as not only a working tool, but also as an instrument of personal expression and creativity. This was part of a much wider cultural message emphasizing the importance of every human being. This brand is partly responsible for initiating the commercialization of an enormous cultural trend. It is reflected by the wide variety of ways regular people can express themselves. Today, many engage in creative activities not because they have an unusual gift, but because it makes them feel good. Regular people can write blogs, broadcast themselves on YouTube, and otherwise express themselves and document their lives with professional quality equipment. The professional-level equipment for every man's use is an important part of this trend (e.g., they can also cook with professional kitchenware). This is only the tip of the iceberg of this important trend.

Lifestyle brands use this method often. Contrary to common belief, lifestyle brands are not the ones shown in commercials featuring pretty people jogging on the beach or passing luxury leisure time in fancy swimming pools. Lifestyle brands are instruments with which consumers can take part in specific lifestyles. These brands support desired lifestyles and aid consumers' participation in them. Creating a public authority or a cultural authority constitutes support of this kind.

Take Vans shoe brand, for example. It built itself around supporting non-institutionalized sports loved by teens, such as skateboarding, surfing, BMX bicycle riding, field motorcycling, and skiing. They built parks for skateboarding. They developed organizations of tournaments, championships, and even musical tours, all the way up to pool parties and other types of events for their brand community. This branding method is also very adaptive to brand communities.

7. Creating the long arm

With the seventh method, branding is about creating an instrument for consumers to act upon objectives that they consider grand or extremely important, which they cannot affect by themselves. Just as Anton Chekhov, the Russian author and playwright wrote, "Man is what he believes."

As I mentioned before, The Body Shop turned shopping at its stores and buying its products into a way to contribute to environmental causes, and as a way to support needy people all over the world. Anita Roddick, who founded this chain in 1976, established a strict policy of working only with suppliers who refrain from experiments on animals and who take measures to protect the environment. She donated generously to humane causes, volunteered herself, and single-handedly designed an organizational culture oriented towards volunteer work and donations to worthy causes. Today this chain has more than 2,000 shops in more than 50 countries.

Another impressive example is Mecca Cola. In 2002, a French businessman (Tunisian by origin), named Tawfik Mathlouthi decided to combine a protest against U.S. behavior towards the Arab world, donations to Palestinian children, and good business. He launched a cola brand that is a proclaimed Coca-Cola imitation. This psychological, and perhaps also social instrument allows consumers to contribute to causes they support while they drink their cola. Between 10 to 20 percent of Mecca Cola's profits are dedicated to these causes. Their slogan: "Don't drink stupid, drink with commitment." It is not surprising that this brand became a hit among Arab consumers in Western Europe. By the way, this method is also fit for creating brand communities.

8. Creating an alter ego

With the eighth method, branding creates a means by which consumers can behave, at least at a fantasy level, in a way desired yet repressed. The brand acts in a specific manner and constitutes an "alter ego" for its customers. By buying the brand, consumers can feel as if they realize the specific desired behavior.

One of the most conspicuous brands of this kind is *Playboy* magazine. Hugh Hefner published the first issue of this magazine in December 1953, with an investment of approximately $8,000 and with Marilyn Monroe as the first centerfold girl. The magazine carried no date because Hefner did not know whether there would be a second issue. The magazine sold approximately 4,000 copies. As the second issue approached, Arthur Paul, who later became the magazine's graphic editor, designed the famous Playboy bunny logo with his tux and bowtie to represent a cultured man who was interested in sex. The term "playboy" was designed to express outgoing sexuality and hedonism combined with intellectualism.

Today only a few people are aware that Playboy endorsed quite a few of America's biggest artists in its time, and that it also organized jazz festivals, supported stand-up comics like Lenny Bruce who engaged in biting social and political commentary, and stood at the front leading heated social battles for causes such as a woman's right to abortion. The Playboy brand became an instrument for the sophisticated and successful man, with which he could experience saucy mischief that he could not allow himself to experience in his real "respectable" life.

Fashion brand Diesel, led since 1985 by Renzo Rosso, is a more recent example. *Select*, the British music and trends magazine, chose Rosso as one of the one hundred most influential people in the world. Diesel's second name is provocation—endless provocation. Its cynical slogan, which is famous by now, "For successful living," accompanies campaigns in which pigs sit around a dinner table, homosexual sailors kiss, Africa is the world's superpower, and nuns wear jeans. Teens, the brand's enthusiastic consumers, can feel as though they themselves are behaving provocatively every time the brand spawns another one of its juicy and far-reaching campaigns.

9. Building an emotional gym

The ninth method is based on the insight that in our relatively safe and protected, civilized way of life we bypass many of our possibilities as human beings. Originally our body was designed for challenges and risks that our current lifestyles do not demand of us most of the time. As it happens, we do not go out hunting for food often, and do not have to fight for our survival. Likewise, we have been designed to experience feelings and emotions in a range much wider than our lifestyle enables. Thus, we are not able to know the whole range of our possibilities. Our life in the modern world is arranged in such a way that most of us experience acute fear or obsessive desire rarely, if at all.

Of course, this means risking degeneration. So we go to work out at the gym in order to prevent our body from becoming soft and weak. Similarly, we watch movies and television shows in order to "work out" these feelings labeled inappropriate and incorporate them into our lives. The "building an emotional gym" branding method builds opportunities for us to exercise our neglected feelings.

Soap operas and reality TV are good at that. "Television without pity" is the description provided by one website which reviews reality TV. Dozens of such popular programs are broadcast, beginning with the "softer" kind like *American Idol* and its counterparts, in which talented youth compete for the chance of becoming instant music mega-stars. *The Apprentice* has contestants compete for a dream job with Donald Trump. In *Wife Swap*, families exchange women for ten days and see what happens. *The Swan* has contestants undergo plastic surgery and physical as well as mental treatments in order to come closer to the ultimate standard of beauty.

When we watch shows such as these, we become excited like our ancestors in the ancient Roman Coliseums who watched gladiators fight each other or wild beasts to the death. Just as they were aroused by real blood back then, we are excited and aroused by real distress today. We watch people emotionally and physically endure extreme situations and knowing that it is real excites us.

Las Vegas (the city and the brand), a good example of the "experience locations" industry, cuts us off from our regular lives and offers us a chance to encounter our extreme emotions—the dreams, the hopes, the ecstasy and loss of control, and even the fear and anxiety.

10. Fantasy support

Slightly different from the previous method, our tenth branding method creates fantasy catalysts for our consumers. These brands are designed according to people's favorite fantasies, some of which we discussed earlier.

In 1973 the name Timberland, meaning "woodland," was given to products from a shoe factory belonging to the Schwartz family from Boston. This brand was designed as an instrument by which consumers could fantasize daring adventures in the face of natural forces. Timberland shoes' fantastic (although seldom needed) durability was used to create a much wider psychological significance when it was introduced as a means to endure extreme climatic and surface conditions. Alaska starred in this brand's advertising for a long time. Then this fantasy was broadened even further, with campaigns for a variety of fashion products marketed under that brand name.

A different brand altogether, Harley-Davidson, still succeeds today in maintaining up to 50 percent of the global heavy motorcycle market! The average Harley rider is nearing 50 years old. The common profile includes white collar professionals and executives. During weekends they ride their Harleys and know that deep inside their mundane, square, and respectable image—known by everyone in their surroundings—hides a wild brute thirsty for adventure. They fantasize about a different life, much more riotous and tempestuous than the one they have.

Dr. Gian Luigi Longinotti-Buitoni, president and CEO of Ferrari North America, wrote a fascinating book on marketing high-end brands called *Selling Dreams* (Simon & Schuster, June 1999). He says about fantasy supporting brands, "The dream is not to own a crown, it is to be a king!"

The common approach of MBA clones is to pile together all these very different types of brands, labeling them with a different trendy term every time, such as added value brands, emotional brands, or Lovemarks. Usually they make a fine salad out of brands that carry experiential-sensuous benefits, tossing them together with brands that carry experiential—emotional, psychological, interpersonal, and social benefits. They make an erroneous distinction between "rational" brands and "emotional" brands. This is as discerning as making a distinction between cheese from cow's milk and goat cheese. In fact, it is even more idiotic than that because there is no such thing as "rational" brands. By this mistaken term they refer to brands whose purchase is characterized by thoughtfulness. However, this contemplation is in fact only one step of the way leading towards imagination and emotion, as explained earlier. This happens because they are very often clueless when it comes to knowing how brands become incorporated into consumers' worlds.

Understanding the various types of added benefits, or intangible instrumentality, as well as understanding ways in which these brands benefit consumers and turn into ways by which they can achieve their goals, makes all the difference in the world between creating brands professionally and creating pseudo-brands amateurishly.

14

Electrifying Marketing vs. Satisfying Marketing

Introducing the Consumer You Haven't Met . . . Yet

Electrifying marketing is based on a different understanding of consumers, as well as their needs and wants. In this chapter I will introduce you to additional consumer facets never exposed to you before, neither by any conventional market research, nor by popular marketing books about consumer behaviors. And despite this, I am certain that you will immediately identify the authenticity of it all because we are all human beings. Once you acknowledge these insights, you will realize how deeply limited the traditional consumer perception is common among MBA clones who are often satisfying marketers. Then, once these limitations are cleared, we will move on to deal with opportunities opened before you by electrifying marketing insights, and methods to find and grab them.

As I told you in Chapter 4, satisfying marketers believe that one must find out what consumers want and deliver it better than the competition. They presume that consumers always know and buy what they want. Big mistake! The truth is consumers often are not sure about what they want. Even when they are sure, consumers only know what they want right this minute, before they bump into that new unfamiliar product which might be better, not to mention tomorrow's products which might not even be imaginable to them right now. Assuming that consumer desires are a given, and one only needs to satisfy them, makes the goal of satisfying marketing a consequence of a shallow and deficient understanding of consumers.

Now, I would like to tell you a few intimate details about consumers and their worlds. What I am about to say is a gross over-generalization. These insights refer to people in their mid-30s and older, men and women alike; they do not refer to children, teens, or young adults. Not every detail will be true about everybody, certainly not when it comes to forcefulness and emphasis. However, most are true about most people, and it is important that you acknowledge it. The picture I am about to present to you is not at all joyful but the opportunity it reveals is very much so. This is not a cynical expression. I think that upon following these insights you will be able to help your consumers attain the benefits they seek in a much deeper way. They, in their turn, will be more than happy to reward you with their purchases.

Some Observations About Consumers and Their Lives

Let us begin with the background. Up until age 20, people live in the fantasy that everything in life will somehow fall into place and be good. Between the early 20s and mid-30s, people come to understand that they need to take action and work to make life turn out the way they want it to. Still, they continue to have a general feeling that they can make life be what they want it to be. Sometime in the course of the second half of their 30s, most people slowly come to realize that their life is not the same as they thought it would be. Nothing, of course, happens abruptly or at a specific age. This is a gradual process that happens almost unnoticed. We would be wrong to say that consumers live this acknowledgement every day of their lives, but it is there, under the surface. What happens to such typical consumers (with many personal variations, of course) is as follows (written in masculine tense for convenience, but refers to men and women alike):

- **The consumer lives a routine, more or less.** The more his life advances, his work life progresses, and his family grows, the more his days are organized and prioritized by obligations and responsibilities. Even when his life is generally a good life (and he has nothing to complain about), in one way or another he is bored, engulfed in a banal everyday reality. No glamour, no magic. He endures, he pulls, he strives, he survives. I want to stress this: most of the time he is far from suffering. He is even happy and thankful about many things in his life. He has days of fulfillment, and even high spirits. And yet he feels that something is lacking. The Czech author Milan Kundera once wrote a book called *Life is Elsewhere*. This is how our consumer feels. He senses an existence of another breed of humans, maybe wealthier, prettier, having different personalities, living in different places, living the "real" life, which is oh, so different from his own.

- **The consumer sometimes feels trapped.** He has dependents—young children, aging parents, employees, superiors, and customers. He has responsibilities, obligations, and is expected to be in control most of the time, sensible, planned; he is not a child anymore. His life offers few possibilities (if any) for letting go, breaking the rules, real excitement, adventure, or risk. He does have periods of awakening and enthusiasm, for various reasons, but there are also times in which he does not really feel alive. When he encounters temptations, he fights to maintain stability, and to keep his safe world intact, but at the price of misgivings and sometimes regrets. He wants to be seduced and to feel temptation growing stronger, enticing and irresistible, but most of the time, he wouldn't dare to give in. Sometimes he hears about friends who reinvented their lives. Secretly he envies them, even though deep inside he knows that he wouldn't really swap lives with them. And yet his shady self wishes them failure and misfortune.

- **Once he dreamed about becoming a person of certain stature, he dreamed about grand achievements—most of them did not materialize.** Once he had hopes that certain things would happen to him in life, but these hopes were disappointed. Even if there is something calming and soothing about concession and acceptance, still he would have preferred that things turned out differently. He remembers that once he was way more alive, and energetic. He misses his childhood and adolescence; he misses living lightly, spontaneously, happily. He misses all that emotional flux, mischief, naïveté and fascination. He especially misses those times when he was free, when he used to have a bright future ahead and all the doors of opportunity were open before him. Not that he took advantage, but still. . . . And now his fantasies are all covert. Somewhere inside him he still hopes that maybe, just maybe, something will happen. Most of the time, however, this hope carries behind it a kind of quiet despair, lurking under the surface (because, as I said before, everything is really quite fine).

- **No matter how much our consumer seems confident to others, deep inside he feels inept, self-doubt, and even emptiness.** He feels less desirable than he would like to be (even if he is well preserved and in shape). He lives with a perpetual doubt about being loved, and being worthy of love. He is busy inflating his self-image, capabilities, achievements, importance, and contribution to other people's lives. He tends to focus on himself, his weaknesses, and his anxieties. He is afraid of abandonment, loneliness, diseases, old age, and death. Paradoxically, he is a self-centered narcissist. He listens only when he, or something relevant to him or his world, happens to be the subject of discussion. He likes to see his views, tastes, and preferences in proclamations made by other people. He connects with these people because this unity gives him confidence, and relaxes his deep anxiety that something basic is wrong with him.

- **He has secret longings, hidden even from those who are closest to him in the world.** He may have a sexual fetish. He is possibly attracted to some unconventional behaviors (and sometimes he seeks a partner for testing limits). He might feel masochistic tendencies, or a desire to render himself a martyr wronged by the unrighteous. Alternatively he may have sadistic inclinations.

Maybe he just feels worn out and longs to be able to surrender, free himself from burden, be dependent on somebody else to take care of him and satisfy his needs. He loves to be sometimes led without knowing where to, and to be surprised by someone strong who knows exactly where he's going.

Get the idea? Although this subject is far from exhausted by this short discussion, by now you should be able to understand consumers better than you did before when you viewed them through the popular lenses of common marketing wisdom. The picture I have painted for you is much more human and realistic. I hope that now you understand the reason why it is so absurd and off-point to treat consumers as being in complete control, as having clear and fully acknowledged needs and desires, and as acting unequivocally upon those needs and desires so as to satisfy them consistently. Consequently, you must recognize now how pointless it is to market just in order to tap into these consumers' expectations. Consumer satisfaction surveys make perfect sense, but if you are guided by their results your product or service would become just another one of those ok-but-boring things in his life. An MBA clone might expect grateful loyalty. You know better (and research overwhelmingly shows that customer satisfaction does not assure loyalty).

Now let us move on to understand how all of this reflects upon our consumer's less obvious and more hidden needs.

Other Needs

Here are some insights on consumer-needs that satisfying marketing does not know how to satisfy:

- An experience of glamour, bigger than life, enchantment
- Refuge from the banality of life and boredom
- A chance to get away from one's own self, be someone else for a while
- A peek of the beyond, mystery, secrets

- A taste of the "real life"

- Adventure, excitement, risk, liveliness

- Being surprised, turned on, entertained

- A chance to be tempted, give in, get carried away

- Something to yearn for, the sweet pain of anticipation

- Playing with the forbidden, "testing limits" without real danger

- A chance to be a child again, to play, have fun, act silly

- An opportunity to be teased, a little bit provoked, stimulated

- Being discovered, exposing new and unfamiliar sides of one's self

- Confirmation of appeal, of being worthy of love

- Confirmation of being valuable, important

Electrifying marketing offers these benefits. Electrifying marketing can be applied in any industry, not only where it is expected, like entertainment. In fact, it will be especially effective where it is less expected. Once unexpected, electrifying marketing will deliver benefits that are "off core," external to your category's core benefits, therefore creating off-core differentiation and opening opportunities for achieving an unfair advantage.

Going Under

In Chapter 6 I told you about Harry Potter's electrifying marketing and also about the reality-based inspiration for the "Soup Nazi" character from *Seinfeld*. Now I want to tell you about electrifying marketing in an even more surprising category—men's underwear. Nick Graham, founder of the Joe Boxer clothing line, says, "The brand is an amusement park, and the product is the souvenir." Graham created one of the most amazing examples ever of an off-core differentiation that became a fantastic business success.

In 1985 at age 27, Graham reached San Francisco and founded a little business that manufactured and marketed ties in innovative designs. He began producing boxer underpants too, and gave his business the name Joe Boxer, implying boxers for every Joe—or every man.

One of his early innovations was boxers made of silk, covered with imprints of $100 bills. Little did he know that using the bills that way was a federal offense, and 1,000 pieces were confiscated. The media rolled on the floor laughing, and Graham learned about the financial value of humor in business. He recalls that it was at that point that he really started thinking about the whole idea of Joe Boxer, and how he was going to offer his customers one healthy dose of fun and wacky humor after another, not only entertaining them, but also creating for them a psychological benefit by supporting their self image ("I wear Joe Boxer; therefore I am a fun, cool guy").

I will only give you some examples, since the brand Joe Boxer was not built on big advertising campaigns (although it did have a few), but rather on a very wide collection of funny and cool initiatives that kept delivering the brand's unique spirit for years. Here are some of the more interesting ones:

- In 1988 the company launched its first glow-in-the-dark boxers for men. When you look at them in daylight, the word NO was printed all over the material. However, in the dark the word YES showed up instead. In 1990, it launched homewear and sleepwear and a long t-shirt with the legend, "Shut up and go to sleep" printed on them. Roseanne Barr thought it was cool and wore it on her TV show. One of the better consequences of electrifying marketing is that celebrities often grow fond of these products and contribute to their success without receiving any compensation in return.

- In 1993 the company began printing a red-tongued smiley-face logo on its products, and dubbed it "Licky Logo," making it the registered trademark of Joe Boxer Corporation. That same year it launched the Joe Boxer Suite at the Triton Hotel in San

Francisco, decorated with Joe Boxer home products, available for guests wanting to spend their vacations in a not-so-ordinary hotel room. The suite stayed intact and in demand for two years.

- Then Joe Boxer sent 100 pairs of underwear to President Bill Clinton to mark his first 100 days in office. The note in the parcel said, "If you're going to change the country, you've got to change your underwear." Little did it know how relevant the gift would turn out to be.

- In 1994, it conducted the first ever in-flight underwear fashion show on a Virgin Airways' flight from London to San Francisco, with the announcement that, "U.S. Customs require that all passengers change their underwear." Then Quentin Tarantino wore Joe Boxer pajamas in *Pulp Fiction*. Madonna wore them in *Truth or Dare* in 1991.

- In 1995, to mark Joe Boxer's 10th anniversary, the company held a mock wedding reception at a Las Vegas wedding chapel, with a fashion show and auction of designer wedding dresses. All the revenues—$14,000—were contributed to the Pediatric AIDS Foundation. Charitable contributions of various types constitute a central component in all Joe Boxer activities.

- That same year, Nick Graham published a book by the name of *A Brief History of Shorts: The Ultimate Guide to Understanding Your Underwear*. Then, a successful collaboration with Timex Corporation yielded Joe Boxer Time—a wristwatch launched at Bloomindale's, and said to have been the most successful watch launch ever.

- Another important principle leading Joe Boxer's way of doing business is the instant bonding that the brand carefully forms with every new trend and every possible technological development. It keeps the brand fresh and relevant. Accordingly, Joe Boxer was the first brand of underwear sold on the web.

- Joe Boxer launched a promotion with Virgin Airways, "Buy Five Pairs and Fly" program (consumers buy five pairs of boxers and get a Virgin companion ticket free to London). For the launch, Graham was suspended 100 feet above Times Square dressed as the Queen of England.

- In the mid 1990s, it rented a huge billboard in Times Square, New York, on which it featured actual messages sent by e-mail to *timessquare@Joeboxer.com*. It wasn't long before the first cyber-wedding rocked New York City. Robert Norris III proposed to Catherine Smylie after meeting her online in an Internet chat-room, via Joe Boxer's largest e-mail box in the world. Graham realized it was love at first byte, and agreed to unite the two in marriage. New York Mayor Giuliani officiated at the wedding of the happy couple.

- By 1997 Joe Boxer launched a promotion with General Mills, accompanied by the slogan, "Breakfast In Your Boxers." More than six million boxes of Frosted Cheerios cereal promoting Joe Boxer were sold. That same year Joe Boxer launched a pair of underwear into space, in the Joe Boxer rocket, together with underwear made by a Russian producer. I guess it all worked, because before the end of that year department stores reported Joe Boxer as the best selling underwear brand in America.

- In 1998 Joe Boxer teamed up with New York radio station Z100 and the Harley-Davidson Café, to create a promotional sweepstakes. Contestants threw balls to knock DJ Greg T into a dunk tank at the Harley-Davidson Café and their names were entered into a ballot box for the chance to leave that night (with a guest) to "See Jerry Seinfeld in Iceland." They also sponsored an American tour for Eddie Izzard, the outgoing English come-dian, giving away underwear with the tickets because customers losing bladder control due to laughter might be in need of a clean pair. Among all other activities that year, Joe Boxer also launched the first underwear vending machines.

I have mentioned only a few of the bright and wacky ideas by Joe Boxer. This brand's history was scattered with such activities until 2001, when Graham sold the company to Windsong Allegiance Group, and the brand was annexed to Kmart. Under its new management it lost much of its madness, but it is still engaging and also successful.

A Small and Soft Success

Another success story of electrifying marketing is that of Ty Warner, the richest toy manufacturer in the world, and inventor of the Beanie Babies. His personal fortune (his company, Ty Inc., issued 100 shares; he owns them all) was estimated by *Forbes* magazine at $4.4 billion in 2006, and most he earned since he launched Beanie Babies in 1994. Although it seems that the Beanie Babies' craze is behind us, the company is still extremely profitable. Ty Warner made his fortune using big-time electrifying marketing.

Warner was born in Chicago, where he still lives today, to a wealthy family. He went to school to study drama, but quit after one year and left for California. He dreamed about becoming a Hollywood star, but all he could accomplish were jobs at a gas station and as a door-to-door camera salesman.

In 1962, Warner settled in San Francisco, and became a sales representative for the Dakin company, a manufacturer of soft stuffed animals. Warner was known for driving a Rolls-Royce convertible, and wearing a fur coat and top hat. Undoubtedly he learned young about the importance of showmanship in business. He worked in this company for eighteen years and learned a lot about marketing toys.

After leaving Dakin, he spent three years in Italy, near Sorrento. During his stay he found beautiful toy kittens, which were soft and huggable, unlike the kind that were popular in America at the time. In 1983, he came back to Chicago, started his company, and began marketing a similar product called Himalayan Cats, manufactured for him in Korea. They came in different colors and sizes and had names, such as Peaches, George, Angel, and Smoky. He did pretty well, and in the following decade his product catalog grew to include a few dozen animals. But it was still not what he was looking for. At age 49, Warner decided to recheck everything experience had taught him. The result was Beanie Babies, his grand success.

His idea was to manufacture hand-sized, stuffed, furry animals with less filling than was common, to make them even softer, and to sell them for $5 so that any kid could buy one from his own weekly allowance. The filling was made of bean-like plastic pieces—hence, Beanie Babies. The animals all received cute names and for each one of them there was a personal story. They were developed as a series in order to encourage collecting. The first series that was marketed, and is considered almost legendary today, included nine animals: Spot the dog, Squealer the pig, Patti the platypus, Cubbie the bear, Chocolate the moose, Pinchers the lobster, Splash the killer whale, Legs the frog, and Flash the dolphin. In the years that followed many more Beanie Babies were launched, some with cute names for children, and others with meaningful names for the older collectors, like Courage the Dog, which was created in honor of the rescue teams, heroes of 9/11.

The product was right and its quality was high. Recognizing children as direct target consumers was original, and the pricing was right too. But what helped complete the picture and made the Beanie Babies a total hysteria, was none other than what I call electrifying marketing:

- Every animal was manufactured only in one series, meaning that either you bought it immediately (if you could make it to the shop on time), or maybe you could find it later in prices beyond imagination (up to $12,000!).

- Beanie Babies could not be found in big toy stores, but only in small shops, especially gift shops. This way the company retained more control over its distribution channels.

- Beanie Babies were never advertised.

- Rumors preceded the launch of every new model, which caused long lines and sometimes even fist fights.

- The company has neither an address (except a post office box) nor a written telephone number. Company offices are located somewhere in one of Chicago's suburbs, but the building has no sign on it.

- Company employees must sign a strict contract not to tell anyone anything about the company, especially not about Ty Warner, and they are forbidden to have social conversations about their company and employer.

- Ty Warner does not talk to the press and keeps his private life under complete secrecy.

The craze around the Beanie Babies was so wild that even books written about them turned into best sellers, including price guides and books for collectors. There are active websites for fans, and collector assemblies run by various community groups. The point that makes this case relevant to our subject of electrifying marketing is that the Beanie Babies are almost as popular with adults as they are with children. Adults are the collectors who pay big money—thousands of dollars—for rare and extinct animals, whereas children are the enthusiastic collectors of the newborns.

Today Ty Warner lives in Oak Brook, Illinois, a suburb of Chicago. He conducts his life like a mystery man, far from the public eye. He contributes to various worthy causes, and invests in real estate and hotels.

Principles of Electrifying Marketing

Here is a summary of the ten central principles of electrifying marketing. The ten principles constitute different ways to implement the basic electrifying marketing approach so you do not need all ten principles for each and every case. If you get most of them, that will do.

1. First and foremost, you need a high quality product and service. Nothing in the world will change this necessity. No marketing or branding "hocus pocus" will do. A product or a service that

stands steadfast compared with those of the competition constitutes your way of delivering the expected core benefits to your consumers. This is your ticket to the competition.

Make sure that your product taps exactly into your consumers' potential desires using the ForeSearch method (Chapter 8), and you will gain "desire leadership." You will have provoked a first-time, unfamiliar desire in your consumers' minds, making them feel that this is exactly what they wanted all along, and didn't realize it until now.

2. Create a differentiated benefit that takes your consumers beyond the borders of their normal lives. There are two kinds of such benefits:

* The benefit of an escape from the ordinary reality into a bigger-than-life existence, a world of fantasy, magic, and delirium. It isn't a coincidence that two of the most successful literary works of the past few years were the Harry Potter books and the *Da Vinci Code*.

* The benefit of experiencing an intense feeling of being alive: excitement, ecstasy, surprise, risk.

3. Deliver a strong sensual or emotional experience for your consumers that taps powerfully into one or more of their senses, evoking a strong emotional response, whether it is fear or any other powerful emotion.

4. Display a rule-shattering, convention-breaking, routine-shaking, marketing-competitive behavior. There are several ways of doing this. You can be any of the following:

* Expectation rockers—surprising

* Provocative

* Rebellious, subversive

* Mad, wacky

* Unreasonable, crazy

5. Use a secretive or mysterious element such as a secret formula, mystery people, something that nobody knows how it's done.

6. Put deliberate limitations on availability or accessibility of your product:

- A limited number (the "now-or-never" factor)

- A limited time (note short-term brands in the next chapter)

- Selectivity (limiting your targets) another type of exclusivity

- Taking the "don't-call-us-we'll-call-you" approach

7. Get your consumers actively involved in some kind of activity, some game or some type of interactive cooperation.

8. Use a "viral" element, meaning that you supply your consumers with reason to talk about your product or service with other people. There are three basic types of viral elements: the wow, the cool, and the Twist, on which we will elaborate in the next chapter.

9. Playfully incorporate elements of fun and entertainment. When you do so, do not take yourself too seriously, do not be heavy, and remember that, hey, this is only marketing after all.

10. Play around with your consumers—mislead them in some positive way (funny and inoffensive), manipulate them, play a joke on them, do something which appears to be one thing at first, but turns out to be something else.

These principles are very close in spirit to the methods we are about to address in the following two chapters: the branding hits formula and the short-term brands, as well as the brand drama approach.

I hope you will enjoy them.

15

How Are Marketing Hits Developed?

Surprise, Surprise—It's Systematic!

From time to time, the marketing world stands in awe in the face of huge, quick, and unexpected successes. These hits are products or services, recreation sites or resort spots, coffee shops, restaurants or bars, shopping centers or specific stores, which manage to gain inexplicable popularity. There are people who turn into sizzling celebrities. There are events and festivals that manage to attract huge crowds. There are housing projects that generate fantastic demand, and there are styles in various areas of our lives that become hot trends. In almost all cases, these are showcases of new brands, embraced warmly in marketing seconds by their target crowds. The Harry Potter books and the *Da Vinci Code* are good examples; Apple's iPod, YouTube, the Hamptons in Long Island, New York; the Scion by Toyota; Crest's electric tooth brush; and many more.

Sometimes the success does not surprise anyone. The success of a product like Viagra which solved a severe problem experienced by millions of men worldwide is completely obvious. Even the success of vacation resorts in Turkey is not surprising. They introduced vacations in a style (accessible until then only to the rich) now affordable to every Joe and Jill.

However, in other cases, sometimes it is completely unclear why one product, service, person, or place succeeds and its rivals do not. We have all witnessed a coffee shop that is constantly and completely packed, while around it others are empty.

Marketing hits research is not a new thing. In various product categories we have enough experience to enable the planning and launching of hits with the high probability of success. In the recreation and entertainment industries, companies like Disney, Warner, HBO, and others have proved this capability time and again (despite occasional lapses) in theaters, television, music, toys, electronic games, and more. A similar capability is also manifest by some in the fashion, fragrance, and retail industries. Usually, all secrets are carefully guarded.

I began to study marketing hits in the course of my work to create a methodology aimed at developing *short term brands* (STBs). STBs constitute the answer of marketing to a new and dominant consumer motivation, on which we will elaborate soon. In the course of this process I analyzed case studies of many hits in a variety of product categories, while at the same time I studied the experience accumulated in product categories that had already learned to develop hits methodically. The result was the *Marketing Hits Formula*, and the method by which it can be implemented. Together they help achieve effective marketing innovations that are easily and immediately embraced by any targeted customers. This formula has two advantages: the first is that it can be implemented in most product categories, and the second is that it does not necessitate huge marketing or advertising budgets that are the traditional way of attempting quick successes.

The Lifetime Customer

MBA clones usually do not take interest in marketing hits, or at least not a major interest. Their goal is, and has been for many years, to try and catch customers for life. It is understandable. Captive customers mean stable revenues and less money and effort on marketing, especially if they make it their habit to put in a good word for you with their friends every so often. Allegedly rival products are less tempting to captive customers; therefore you get more time to respond to competitors' innovations. They are not so price-sensitive; therefore you can afford to charge them a little more, and so forth. This is why MBA clones please themselves with terms of all kinds, starting with the good old "conquering market share," and "achieving share of customer/wallet/mind" and ending with the more recent "lifetime customers," "relationship marketing," "brand loyalty," and so forth.

In light of the above, did you ever stop and ask yourself about the nature of the latent assumptions they've been making about your customers? Average consumers who fit this portrait are conservative and tend to enjoy the familiar; they are calm, slow, and loyal by nature. Does that description sound like consumers of the 21st century? In one word: No. I have doubts about whether customers have ever been loyal. We generally take every consumer habit of purchase, which reflects lack of interest in other quite identical brands and products, as "loyalty," but this is a misnaming, and a big one at that. Even if consumers were loyal once upon a time, there is more than enough evidence to support the conviction that today they are not. Data from most countries leave no doubt. In 2004, even bank managers (and banking is a highly "loyal" product category) in Europe reported "loyalty bankruptcy" as the number one problem on their list (according to Datamonitor research).

We live in the post-customer-loyalty era. Nevertheless, your rivals are still deluding themselves, and not only about this matter. Lately launches of new products, and even brands, rise to success much quicker and higher than they did in the past (albeit for shorter time periods). Following these successes, there are more than a few marketers who walk around glowing with contentment. After all, they single-handedly achieved dramatic successes. However, a true perspective does require some humility. Marketing guru Seth Godin observed some years ago, "It took 40 years for radio to have 10 million users. It took 15 years for TV to have 10 million users. It only took 3 years for Netscape to get to 10 million, and it took Hotmail and Napster less than a year."

What is really happening here is an unprecedented readiness of consumers to try new products and brands. It's a little ironic, but these achievements that marketers are so proud of are nothing but a direct result of this very development—this one behavioral pattern that has been lately hammering the final nail into the coffin of the long deceased marketing loyalty.

As it turns out, in many cases marketers attempt to achieve one thing, while consumers of today need another. Thus marketers find their efforts are thwarted quite regularly. Contrary to MBA clones' best intentions to keep them loyal, consumers today take a highly watchful interest in changing objects of desire, that is to say, hits.

The rest of this chapter is divided into two parts:

First, we will understand what is happening to our consumers. We will talk about motivations and psychological mechanisms that render hits so central in contemporary strategic management. Second, we will see how perceptions and methods, which used to do the work in the past, are useless today and do not have the anticipated impact on the changed consumers of the 21st century. You will be introduced to the short term brands (STBs), and the Marketing Hits Formula (MHF), which will help you win in the new reality.

The FoMO-Plagued Consumer

Consumers have become serial adopters of innovations in every category that offers them worthwhile ones. This readiness is strengthening as time goes by. In the second half of the 1990s I identified this radical change in consumer behavior and its dramatic rise driven by a new and very powerful motivation I named The Fear of Missing Out, or in short, FoMO. In 2001, I developed a questionnaire for measuring levels of FoMO and discovered that this motivation exists at various levels in more than two-thirds of the consumers living in developed countries, and in half of these consumers it exists at high levels.

Join me on a short historical tour, just so that you can understand what really happened here. Up until the 19th century, most people rarely got to choose anything in their lives. They were born into a certain living situation, and usually stayed there all their lives. Men inherited their fathers' vocation and socioeconomic status, and women were in charge of their house. Dress was dictated by the local culture, with few variations allowed. Marriages were a result of arrangements, lifestyle was uniform; there was only one right way to go about things, one God, and one outlook on life.

Moving into the 20th century, people began to exercise more freedom in their lives as a result of several technological, cultural and social revolutions, new ideologies, and demographic changes. The transportation revolution (cars, planes), the communications revolution (telephony, television, and satellites), and the information revolution (computers, Internet) exposed people to new possibilities and increased options in every area of life. In the first half of the 20th century, most people were at a loss, and were not equipped mentally to deal with this newly acquired freedom and with the overabundance of possibilities.

In 1941, psychologist and philosopher Erich Fromm wrote a book called *Escape from Freedom* (Owl Books, 1994) in which he explained how a dictator like Hitler was elected in a democracy, claiming that people were trying to escape the freedom that was given to them. By the second half of the 20th century, this very freedom increased even further, widening the scope of what is considered legitimate. Possibilities multiplied (global commerce and rising competition added fuel to the fire too) but also people's freedom of choice increased and rose to a new level.

Today we are expected to choose almost everything about our existence—where we live, what we do, who we marry, what we believe in (if we choose to believe at all), our lifestyle, our identity, and finally, our products, services, and brands. The cultural focus today highlights the individual who wishes to self-develop, self-design, self-enhance and self-broadcast. There is no doubt about it: we've finally learned to deal with variety and choice. "Learned," I said? That's an understatement if there ever was one. We've become addicted to the feeling of having options and open possibilities. This is how FoMO has developed as a major motivation in our lives.

Contemporary consumers are drunk with possibilities. Choices are everywhere, and everything seems very much within reach. We want it all, or conversely, do not wish to miss out on anything. Therefore our lives are crazily paced and diverse, yet loaded with stimuli. We want everything and we want it now. We lead a hectic lifestyle in an attempt to squeeze as much as possible into our limited time. We're always reachable, up-to-date, open to new things, and not afraid of change. Oops, let me rephrase that; we crave change. We spend much less time than was acceptable even a decade ago at the same apartment, same job, and same marriage (if we do not belong to the eternal singles group). We have fewer long-lasting habits.

Once, having "character" was considered important. Today, consumers feel the need to maintain flexibility and to develop constantly throughout their lives. People are considered more interesting when they demonstrate contrasts, and if they behave differently and even contradictorily in various situations. (For instance, we may be in sync with our feelings and a warm personality in our personal life, a real killer in the business world, culturally attuned in concert halls, but loud and crude at the football stadium.) We like to change our appearance every so often.

On the Internet, if not (yet) in reality, we can live second lives and in our ever more complex communication with others we can assume multiple identities. That's normal now.

Today's consumers are all for fusing together combinations previously unthinkable, to have even more options. They like fusion not only in their food, their home living room, and clothing, but also in their identities and in their lives. A person who is an engineer, who paints pictures, practices Kundalini Yoga, and manages an investment portfolio over the Internet is a versatile and interesting person. By versatile, I mean this person can be more and probably this person also wants to stay young as long as possible because old age means *missing out*.

Another phenomenon that is closely related to FoMO is multitasking. It is growing stronger from one generation to the next. It is the inclination and the ability to do several things simultaneously. It is not unusual to see a young mother nursing her baby while working on her laptop, speaking on her mobile, and switching channels on her TV, perhaps following several television programs broadcast on several channels all at once.

FoMO is Crunching Loyalty

Naturally, consumers who are afraid of missing out are much less loyal to brands than before.

If you have children, especially boys, you probably know that whereas life these days may be revolving around X cards, a few months ago life revolved around Y cards. They went to sleep with them and any momentary separation was considered a crisis, even if it was for the purpose of taking a shower. But then things changed. Suddenly that same pack of Y cards was forsaken in the corner of the room. A few more weeks passed and nobody knows where it disappeared to, but who cares? Six months ago, Z cards were the hottest trend, but today, who remembers? I do not mention any names because I know that by the time you'll be reading this, these cards will be ancient history. Incidentally, it does not have to be cards; it can be the same with any computer game or other toy. And all I can say is: where are the days of Monopoly, Scrabble, Checkers, and Chess?

And if you are parents of girls, you are not exempt. Your lives have been lately taken over by Bratz dolls, which may be threatening ageless Barbie's formerly unbeatable status. Don't count on it. It is more than probable that a few years from now, everybody will be asking, "Bratz who?"

Kids, you say. They forget as easily as they are pleased. But what about adults? Let us for a moment ignore passing fashion quirks, momentary musical hits, dance styles that sweep us all and then and disappear just as instantly, television shows loved and forgotten, snacks, ice cream brands, popping up and vanishing cellular and PDA models. We are used to all of these already, and we see their short-lived nature as an obvious thing. Scents are not so obvious. Once there were classic fragrances like Chanel N°5 (since 1921!). Today we love to "nose" around in drugstores and perfumeries and sniff what's new.

And what about recreation spots? Once we had our little coffee house, and our favorite local restaurant. Today we turn to our local radio station or newspaper or to the web to search for new places. We also used to have our favorite vacation resort, but not anymore. Where is everybody going this year? Where will the hottest place be next summer? Surely not the same locale as last year.

And on the road, what happened to car models such as the Ford Fiesta and the Renault 5 which stood by us for so many decades, wanted and appreciated? The biggest hits of recent years, such as the new VW Beetle, or the cool PT Cruiser, are already barely in this year's competition, pushed by massive sales activities. In the more popular sector, how many years did the Mazda Lantis have with us before Mazda3 took over? New is fun, and even diamonds aren't forever anymore. (Wow! Isn't that taken from an expression as old as dinosaurs?)

Our customers embrace new products and brands at frantic speed. But, as quickly as they do, they abandon those for newer ones. And do not forget that by embracing your brand a minute ago, they have forsaken some other brand that was lucky before you—for a second.

Multi-Satisfiable Recurring Motivations

In Chapter 11 I mentioned how most benefits people seek are multi-satisfiable; they originate in recurring motivations and require recurring satisfactions, meaning that we feel the need to get more of the same benefit over and over again, possibly from the same products and brands, possibly from others. However, there are some recurring motivations that cannot be satisfied repeatedly by the same products and brands. These are what I call regenerating motivations and unsatisfiable motivations. It is essential to be aware of these needs. Their relative significance among the full "mix of motivations" is increasingly high, especially with contemporary consumers who are motivated by FoMO. These motivations drive consumers to look for new brands and new products all the time. On the one hand, these needs do indeed sabotage what is generally called "loyalty." However, on the other hand, they open up grand opportunities where this chapter is concerned: the developing and marketing of hits and successful brands for the short term.

There are two types of such motivations:

1. **Unsatisfiable motivations** are desires that cannot be realized, but will always be pursued by humans, who, despite repeated failures, will keep on deluding themselves that it is possible. Essentially, these futile attempts only enable our consumers to enjoy the realization of these needs in fantasy. We discussed

this in Chapter 13. Consumers love to fantasize about eternal youth, shapely bodies, personality and behavioral metamorphoses, endless sex-appeal, fateful romantic encounters, adventure, power, eminence, glory, and other general goals that are unattainable or very difficult, costly or risky to attain. The fantasy is pleasant, comforting and encouraging. Therefore it is valuable by its own right. Most consumers do not let it hurt their lives in any way. Brands that support such fantasies (wonder diets, anti-aging elixirs, and aphrodisiacs) are disappointing, which means that consumers need new ones to replace them. Irrational behavior? Only in the eyes of someone who doesn't understand them. Consumer fraud? No. We only provide them with means by which they can carry on doing what they were about to do anyway, with us or without us.

Another **unsatisfiable motivation** is the "unanswerable question" and it has to do with other issues we have discussed in the previous chapter. Every person has at least one facet in life in which they feel a deep void, deficiency, or flaw. It originated in early childhood. Every person asks his or her unanswerable question again and again, usually without even being aware of it. The question is asked implicitly, indirectly, suggestively: "Am I lovable?" "Am I worthy?" "I am not stupid, am I?" There are quite a few of those. Each and every person has a central unanswerable question. No matter how many times this question is answered, the need to hear the answer again and again will not be relieved, and will not diminish ever. From time to time there will be brands or products that deliver the answer. If you look sensitively at the people around you, you can identify their questions. If you look bravely at yourself, you may be able to identify your own.

2. **Regenerating motivations** are needs that demand new satisfaction agents every time in order to offer regenerating satisfaction. Therefore, products and brands that deliver wanted benefits lose their ability to satisfy and must be replaced, time after time.

Among these we can find regenerating interpersonal motivations, including the need to win attention and acknowledgement from one's surroundings, and regenerating psychological motivations such as the motivation for renewal, discovery, and seduction. Can you see why we need new brands and products all the time?

There are also social regenerating motivations such as the motivation to signal to others your continuous involvement, being up-to-date and in sync with what's going on, the motivation to signal youth and openness, and sometimes the motivation to be a trend setter and influence other people.

Finally, there are regenerating sensuous and experiential needs that demand new satisfactions, revolving around the central need to be aroused through fresh sensuous experiences. As we all know, our system becomes accustomed to stimulations that then lose their strength. Therefore we need new smells, flavors, sounds, and textures in order to experience our senses to their full capacity. I include here also the motivation for emotional exercise, and the imaginary preparation for any future event.

The Cycle of Desire

Consumers shop for two main reasons: the first one is in order to stop or prevent any damage, lack of comfort, unpleasantness, embarrassment, pain, grief, remorse, regret, and other negative emotions or undesirable experiences. Sometimes we call these purchases "motivated by necessity." The array is wide. It begins with insurance or medicine, moves on to routine food shopping, and ends with planning a family vacation, but not of the kind consumers generally get excited about. Sometimes we say that these are "rational" purchases because the purchasing process is characterized by reasoning, in an attempt to limit your spending. Of course, every purchase has an emotional element to it because where there is no emotion there is no motivation. Reasoned purchases are typically driven by obligation, duty and underlying concerns, anxieties and even fears, often too mild to be actually noticeable. Normally, emotion is not the center of attention in this type of purchase.

There is also another type of shopping. This type is intended to create or to attain a wanted situation, or to bring about positive emotions or pleasant sensations or experiences. These are purchases motivated by desire. They have elements of fantasy, anticipation, and longing. Here too the array of possibilities is wide, beginning with a wonderful cake from a top pastry shop, through clothes, perfumes, jewelry, and gadgets, and up to cars and houses. Despite these examples, notice that what determines the type of purchase is not the product but rather the consumer's attitude towards the purchase. The purchase of the same product (a car, for instance) could be motivated by necessity for one person, and be a purchase of desire for another.

And still, each of the two types of purchase behavior is more typical of some categories and less typical of others. It is hard to imagine a desire-motivated purchase of toilet paper (but not impossible, since recently a brand of black stylish toilet paper was launched), just as much as it is difficult to see a purchase of music motivated by necessity. And one more thing: these two types of purchasing constitute two ends on a continuous axis, along which we can trace all purchases in general.

Where desire-motivated purchases are concerned, there is often a psychological cycle at work, which I named *The Cycle of Desire*. The cycle of desire is directly related to the multi-satisfiable needs we discussed earlier. It is also related to the consumer's need for electrifying marketing, the central issue in the previous chapter.

The cycle of desire begins with a feeling of dissatisfaction, boredom, or disgust (for example, a feeling that you cannot stand your cellular phone anymore). Sometimes this stage is not entirely conscious but rather it takes the form of some vague feeling that lingers in the background. The next stage happens when you suddenly bump into a new and hot product, model, or design. It could happen upon seeing an ad, or at a friend's, house, or while window shopping at the mall. This new product ignites your imagination. You are quite sure that once you have it, once you do it, once you consume it, things will be wonderful!

The cycle of desire, as the name implies, is a cyclical phenomenon. It begins with a feeling of discontent which leads, sooner or later, to a discovery of a new cool option (a new brand, for instance). The rest of this process consists of self seduction using obsessive fantasizing (to some degree) about the wonders which will be yours upon purchase. The more conflict the purchase raises in you, the sweeter the torments will be that accompany your anticipation. Giving in to desire and going on with the purchase will bring about a feeling of indulgence, dazzling but short lived.

If the purchase itself is no big deal for you, you just buy it and pass on the real fun. If the purchase is not so simple for you for one reason or another (too expensive right now, your spouse will not appreciate it), then begins the stage of your self-seduction. You torment yourself about this decision for minutes, for hours, or for days. You really want this thing but you are hesitant. You have fun fantasizing about the good things it may bring you, but you dread the possible consequences. There is drama. You feel simultaneous craving and pangs of guilt. Usually, you end up buying. You feel it is stronger than you. You rationalize (it's your birthday, it's on sale, and so forth).

After having bought it, you're in heaven. Such a sweet delight. You wanted this so much; you are really happy that you have decided to buy it. However, this is a fleeting feeling. It is not long before you feel that although it was a good experience, you are not so enthusiastic anymore. Here you are back to that gnawing feeling of dissatisfaction, boredom, or disgust. The cycle begins again.

The Psychology of Temptation

Temptation is crucial to consumers because many purchases are hard to justify (since the benefits they deliver are not always legitimate ones given specific circumstances or prices). The seduction is an unconscious game. The covert purpose is to give in to something stronger than you. Why? There are two central benefits: the first one is to feel strong vital feelings (the feeling of life), the second is to do something you really want to, even though it is not legitimate or appropriate (in the eyes of your responsible side, or your surroundings), and despite all the good reasons on the "don't do" side.

Seduction is often necessary when it comes to short-term brands (STBs), which you will get to know in a minute, since it is obvious that any benefit to be attained is short term, making it even less justified.

The enticing marketer plays the game with his customers using principles of hypnotic marketing, which we will discuss in detail in the next chapter.

Up until now, we have dealt with the psychologically fertile ground of STBs and marketing hits. Now let us understand what they are and how to use them.

Some Marketers Are Already Thinking Short

How did it all begin? Lately marketers have found that their new brands, even when successful, last a much shorter time than they had hoped. When planning a long-term brand that is rendered short term (even when successful) by consumers, the result is a painful loss. Smart marketers understand that if consumers render their brands short term anyway, then they might as well plan them that way to begin with. One after another, marketers in dozens of categories have begun experimenting with creating marketing hits and launching short-term brands, even before this term was ever created. Although many managers and marketing experts are still fighting courageously and almost religiously in the lost battle for loyalty, a large number already understand that it's a matter of changing thinking paradigms. If the traditional long-term brand strives to "marry" its consumers "until death do us part," then the short-term brand invites consumers for an exciting, thrilling "one night stand," knowing that it will be short and sweet.

After years of exclusive featuring of long-term brands (LTBs), Disney's cartoon factory began to neglect good old Mickey Mouse and friends. If we look at recent years and plans for the near future, we can see that each year the studios released or plan to release at least one hit:

2001   *Atlantis: The Lost Empire* (and *Monsters, Inc.* by Pixar)

2002   *Lilo & Stitch* and *Treasure Planet*

2003   *Brother Bear* (and *Finding Nemo* by Pixar)

2004   *The Incredibles* by Pixar

2005   *Home on the Range*

2006   *Chicken Little* (and *Cars* by Pixar)

2007   *Ratatouille* by Pixar

2008   *Meet the Robinsons* (and *Wall-E* by Pixar)

2009   *American Dog*

The entertainment industry (theater, television, music) is not the only product category that has been thinking along the lines of "hits" lately. This way of thinking is true in many other categories: toys and games, medicine, cosmetics, hygiene and grooming, fashion, cars, building projects, computers, gadgets, cellular devices, vacation resorts, books, and indeed in almost every category known. Look at Microsoft and its Windows versions. Once they were named after the year of launch. After that they were called XP and Millennium. The new Windows is already called Vista, and is being treated marketing-wise unmistakably like an STB. Windows is background matter. Vista is worthy of the spotlight.

Start-up companies began arousing incredible interest since the happy days of the hi-tech boom back in the 1990s. Most of them are designed to do their thing and be sold or IPO'd, according to a predetermined time schedule. The term "exit strategy" was coined around these companies, meaning cashing in the investment and profits, which is preplanned. They are short-term brands.

Managerial theories are surely also short-term brands. Once every few years a new approach or method, behind a new guru, turns into the contemporary, absolutely irrefutable, "must-do" thing, only until a new one comes along. Do you care for some examples? MBO, SCM, TQM, EFQM, BPM, PMM, SFO, CRM, CPM, CFO, BSC, QFD, ERP, 6 Sigma, Balanced Scorecard, Reengineering, Lean Management, Strategy Maps, ABS Costing, Performance Prism. . . . Need I say more?

Short-Term Stores

One of the most surprising expressions of the short-term managerial thinking is the emergence of pop-up stores and of stores on wheels that move around. The phenomenon began in mid-2003, and apparently has been turning into an effective way to turn customers on to your brand and create a serious buzz.

Target opened a store in Rockefeller Center in order to launch the new women's fashion line designed by Isaac Mizrahi. The store was active for only ten days. Six months later, the chain opened a store in the Hamptons on Long Island for a month and a week. After several more months they did it again in Times Square in Manhattan. These temporary Target shops, that highlight a new product line every time, turn out to be a regular way of doing business and promotion at once.

Vacant fashion brand regularly opens one-month shops in New York, Los Angeles, and ten more cities in the United States, as well as in London, Paris, Berlin, Stockholm, Shanghai, and Tokyo. These shops usually feature limited lines of fashion. The chain, by the way, has been working according to electrifying marketing principles. Not only does it produce small series, but not every piece that is presented at the stores is for sale, and only registered Vacant Club members get an early announcement about the stores' locations.

Comme des Garçons, the fashion and perfume brand, opened short-term stores in Berlin and Tokyo, and from what I hear, they are planning to continue in other cities as well.

Detergent and toiletry brand Method, "People Against Dirty," offers products that are scented, colorful and exquisitely designed (it is worthwhile to see their website *www.methodhome.com*). Method opened a store for three months in Union Square in San Francisco. The store looked like a gallery and demonstrated the sensuous feeling that is offered to consumers by this brand, whether they are cleansing their bodies, doing laundry, or cleaning their kitchen stove.

Other brands that are also worth mentioning are Meow Mix Café, which was open for a week, offering cat-delicacies; Suave's hairstyle shops which opened for one month in New York, Chicago, and Minneapolis; and Lancome Peeling Centers which opened in Milan for two weeks. The list of brands and chains that use this new method is getting longer by the minute and includes names such as Adidas, MTV, Levi's, Nike, JCPenney, and many others.

In the shops on wheels arena, another form of temporary presence, there is the London Fashion Bus, which offers 1,400 pieces by 40 designers; Vacant's Hummer H2–accommodated shop; and Brazilian cosmetic company Oceanic's Fiat Dublo–accommodated shop.

The popular web-magazine *Trendwatching.com* gave this phenomenon the very appropriate name of pop-up retail.

Short-Term Brands

As often happens, a select minority of quick marketers did not wait idly for a methodology to come along theorizing short-term branding. They began experimenting pretty much intuitively. I observed this experimentation at the end of the 1990s at the same time I was researching FoMO. I began working on a method of planning, launching, and managing such brands. In 2000 I published an article in the *Journal of Brand Management* in which I coined the term short-term brands, or STBs. The article articulated for the first time some principles of developing short-term brands and the economic logic behind it. London Business School included this article in its list of recommended articles on marketing. Since then I have developed this method further and recently completed a book that will serve as a field guide for marketers developing STBs. Here are some of its principles.

STBs are successes planned for the short term. STBs are hits. They are successes based on unsatisfiable or regenerating motivations, FoMO, the circle of desire, the psychology of seduction, and also the other psychological phenomena related to electrifying marketing that we talked about in the previous chapter. When you develop an STB you exploit (in the positive sense of the word) opportunities for success. You do it by delivering benefits to consumers, even if these are not the same benefits which are dealt with in regular marketing literature. However, you must keep in mind that the nature of these benefits causes successes to be short-lived. So long as you take this into account, STBs can be very profitable.

Do not mistake STBs for failed long-term brands. Short-term brands are not failures. On the contrary, they are huge successes, even though they exist for a short time. In order to achieve such successes, marketing veterans need to learn some new tricks.

I'm sure you are asking, "Why not stay with a fixed long-term brand and innovate on the product line?" The answer is that launches of new products and new improved product versions are not enough. A new brand signals "new" better than a new product under an old brand. Moreover, when we are talking about benefits that are psychological or social, the need for a new brand, rather than just a new product, is even more apparent. Today, when consumers are ready and willing to try new brands and embrace them quickly, many past obstacles are gone.

I'm not claiming that there are no classics. Of course we have our all-time favorites like Coca-Cola, but still we're glad to try out their new stuff, like Diet Coke with Lemon or the recent Coca-Cola Zero. We will always have Paris, McDonald's, and Harley-Davidson, among many others; in fact, even local classics are still loved and cherished. However, the list of classics is more or less a closed list, and any additions to that list are rare. The youngest brand listed among the 20 biggest world brands (from Interbrand's 100 Best Global Brands list) is Microsoft, and it was founded in 1975.

I want to be clear about this. I am not saying that there is absolutely no sense in launching long-term brands. Not at all. But I am saying that long-term branding today is harder to achieve than it used to be, whereas short-term branding opens up great opportunities Short-term brands offer consumers benefits which cannot be provided, by definition, by long-term brands. The STB is simply better at tapping into the new consumers' state of existence, with their hectic lifestyles, their ever-changing realities, and their constant yearning for the "new-new." Moreover, today we tend to brand not only products and services but also projects, events, processes, campaigns, and contests, all of which are short term by their nature. If nothing else, at least for the purpose of managing such brands, marketers need to develop their STB abilities.

The definition of "short" depends on the category. In some categories, like films, short implies several weeks or months. For other categories, like cars for instance, short now means somewhere between six to seven years. The brand Harry Potter was pre-planned to include only seven books. This is STB logic. The sixth book in the series was published in July 2005, with more than 250 million copies sold in advance. In research conducted by Martin Lindstrom in collaboration with Millward Brown, which covered 20,000 children aged 7 to 12, in

18 countries, it was found that 69 percent do not consider this brand to be so interesting any more. Lucky for J.K. Rowling, she finished the series in mid-2007. The success of *Harry Potter and the Deathly Hallows*, launched on July 21, is heightened by the fact that this is the seventh and final book in the series.

An STB is sometimes launched as a stand-alone brand (the Beyblade for instance), but in many cases it is launched along with a long standing LTB (like Fusion shaving system by Gillette). When combined, the marketing celebration should be focused on the STB. The LTB takes on the role of a reassuring background brand. STBs help LTBs preserve their freshness, contemporariness and relevance. They also enable a gradual continuous updating of the long-term brand's significance and promise to consumers. Surprisingly, STBs help maintain consumer loyalty to the LTB because they evoke renewed interest in the brand every time.

The economic logic of STBs starts with the fact that they potentially achieve, though for a short term, a markedly higher market share compared with typical LTBs in the same category. Over time, planned launching of one STB after the other will achieve a mean market share that can be considerably higher than the average market shares of similar LTBs. But aren't these launches too expensive? According to my experience, and in light of all the changes that have occurred in consumer behavior, many launches of products and new brands are grossly over-invested. A well-planned STB will not require such extravagance.

If the best metaphor for long-term branding is building a skyscraper, one floor after another, then the best metaphor for short-term branding is lighting a fire. The STBs life cycle is composed of three typical stages:

1. The pre-launch stage, the preparation of the wood pile, all ready for the match to light it

2. The launch's big bang, or adding a fire starter to the pile of wood

3. A viral spreading of the news from one consumer to another, and the spreading of the fire which catches on to the entirety of the wood pile until it is all burned out, the sales go down, and the fire dies

An interesting variation of the STB is the short-term consumer. In some cases it will be wise to keep your brand static, but change its target consumers. One good example for such a brand would be the marketing of vacation resorts. A vacation resort can switch the focus of its main marketing efforts to different places in the world every year or few years, thus rendering itself relevant to tourists from different places every time. By doing so, it will answer the current tourists' need to achieve variety in their vacation consumption. Another example is children's toy brands. These brands that are usually targeted at a certain age group enjoy new waves of target consumers (the children and their parents), enabling renewed launches of these brands once every several years.

I also want to tell you about The Law of Exciting Brands. It proclaims that when a brand penetrates a market and arouses excitement and great interest, then by definition it is bound to be an STB, no matter the original intent of its creators. The reason is simple: excitement tends to be short-lived. LTBs are based on security and trust. The excitement is saved for STBs.

How is an STB Created?

The development of an STB is roughly a four-stage process (a more elaborate 10 step process is detailed in my book about STBs).

1. The first stage is choosing the right timing for launch. There are three main signs for "ripe" timing. The first one is called "mature replacement cycle," which refers to the feeling sensed by our consumers (whom we identify using market research) that the previous hit, or the current brand, has already lost its attractiveness. The second is called "seasonal readiness" which is

relevant in some categories beginning with swimwear, and going to other seasonal foods and beverages, sports, and activities. The third sign is called "situational readiness" and it refers to the identification of your rival's weaknesses.

2. The second stage is the methodical scanning, mapping, and evaluating of opportunities for marketing innovation. You can use the "What's next?" process and the O-Scan method, which I described in Chapters 6 through 10, for spotting opportunities for new STB launchings.

3. The third stage consists of developing the new hit concept according to the Marketing Hits Formula, which I will describe to you shortly.

4. The fourth stage consists of developing a launch plan based on the concentration of a short and intense effort in advertising, promotion, and other activities that are designed to develop a viral effect, i.e., word of mouth.

An important decision is whether to launch an STB as a stand alone or in combination with an LTB. Around STBs and their integration with LTBs, two new brand architectures have developed, which will be worth your while to examine. The first is the *background-foreground architecture*. Within this architecture the LTB stands in the background, and its role is to reassure consumers that their "bride" is from a good home. The STB stands in the front, and gets all the merrymaking. It is what consumers get excited about, and it is what they buy. Think about BMW and the Mini.

The second architecture is the *star-satellite architecture* where the LTB is the main thing bought by consumers. The STB is the solution for X which stands for a certain issue pertaining to the said LTB. A great example would be C2 launched in 2004 by Coca-Cola, first in Japan and then in the U.S., in light of the no- or low-carb diet crazes like Atkins.

The Process of Developing a Marketing Hit

The process of developing a new marketing hit includes, before anything else, identification of a fitting opportunity: consumers whose attitudes have matured to move on to the next big thing, and also seasonality or situational readiness. The following step is the spotting of the right opportunity to develop a product and a brand which will be embraced enthusiastically by target consumers. Designing the product that you are offering your consumers should be based 80 percent on a previously successful template, and only 20 percent on innovation.

It is also necessary to decide upon the type and degree of correlation between the various STBs you are about to launch.

• A one-time STB: you could launch one from time to time without any linkage between them.

- A developing series in which there is a factor of continuance and development, like Windows by Microsoft, or the *Lord of the Rings* trilogy.

- A non-developing series in which every STB has to obey the same basic rules, but it is not dependent on its predecessors or followers, like the James Bond films and Beanie Babies.

The Marketing Hits Formula

Every STB is designed to be a marketing hit. Hits are by nature short-term successes, and they are replaced in a certain frequency with new hits. The formula I have developed determines that a marketing hit complies with four rules. Use them in order to develop your marketing hits.

Rule One says that the product, service, or place has to be based 80 percent on a previously successful "recipe," which has been known to succeed many times before in the same category. This recipe assures consumer satisfaction, and prevents unnecessary hassle, learning, adapting or other efforts in the process of embracing the new hit. This is one of the surprises hidden in this formula, and it refutes most of the talk you hear these days about innovation in marketing. Whether it is a bar or vacation resort, a food product or new software, you should build it around a strongly familiar base, so that consumers who used previous hits from the same "home" can find in your product all the core benefits they expected to find, in addition to the added value of the innovation.

Rule Two says that approximately 20 percent should constitute the innovation factor. The novelty offers an added benefit, an improvement, a unique experience, a fashionable and current element, or at least an opportunity for the consumers to feel renewal, freshness, or being up-to-date. This "new" factor will comply with rules 3 and 4 below.

Rule Three states the product's "new" factor will cater to at least one of the unsatisfiable or regenerating motivations. (See the beginning of this chapter.)

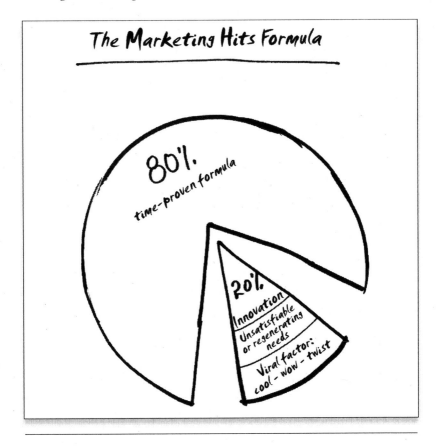

The Marketing Hits Formula suggests that hits are not based on a high level of innovation. Hits are based on a low novelty factor, which does not exceed 20 percent of the whole. This factor complies with two important rules: it caters to a regenerating or unsatisfiable motivation, and it contains a viral element that is designed to deliver a good reason for consumers to talk about the product with other potentials and nurture its spreading.

Finally, Rule Four says the "new" factor in your product should contain an element of cool, wow, or twist, which will constitute its viral engine. In other words, it will supply the product's buyers with a good reason to pass on the exciting news to other potential buyers.

This good reason has to do with benefits derived from the telling. The innovative factor is such that their stories will win them attention and will also help them appear to be up-to-date and in-the-know. Their listeners will be interested and grateful. Why? Because cool means trendy, maybe even a little bit bold. Wow means arousing wonder because of an amazing design or an impressive performance. Twist means weird or unexpected.

In order to see how it works, let us look at Apple's iPod, which was responsible for the company's dramatic upturn in sales.

1. The iPod is a mobile music player, hardly a new idea at the time it was launched. Ever since Sony's Walkman, through digital players of recent years, we have gotten pretty accustomed to carrying our music with us wherever we go. That's the 80 percent. That's the proven recipe.

2. The major innovation of the iPod is the combination of several elements. First, high storage volumes in small physical size (previous mobile players had the customers choosing between the two). In addition to that, the innovation includes the amazing and unusual designs, the simplicity and easy user interface, the quick connection to any PC or Mac, and the iTunes website, each of which constitutes an additional novelty. That's the 20 percent.

3. For early users, the iPod answers the regenerating motivation to win attention from the surroundings. One cannot mistake the conspicuous white headphones or iPod's unique design. For the wider market iPod's millions of users answers the regenerating motivation to be up-to-date, to belong to the right group, even before the pleasure that music delivers, which is a self-evident core benefit.

4. The major viral element in the iPod is the unmistakable design. This is a sure wow element. The huge storage volume is also a wow in itself. Another viral element is that iTunes delivers intra-iPod users folklore, reserved only for them.

16

How to Drive Consumers Crazy about your Brand

How Do Consumers Discover a Brand?

After you have developed a strategy to achieve your strong competitive advantage, and after, as an integral part of this strategy, you also have developed your brand's concept, you will need to get consumers excited enough about your brand to want to buy it. This is what this chapter is all about. Incidentally, please note that the methods in this chapter can be used for LTBs (especially those that offer consumers intangible instrumentality), as well as STBs or short-term marketing hits.

There's an old chauvinist saying, "A man chases a woman until she catches him." At least when it comes to brands, this is a pretty good way to put it. Marketers do what they do, and invest what they invest, all so that consumers will discover their brand. This is the only way it works.

Consumers live their lives, and in the frame of everything they do and go through they are constantly on the lookout for new opportunities to improve their existence. They search for solutions to their problems, ways to prevent unwanted situations and experiences, opportunities to develop, improve, and advance themselves and their circumstances, and chances to have fun and enjoy life with their loved ones. We have dealt with various aspects of what consumers want in life, and what benefits they are looking for. All of these can add up to the term *consumer pre-readiness*. It is a kind of flammability. It is what determines whether or not your consumers will be "brand affectable" or turned on by your brand.

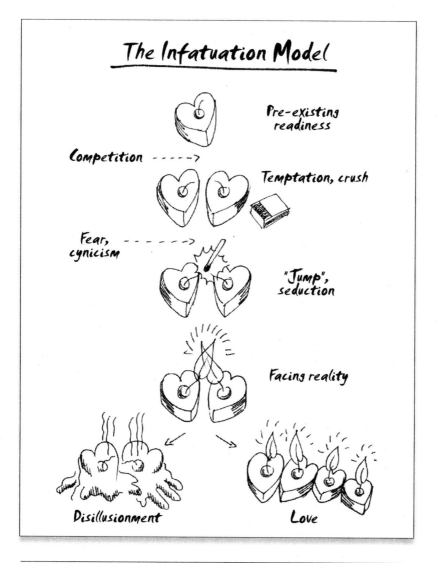

The Infatuation Model

Pre-existing readiness

Competition ----->

Temptation, crush

Fear, cynicism ------>

"Jump", seduction

Facing reality

Disillusionment

Love

According to the infatuation model, a turn-on can occur only when pre-readiness exists. When we identify (without being aware of it) someone we meet as similar to our internal image of "the loved one" who will supposedly bring us happiness, then we have a turn-on. The feeling of "finding" and the excited anticipation is "falling in love." The "leap" into a relationship is what leads to the encounter with the real person. The result is either an experience of disillusionment or of true love.

I suggest that in order to understand this process better, we should borrow a psychological model that I developed to depict the process of infatuation. You already know that I do not think that people fall in love with brands. The reason for using this model is that it helps you understand how people become "turned on" to something or someone in general.

According to this model, the basis for falling in love is the state of pre-readiness. It is what determines whether or not a person is indeed open and prone to the possibility of falling in love, and if the answer is yes, then with whom. This pre-readiness really consists of benefits that people seek, whether consciously or not. These benefits are not abstract but rather they exist as images and even scenarios that are fantasized reality scenes and stories, living in people's imagination. They portray the perfect and desired life and relationship, and how they might come to be.

These images are constructed from the person's surrounding culture and personal history; from continuous exposure to television, newspapers, magazines, radio, the web, advertisements, books, movies, and personal stories of other people's lives, celebrities as well as friends and family. All of these form and shape our pre-readiness. Without our being aware of it, we constantly collect fantasy scenarios of "the good life," of love, pleasure, fun, and happiness. These possibilities live in our imagination and construct a template of our own beliefs regarding what is good for us and how we could attain the benefits we seek. All of these become entangled (there is no requirement for internal consistency) and are weighted with our beliefs about ourselves, our worth, our abilities, and our identities.

A relatively large part of this pre-readiness is common to many people sharing the same cultures or social groups. Therefore, our aspirations and lifestyles, like those of many people around us, often constitute variations of "like mixes," put together from the same pool of options as those of our peers. The other component of pre-readiness is personal. Of course we find great interest in our shared pre-readiness and it is certainly related to the shared realities that we discussed in Chapter 13.

The infatuation model says that embodied within our pre-readiness state lies the subconscious image of a lover who will make us happy, and also scenes and stories telling us how we shall meet them, fall in love, and live happily ever after, or any other scenario that fits our image of utopia. Regretfully, this pre-readiness does not have prophetic powers. It is only a bunch of beliefs that were collected and formed subconsciously during the course of our lives. When we encounter, in reality, a candidate who resembles this image, or we meet him or her in circumstances that resemble our subconscious story or situation, then we have a match. We identify something familiar, similar to what we have in our imagination. It all happens subconsciously and instantly and therefore we do not even know why he or she seems so familiar. We undergo a "eureka" experience without being able to provide any explanation. It seems like magic. This is how we become turned on. We meet someone whom we confidently perceive as a way to achieve the good life we seek.

Similarly, consumers also feel that they are turned on when a brand they encounter transmits to them a promise to realize the good things they seek within the frame of their pre-readiness template. Some brands communicate something that seems to be the realization of our more or less conscious images. But here is the problem. All marketers know many of the common pre-readiness templates, and they all attempt to communicate similar promises. After all, MBA clones think alike, research consumers with the same methods, use the same skills to develop their products and brands, their campaigns and promos, and also market the same way. We have already discussed this at length; I'm only tying the ends for you right now.

This problem leads to two results. The first one maintains that consumers do not believe anyone anymore due to myriad over-promising that is dispersed continuously around them. The second is that consumers do believe the less extravagant promises, but think that everyone can deliver the same benefits exactly and are therefore indifferent and disloyal.

From time to time some marketer bursts forth and manages to upstage his rivals using super-creative marketing tactics and communication. For a while this marketer manages to attract extra attention for his brand. From time to time a marketer can launch a product or service that constitutes an opening of a gap between him and his competition by offering better benefits. It definitely arouses public attention from some consumers, until the competition closes that gap.

So how do you escape this trap? There are a few ways that I described earlier and here they are again in brief:

1. You use the methods detailed in Chapters 7 though 10 (especially the ForeSearch) to identify not only what already exists in the concrete part of the states of pre-readiness, but also what could exist but is not there yet. On this basis you create differentiation. Differentiation always means showing consumers options they are not familiar with that will enable them to obtain the benefits they seek. Of course, an off-core differentiation is always better, offering consumers unexpected benefits that perhaps are part of the consumer's pre-readiness in other product categories but not in yours. Because this is not a core benefit, your competition will find it awkward or difficult to imitate you and will usually not do so.

2. You use the ForeSearch and other methods I mentioned in order to identify new elements of pre-readiness that are just beginning to form (e.g., as a result of an emerging trend). You pay special attention to unsatisfiable and regenerating motivations. You do this prior to your competitors and then develop a marketing hit on the basis of this discovery.

3. You understand your customers and research realms better than your rivals. These are typically neglected by your MBA-clone competition. Usually this means researching aspects such as enriched realities, FoMO, the circle of desire, and other phenomena we've dealt with. Then you use them in order to create electrifying marketing.

When you manage to embed yourself into your consumers' awareness, and to be perceived by them as offering a unique benefit (not better or cheaper than your competition, but a different benefit altogether), then the result would be that "eureka" experience I mentioned earlier. I call it "just on desire." This is how you manage to turn your customers on.

The branding aspect of your strategic thinking (alongside your competitive strategy and your business model) is the creation of this consumer turn-on for your brand. It has two parts. The first consists of building a unique benefit into your brand strategy and making it deliver. If it is an intangible benefit, realizing it would include shaping the brand experience and fine-tuning its marketing communications, with all its layers and flavors, to provide the benefit on the experiential, social, or psychological levels. The second part consists of communicating your brand promise to your customers.

Note also the next stages in the infatuation model. After the turn-on, there is the leap that is an accelerated involvement in a relationship, or in our case, a first purchase to actually try the product. This trial may develop into love, or in our modest case, into repeat purchases and excitement. This trial may also lead to disenchantment and disappointment. With good and knowledgeable management, the first scenario will occur, not the second.

Leading Them by Their Noses

I would like to share a brand story with you. It is an odd story, yet it carries an important lesson.

Since 1983, Unilever had been marketing a deodorant for men called Axe (in some countries it is known as Lynx). It was a decent brand, but going nowhere. In 2002, Unilever decided to launch it in the American market and turn it into a global hit at the same time. Target customers were defined as young men, aged 18 to 24. This customers' typical fantasy is well-known. The idea to introduce a hygiene product as a way to increase one's sex appeal is certainly *not* a new idea, but managers behind Axe identified an interesting fact. Marketers are usually serious and responsible people; therefore, in the past, the promise to increase a user's sex appeal was always communicated implicitly or suggestively. They didn't want to be held responsible for a promise that nobody really meant seriously anyway.

The Axe team decided to go with a different approach, and to communicate a bold promise that would be like a direct infusion into the veins, pumping blood into fantasies. Young men were told directly and boldly: use Axe and get the ladies, and not just one, but many. They named it the Axe Effect. This is not just talking to targets' pre-readiness; this is screaming it out! On its website, Axe declared that just like Keanu Reeves decided to take the red pill in *The Matrix*, the brand Axe decided to take the red pill too. In this case, the identification of the pre-readiness state did not entail any sophistication at all. Their differentiation was based on a boldness that was never witnessed before. Their bet was that this powerfulness would inflate the fantasy so strongly that it would crush any resistance or doubt at once. However, there's still a way out. If the consumer is cynical, he can still interpret it all as cool and wild humor.

Axe delivered all four conditions of the Marketing Hit's Formula: the 80 percent proven formula was the spray deodorant since everybody knows what it is; the 20 percent innovative factor was not just a deodorant spray but a new category altogether—a body perfume to be sprayed all over the body (using semi-ritualistic motions as featured in the commercial); catering to an unsatisfiable motivation of the fantasy of endless sex appeal; and finally, the viral twist factor was a popular conversation starter with friends: "Is it true? Does it really work? Did you try it? Did it happen?"

They played high stakes. They went for it all: a two year advertising budget of $100 million and commercials that are at times grotesquely direct, but at other times really cool and award-winning. One of the better ones is called "Getting Dressed." A couple gets out of bed, and it is instantly apparent that whatever happened there was truly wonderful. Their clothes are spread everywhere, and they walk around, collecting them, wearing each item as they retrieve it. They walk out to the street where they also find clothing items marking the path all the way down to the supermarket, and inside too, until they reach two heavily loaded carts, positioned at one of the aisles, one next to the other, where their final items still rest. Each one of them approaches his or her cart, and to your surprise they walk backwards, and away from each other. Suddenly you get it. It was as if it were run backwards! You've been played with a little, but it was brilliant.

Furthermore, advertising was not the whole campaign. Girls walked around in supermarkets, lifting up young men's shirts and spraying them with Axe. They also used the Internet brilliantly. Take a peek: *www.theaxeeffect.com*, and *www.evanandgareth.com*.

The result? A market share exceeding 80 percent of the target segment. Can you believe it? And people are buying loads of it! I will not be surprised if soon we'll see Axe offered in 6-packs!

Brand Trance

When a brand delivers an intangible benefit in addition to the core benefit that the product or service can deliver, and supports its consumers' enriched realities as described in Chapter 13, something really interesting happens. The brand's power to deliver the benefit is magical. Consumers enter a certain type of trance, i.e., they live some kind of "un-reality." This may sound scary, but it is not at all unusual. All people experience trances during their everyday existence. In its mundane version, this trance is momentary. During our day we go into and out of various kinds of trance states, and we do it many times. At those moments when we are "in it," we exhibit the following trance characteristics:

- We focus our attention on one source or idea which becomes central

- We "filter out" parts of our reality that are not relevant at that moment or consistent with our trance

- Our imagination is intensely active and lifelike

- We relate to concrete and not to abstract ideas

- We think in tangible images, symbols, and metaphors

- We lessen our judgment and criticism relating to our trance's central source

- We are willing to accept some non-reality as completely real

- We exhibit strong and immediate emotional reactions

One of the easier and most common forms of trance to understand is what we experience each time we watch a movie and become immersed in it. People may talk to us, sometimes we even reward them with our answer, and we do not have the slightest awareness that this is happening. When the movie is not entirely realistic, we do not have any problem with that. We go with the flow and accept its internal logic as natural. This is called trance logic. Every trance has its own trance logic.

Every type of enriched reality requires trance because it requires that people accept and live some un-reality. This is true for all the varieties of enriched reality: personal (distortion of reality, self deception, and fantasy), interpersonal (shared and coordinated interpretation of reality, relationship patterns), and socio-cultural (religion, ideology, values, norms, behavioral code, trends, fashion). Going back to consumer contexts, there are several generic types of trance, such as prestige, gourmet, agelessness, and so forth. Numerous brands channel such generic trances into specific trance experiences, according to the positioning and differentiation of their brand promise. For example, Mercedes-Benz was for many years, and still is, a "heavy luxury" brand. This brand's trance is "limitless power," a world in which things get done upon your word. These massive and fancy machines enable their owners to communicate to their surroundings a message of might, political or economic.

If your brand's strategy is based on an intangible benefit, you will need to define your brand's trance. Consumers derive intangible brand benefits only when they are in a brand's trance. After you have reached your strategic decision regarding

- the extent of your branding (Chapter 13),

- the benefits which your brand will offer to its consumers, and

- the instrumentality your brand will have within your customer's inner world, lifestyle, and relationships,

then it's time to move on to the stage where you determine your brand's trance definition.

A brand's trance constitutes the specific enriched reality that your consumers need in order for the brand to be effective. Nike's trance is a world in which everything is possible, a world in which once you dare to do something you win, a world in which any effort will lead to results, and to the realization of wishes. This is the internal logic of Nike's trance. This is the not-quite-reality that consumers need to accept and live for this brand to work. Which world (not entirely realistic) is your brand's world? What happens in it to your customers, which does not happen to them in their actual realities? What can your consumers accomplish there that is not possible in their actual reality? What are this world's rules? What is its internal logic?

After defining your brand's trance, you must analyze and list all elements of your marketing and service that you will have to manage strictly in order to create a system that induces your consumers' trance, deepens it, enriches it beyond one simple purchase, or even one brand category, and maintain it over time. These include actions to be taken, a behavioral code for your employees, the required atmosphere in your service centers or selling points or website. The entirety of the consumer experience is your brand's trance-makers or inducers.

At the same time, it will also be worth your while to identify which elements can break your brand's trance (for instance, an atmosphere at points of purchase that is inconsistent with the brand's trance and does not support it, or sales people and service providers who do not behave according to the trance's internal logic). These are your brand's trance-breakers or busters.

If we go back to the Mercedes-Benz example, some bad things have been happening to this brand lately. Excluding the fact that heavy luxury is now definitely not the "in-thing" for the young and the rich, there are some problematic groups that have become identified with Mercedes. Among these are drug dealers in South America, cab drivers in all sorts of places, and Russian mafiosos. These are trance bust-ers, so the brand slowly began losing legitimacy within its traditional target segment. Mercedes-Benz' managers worked hard to reverse this trend, but they also began milking their brand by launching cheaper series, designed to lengthen its life-span, and simultaneously, they began developing their next dream brand: the Maybach.

As you can see, a brand invites its target customers to enter its trance and encourages them to embrace it as a means by which they can attain a sought-after promised benefit. I want to emphasize the term invitation, in order to make it clear that there is no manipulation, deceit, or brainwashing here. Since your consumers' ability to extract the benefits offered by your brand depends to a certain extent on a type of self-seduction (an issue discussed in Chapter 15), this invitation must follow some principles called the principles of hypnotic branding.

The Principles of Hypnotic Branding

Why hypnotic? Because the hypnotic process creates a trance. You can relax, we're not talking here about the things you see in the movies or on TV or stage shows. You will not swing a pendulum in front of your consumers' eyes and say, "You're feeling sleeeeepy . . . ," and they will not close their eyes and follow your ridiculous orders. I'm talking here about using psychological principles of trance-inducement. In our case, it is your brand's trance.

The principles I will share in a moment constitute stages in a process that leads your consumers into your brand's trance, and then strength-ens it and deepens it. How will you use them? This process, adapted step-by-step to your specific brand's trance requirements, needs to be applied to the planning of your sales process, service process, advertis-ing, website, and any other contact you have with your consumers.

Hypnotic branding is the complete opposite of the hard sell approach, and it is several times more effective and profitable. But notice, it is intended only for brands with intangible instrumentality.

These are the ten principles of hypnotic branding:

1. First, make a personal contact, exhibit understanding, sensitivity, and empathy. Consumers need to know that you understand what they are going through. This stage's purpose is to calm everybody down, create rapport, and inspire openness.

2. Focus attention, using relevance, some reference to their self perception, the way they perceive their current situation, or to a solution or some benefit they seek and that you are offering to deliver. You have to prove that you are worth looking into.

3. Evoke and inflame desire for the certain benefit by triggering and activating the consumer's goal. The purpose is to make their imagined experience of attaining this benefit as vivid and desirable as possible. It is necessary so you can present your brand as a means to attain the benefit.

4. Do not make any explicit claims, do not argue, and refrain as much as possible from words, not to mention data or bold statements. Instead, make them imagine the possibility of attaining that benefit. What you want is to empower your consumers to seduce themselves.

5. Design and shape this possibility in your consumers' imagination. Use pictures, stories, demonstrations, examples, and metaphors. Be dreamy. Approach their imagination and not their thinking. Do not be overly sophisticated and do not use humor. These are thought provokers.

6. Be implicit and indirect; be suggestive and not directive. The possibility of attaining benefits that you have been seeding in their imagination will, by itself, provoke feelings and physical reactions of pleasure and enjoyment. These in turn will awaken anticipation.

7. Create strong expectations and these will direct the brand consumption experience.

8. Do not provide explanations or justifications. After their unconscious self-seduction, consumers will find by themselves all the explanations and rationalizations they need to justify anything. At the most, surrender your arguments passively at their disposal, without pushing too hard.

9. If you expect skepticism or rejection, use the "yes set." According to this method, you should build a progressive track of acceptance, with which you ask your consumers to comply. You will ask for their consent to options that are easily acceptable before you present options that are harder to accept. Dismantle your brand trance, and arrange the resulting components as possibilities beginning with the easiest ones to accept and digest, and ending with the hardest ones. First you want to achieve the light trance before you try for the deep trance.

10. Gently, sensitively, and methodically manage away all resistance and obstacles your consumers may express or even think of. Make it possible for them. Deal with their resistance by offering solutions for problems using a soft approach. Show them understanding, acceptance, and consideration. Avoid entirely any aggressiveness, powerfulness, or flamboyance, in any possible sense.

Putting these principles to work is not a simple thing to do. It entails profundity, and a lot of thought and effort. You are leading your consumers, patiently, sensitively, and sophisticatedly into a state of trance. You have a lot to gain. You are creating a brand that can deliver benefits that stretch far beyond its physical attributes.

The Brand Drama

Drama is one of the best ways to lead any person into a state of trance, as I demonstrated with the example of a person watching a movie. During the course of more than 2,500 years, theories and experience in drama have formed principles and methods for creating involvement and emotional impact. It is natural to take advantage of this huge pool of knowledge for the sake of building brands.

The drama theory begins with the following principle: At the heart of every drama there is some person who badly desires something that is very hard to obtain. Think *Romeo and Juliet* and thousands of other dramas we see at the theaters, in literature, in movies, and on television. We can distinguish them from one another with questions like: "Who is that person? What do they want? Why? Why is it not simply attained?" And beyond that, dramas can also be distinguished by questions like, "At what stage do we get to meet them? What happened before? How will the story develop? What will be the consequence?"

Now back to brands. A brand is a means that we create for someone (target customers) so that they can obtain something desirable that is apparently difficult to obtain.

When you place these two statements next to each other, the relevancy of drama theory to brand development becomes clear.

Your brand's drama is a drama in the lives of your target prospects. In it, your brand is an active participant. Its role in the drama is its role in your consumers' lives. The brand drama approach adds an unfolding dimension of time and process to the brand experience. Dramatization of your brand's story helps your customers grasp the benefit-potential embodied in your brand. Brand drama tools enable you to analyze your customers' psychology and behavior in dramatic terms. Furthermore, they let you create your marketing and branding activities as drama, thus maintaining high involvement and leading consumers into your brand's trance.

The brand-trance method, together with hypnotic branding and brand drama, provide a complete and systematic working process, as well as rules and tools for creating an integrated creative approach for a brand which is applicable to shaping the buying process, your service model, the product usage experience, all marketing communication campaigns, the various promotional activities, the activities of brand communities, and the innovative processes that realize the brand promise time and again. This creative approach serves the task of translating your brand's strategy into effective branding and marketing activities which build your consumers' awareness of your brand and enable them to embrace it and use it as a means to obtain sometimes evasive, inaccessible, but vital benefits.

Your Brand's Drama Analysis

Your brand's drama analysis is the first, and perhaps the most important tool of the brand drama approach. It is the understanding of your customer's quest to find the benefit that your brand is offering, in terms of a conflict between two forces.

The first force (known as the protagonist) is your consumer and every helping factor on his quest, such as people in his life, internal powers, external circumstances, opportunities, and your brand. The opposing force (known as the antagonist) is anything that works against him, blocking him, thwarting his efforts to obtain that benefit. This force can comprise people, organizations and institutions, personal traits, internal inhibitions and fears, erroneous beliefs, external constraints, and sometimes other brands. (Some brands use a tactic of marking a certain competing brand as "the enemy" who embodies values that are in complete contradiction with their own preferable ones. This tactic helps them differentiate themselves in the eyes of consumers.)

The drama analysis identifies these two sides and understands the conflict between them and its dynamics as it plays out in your consumers' lives. The dramatic plots constitute the stories of the development and the persistence of this conflict until finally your brand brings it to a satisfactory resolution.

Drama analysis can be performed using the following questions:

1. Who's the hero in this story (your customer)?

When answering this question, emphasis should be put not on profiling your typical consumer, but rather on reaching insights regarding his deepest motivations leading him to seek this specific benefit.

2. What does he desire (your brand's promised benefit)?

How will attaining this benefit be manifested? How will this consumer experience it? How will it affect his life? What will change in his life? What will be different about him? What will be made possible that was impossible before? In this context, we must also consider *levels of benefit.* In most cases you can see how a benefit attained by a consumer through buying a product or a brand has several levels, from concrete and practical to abstract and psychological. Think for a moment about buying a pair of Nike Soccer shoes. On the basic level, you have the same benefit of actually playing the game, offered by many fine soccer shoes. Above it you can find the benefit of experiencing winning (independent of any specific game or any specific win). Still above that lies a benefit of feeling mighty. The benefit at each level is a means for achieving the benefit, which waits at the higher level. So you have a choice of which level to make the promise of your brand. A simple rule says that in a competitive market, you want to define your brand's central promised benefit at the level in which this benefit becomes not trivial and even difficult to obtain. Nike's brand promise is at the level at which the promised benefit is the consumer's capability to "just do it" and get what he wants.

3. Why doesn't he just go out and get it? Why is it difficult?

Here you must be aware of the opposing parties. Who are they? What are the internal and external factors blocking consumers, thwarting their efforts, or damaging their capability? Everything, of course, must stay within the context of searching after the benefit we are talking about.

4. What is our hero doing in order to get what he wants to get?

This question invites you to explore and think deeply about the past and present of your customer's attempts to obtain the benefit. What did he do? What is he doing? What are his actions and behavioral patterns? And also, who takes part in his attempts? Who assists him? Who and what belongs to his camp?

5. **What has been happening to your consumer in the course of his attempts? How and where does he encounter opposing forces?**

Here it is important to become acquainted with real situations in your consumer's life, in which he takes action to obtain this benefit and encounters his opposing forces. What are those situations? What happens in them? How does your consumer fail? What does he experience? How does he feel?

6. **How can your brand help your consumer realize his purpose?**

This question brings us right back to your strategy. How can your brand help? How exactly does this happen? Who does what? Who says what? What does your consumer say to himself? What does he experience? What is he going through?

7. **What is the happy ending?**

Every brand drama must have a happy ending. What is this happy ending in the case of your brand? How does it happen? What exactly happens? How does your consumer experience all this?

Note that your brand drama (just like its trance) is a way to think about the context of your brand's realization in its entirety, and not only its marketing communication.

Let's look at the example of Starbucks, the successful coffee chain with more than 10,000 shops in the U.S. and many other countries. We can see that this brand brought the neighborhood hangout, long known to European urbanites, to American cities. Inspired by the European espresso bars, pubs, cafés, brasseries, and taverns, founder Howard Schultz created the "third place" for Americans, to be added to their first and second places, home and work. Starbucks was designed to echo Italian coffee culture. Starbucks shops are located on almost every block in big cities, and are equipped with sofas and couches, newspapers and magazines, and Internet connections, functioning as a neighborhood "living room."

Let's analyze the brand drama of Starbucks in its initial stage of success (before it became yet another symbol of America for many worldwide), using the set of questions above.

1. Who's the hero in this story?

- Someone living in a big city
- In many cases, living alone
- Without a large family base or an organic community

2. What does he desire?

What is this brand offering to the consumer? Let us examine some of its levels of benefit, going from the tangible to the abstract:

- "To go out" (but not too far out, without really "going out")
- "To meet people I know"
- "To be known, to be noticed"
- "To feel connected to life around me"

3. Why doesn't he just go out and get it? Why is it difficult?

In this case too there is no one enemy or rival, but several factors exist, external as well as internal:

- Living in an estranged community
- Leading a busy and stressful lifestyle
- Suffering from fear of rejection and shyness, prone to embarrassment
- Overshadowed by more charismatic people

4. What does our hero do in order to get what he wants?

In his camp you can find some family members, friends, and colleagues

- Makes appointments with family, friends, and acquaintances
- Organizes activities together with them
- Active for various causes, in various organizations
- Participates in communities, real and virtual

5. How and where does he encounter the difficulty?

- People are busy, they have their private lives and no time
- He can't get enough courage to turn to people of the same or opposite sex
- He is afraid of nuts and cons on the Internet
- He spends more hours alone than he wants to

6. How does the Starbucks brand help the consumer reach his purpose?

- He's got a place to go, close and accessible
- There are regulars there who recognize him
- Natural encounters occur

7. What is the happy ending?

- He has a community that meets without the need to initiate action or plan anything
- Those who are less shy than him start conversations with him
- He finds a lover who lives really close by

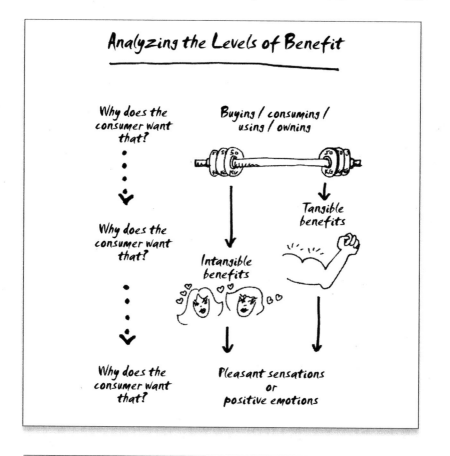

One of the ways to uncover and understand the various levels of a benefit is by using a slightly annoying series of questions you ask consumers in personal interviews. The basic question would be, "Why are you buying this product? What's in it for you?" After every answer you get from the consumer you must ask further, "But why do you want it? What good does it do that you want to have?" Again and again, until the consumer answers angrily, "What do you mean, why do I want it? Isn't it obvious already?" Every round of probing reveals a level of benefit. Only very patient interviewees will go with you all the way to the ultimate level which is always a pleasant physical feeling or positive emotions that are purposes within themselves.

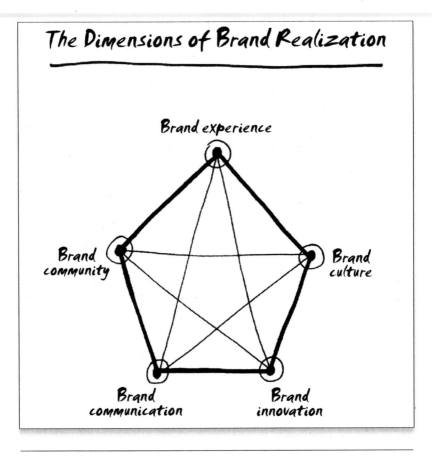

The Dimensions of Brand Realization

Brand experience

Brand community

Brand culture

Brand communication

Brand innovation

The actualization of strong brands is achieved in five different yet integrated dimensions. The first is the consistent and characteristic brand experience offered by your brand in all points of contact, direct (e.g., service) or indirect (e.g., advertising), between consumers and the brand. The second is the intra-company brand culture or the manner in which your company and workers live their commitment to deliver benefits promised by your brand. The third is the brand community, initiated and orchestrated opportunities with consumer meetings, encounters and interactions, via the Internet or face-to-face. Informal community interactions are also encouraged and supported. The fourth is brand-reaffirming innovation, which fulfills the brand promise time and again. The fifth is marketing communications, which sometimes are not only a way to communicate the brand promise but also contribute to realizing that promise (e.g., by being funny when the brand promise is fun).

I hope you can see how an analysis like this enables you to place your strategy in your customer's actual life and understanding what it implies. This type of analysis is much more effective than the usual briefing of your advertising agency or design studio. My experience has proven to me that after a few conversations about strategy using drama theory, creative teams in advertising agencies, product designers, and those who design visual identities, spaces, and experiences, can better understand and develop the creative universe and language of a brand.

Every story has an infinite number of possible dramatizations. If you think of *Romeo and Juliet*, you will see that this same theme, involving two lovers pulled apart by familial and social powers that prevent them from realizing their love, has been the subject of myriad plots and stories in every single medium of dramatization known today. Likewise, the scope and limitations affecting the dramatization of your own brand drama is none other than the scope and limitation of your imagination, creativity, and guts.

Let us end this book with this strong conviction, and wish you lots of success and the achievement of an unfair advantage over your competitors.

Index

4X4 vehicles, 6

A

Abercrombie & Fitch, 163
Absolut vodka, 10, 113–114, 186
added value, 9, 30–31,
    59,71,161,184, 230
advantagizing approach, 19, 32
Aaker, David, 2–4
Amazon.com, 164, 168
American Express, 166
American Idol, 191
American Organization of Quality
    Control, 38
Apple, 40, 42, 47, 65–66, 149,
    187–188
    iPod, 40, 47, 232
    iTunes, 40
Armstrong, Lance, 182
Autonation, 121
Axe (deodorant), 238–240

B

Bacardi & Co., 115
Bagir, 155
Beanie Babies, 203–204
Béhar, Yves (designer), 13
behavioral economics, 37
Belvedere, 10
benefits, 14–15, 70, 253
    attribution of, 171
    brands, 144–145
    connection to tangible, 183
    enriching consumer, 108,
    experiential-emotional, 109,
    139–140, 170
    experiential-sensory, 109, 139–140,
    170

intangible, 31–32, 175, 183
    ten methods for attaining,
    183–193
interpersonal, 109–110, 139,
    142–143, 170
local and timely, 144
new, in category, 120, 123–125
psychological, 110, 139, 141, 170
significant and rare, 14–15
social, 110, 130, 143, 170
Bert, Albert, 73
Bezos, Jeff, 164
Birkenstock, 12–14
    Architect Collection, The, 13
    Karl, 12
    Konrad, 12
    Urban Design, 13
Blackberry, 69
Blahnik, Manolo shoes, 71
Blue Ocean Strategy (book), 34–35
BMW, 4, 42
Boscolo, Rosano, 112
brands, 28–30, 173–193
    abstraction, 48–49
    added-value, 9, 31
    anticipation, 168–169
    as alter ego, 189–190
    as instruments, 168, 242
    benefits of, 144–145
    choices, 149–150
    concept, 173
    consumer use of, 30
    definitions, 173
    design, 30
    drama, 246–255
    emotional attitudes towards,
    148,171

experiential, 31
extension, 48–49
identity, 162
mental gym, 191–192
names, 163–165
perceived advantage, 174–175
personality, 165
promise, 93, 153, 171
relationships, 167–168
social-cultural authority, 187–188
strategy, 153–154, 173
success, 41–43
trance, 240–143
values, 5, 57, 165, 174
brand abstraction
definition of, 48–49
Branson, Richard, 47–49
British Airways, 47, 49–50
BT Cellnet, 158
Built to Last (book), 55

C
Calvin Klein, 31–32
CarChoice, 121
CarMax, 121
cars
new vs. used, 121
category
creating new, 119–120
substitute, 120–121
complementary, 121–122
suppliers, 122–123
intermediate customers, 122–123
Cellcom, 162
cellular phones, 1, 6, 24, 45, 51, 69,
98–99, 158–161
Cemex, 128–129
Chanel, 70
Chrysler PT Cruiser, 95–96,
cigars, 10
Claeys-Vereecke, Rose, 73
Clorox Company, 109
Club Med, 184

Cobain, Kurt, 178
Coca-Cola, 1, 41–42, 163, 225, 228
history of, 42
Cohiba Esplendidos, 10
Cole Haan, 14
Colgate-Palmolive Co., 46
Collins, Jim, 55
Commoditization of Brands, The
(article), 3
competitive advantage, 2, 8–9, 18–19,
21, 32, 34–44
loss of, 21
myths about, 34–35
competitive approach
vs. marketing approach (illustration), 58
competitive autism, 56–57
competitive strategy, 56–58, 174–175
hidden rules of industry, 110–113
consumers
beliefs based on facts, 98–99,
147–148, 151–153
characterization of, 87–88
consumption process analysis,
106–107
eclectic, 89
emotions, 14–15, 22
expectations, 169, 185–186
gut responses, 137–138
in 21st century, 209–210
loyalty model (illustration), 17
loyalty, 16–17, 210
motivations, 36–37, 136
needs, 195–199
pain points, 107–108
pre-readiness, 233–234
psychology, 36
satisfactions, 145–146, 170–171
stereotypes, failure of, 88
consumption process analysis,
105–135
15 stages of consumer, 106–107
Cooper, Dr. Martin, 51
Copernicus Marketing Consulting, 2

core benefits, 45–46
Cotter, Erin, 69–70
Crawford, Fred, 38
Crest electric toothbrush, 208
Crest, 46
customer relationship management, 38
customer satisfaction, 16, 38–39
customer segmentation, 34–35
cycle of desire (illustration), 219–220

D
Da Vinci Code, 208
Dakin, 203
Dalai Lama, 176
data, role of, 65–66
De Beers, 187
Dell, Michael, 52
demographics, 26
design, importance of, 66
development of marketing hits (illustration), 229
Diageo, 11–12
Diesel, 190
differentiation, 10, 18–19, 22, 38,
    45–54, 112, 154–155, 172, 237
    5 percent, 23–24,43, 47
    as part of strategy, 20–21
    circumstantial, 18
    creating, 16–17
    losing, 14
    off-core, 45,48, 50–52, 155
    temporary, 18
Dinner Helpers, 123
Dolce & Gabbana, 109
Dream Dinners, 123
Dubner, Stephan, 37
Ketel One, 113–114

E
The Elder Scrolls Game, 31
electrifying marketing, 39–40
    principles of, 205–207
    vs. satisfying marketing, 194–207

ElekTex, 156
Ernst & Young, 38
Escape from Freedom (book), 212

F
false assumptions
    in strategic planning, 61–63
fantasies, 179
Febreze, 69
Ferrari North America, 10, 192
Fiba, Marco (designer), 113
Filo, David, 164
FirstMatter, 38
FoMo (Fear of Missing Out), 211–215,
    238
ForeSearch, 86, 95–104, 237
    bank research, 98
    benefits of, 99
    G. Zalman's ZMET, 97
    how to conduct, 100–104
    interview methods, 100–104
    lottery research, 103
    mapping consumer associations, 97
    Means-End model, 97
Forum (research institute), 38–39
Fraizer, Margot, 12
Frank, Sidney, 113–115
Freakonomics (book), 37
Fromm, Erich, 212

G
Galbraith, John Kenneth, 59
Gallup, 38
gap analysis, 61, 72–73
generative thinking exercises, 82–83
gift shopping, 25–26
Gillette, 226
Godin, Seth, 210
Google, 50
Graham, Nick, 199–203
Grey Goose, 114–115
GSM, 159
Guinness, 11–12

Guinness, Arthur, 11

H
Habanos, 10
Harley-Davidson, 192, 225
Harry Potter books, 39–40, 169, 199, 208, 225
Hefner, Hugh, 189
Hennes & Mauritz, 70
hierarchy of needs, 36
Hilton hotels, 184–185
Himalayan cats, 203
Hutchison, 159
hypnotic branding, 243–246
principles of, 244–245
Hyundai, 175

I
IBM, 1, 42, 52, 113,163
ICICI bank, 127
identity, 186
IKEA, 38, 163, 165–166
image, 29–30
In Search of Excellence, 7
infatuation model (illustration), 235
Institute of Culinary Studies *Boscolo Etoile*, 112

J–K
Jacuzzi, 5, 154
Jobs, Steve, 40, 66, 149, 160, 164
Joe Boxer, 71, 199–203
Jones, Chuck (designer), 122
Jordan, Michael, 182
Just-on-Desire Branding (book), 7
K8 (Norwegian design firm), 124
Kaaba, 176
Kahneman, Daniel, 36–37
Kendler, Assa, 42
Kim, W. Chan, 34–35
Kinepolis, 73
Klum, Heidi (designer), 13
Konopizza (chain), 112
Kotler, Philip, 2–4, 5, 57

L
Lamborghini, 175
Langerfeld, Karl (designer), 70
Law of Exciting Brands, 227
Lenova, 42
Let's Dish, 123
Levi Strauss & Co., 1
Levitt, Steven, 37
Levitt, Ted, 108
lifestyle perception (illustrations), 90, 91, 92
Lindstrom, Martin, 225
Lipsticket, 69–70
Longinotti-Buitoni, Gian Luigi, 192
Lufthansa, 49

M
marketing communications, 31–32
marketing hits
development of, 208–232, 239
formula, 209
marketing rules, 4–5
Marketing Science Institute, 22
Martin Luther King, 56
Maslow, 36
mass market product, 5–6
Matthews, Ryan, 38
Mauborgne, Rene, 34–35
MBA clones, 2–4
weakness in thinking, 33
McCartney, Stella (designer), 70
McDonald's, 1, 109, 163, 225
McGann, Meredith 69–70
McKinsey & Company, 6–7
Mecca Cola, 189
Mercedes-Benz, 1, 4, 42, 139, 243
Mercury One on One, 159
Microsoft, 47, 52, 127, 149, 222, 225
Microtel, 159
Millward Brown, 225
Mizrahi, Isaac, 222
Montblanc pens, 31
Morgans Hotel Group, 184

motivations
   desires, 139, 172, 217–219
   unsatisfied, 215–216
   regenerating, 71, 216–217
Motorola, 51–52

N
Naked News, 25, 46
Nestle, 31–32
niche product, 5–6
Nike, 14, 110, 181–183, 242
Nirvana, 178
Nokia, 1, 51–52
N.W. Ayer, 187

O
Oakley sunglasses, 152
off-core differentiation, 51 (see also differentiation)
Open your I's, 64
opportunities
   management by, 60, 63
   mapping, 83
   searching methods, 126–129
   strategic, 60, 83
   tactical, 60, 69, 83
opportunity scan (O-Scan), 61, 64, 68–85
   competition, 77–78,80, 118, 119
   competitive analysis, 118–119
   consumers, 77, 80, 118
   consumption process analysis, 105–135
   context, 76–77, 80, 118
   exercises, 79–80, 129–130, 131–133
   market, 77,80, 118
   methodology (tools), 75–76, 86–104, 125–129
   self-analysis, 119
   strategy creation (illustration), 117
   us, 78, 80, 118, 130–131
   zoom in, 74–75, 79
   zoom out, 75
Orange, 158–161, 162–163, 185

P
Paul, Arthur (designer), 190
Pemberton, Dr. John S., 42
Peters, Tom, 6, 66
Peugeot, 175
Playboy magazine, 189
PlayStation 3, 31–32
pop-up retail, 223
Porras, Larry, 55
Porsche, 10
Porter, Michael, 2–4, 23
positioning, 5, 153–154
potential customers, 26–27
   common characteristics, 26
Powerbook, 47
prestigious brands, 4
price-driven market, 8–9
private monopoly, 10–11, 14–15, 16–17, 42, 52
promotional campaigns
   failure of, 22
psycho-babble, 36

R
Rapaille, Clotaire, 95
reality enrichment, 175–178, 241
   culture, 176, 181
   distortions, 178
   personal interpretation, 177
   religion, 176
   self-deception, 178
   shared and coordinated, 176
Red Envelope, 26
Reeves, Keanu, 239
reputation, 29
Rhodes, Cecil, 187
Ries, Al, 2–4
risk avoidance, 21
Robinson, Frank, 42
Rosso, Renzo, 190
Rowling, J.K., 226

S
Samsung, 51

satisfactions, 70–72, 144–145

Scent Stories, 69

Scully. John, 65

seduction, 220

segmentation

characterization, 87

contextual, 86, 93–95, 126–127

Seinfeld, 40, 199

Selling Dreams (book), 192

Sex and the City, 115

shoe manufacturing, 12–14

short-term brands, 209, 210, 220, 224–230

background-foreground architecture, 228

development of, 227–228

movies, 221

pop-up retails, 222–223

rules for, 226, 230–232

star-satellite architecture, 228

short-term stores, 222–223

Sisyphus, 41

Six Sigma, 38

Skyy, 113

Smart Roadster, 139

Smirnoff, 113–114

Soup Kitchen International, 40

Starbucks, 46

Wozniak, Steve 160

Stokke, 124

strategic analysis triangle, 80–81

strategic consulting, 22–23

strategic thinking, 64–67

strategy statement, 84–85

strategy, 20–33

adapting, changing, 2

branding, 29–30

competitive marketing, 25–27

confusion with goals, 27–28

differentiation, 18–19, 24, 28

emotions and, 29–30

giving up something, 20

long-term, 1–2

short-term, 2

strategophobia, 20, 22, 56

Super Fast Pizza, 123

Swatch, 50

SWOT, 63

T

Tartino, Quentin, 168

The Apprentice, 191

The Body Shop, 10, 50, 189

The Swan, 191

The Wall Street Journal, 114

Timberland, 192

Toyota, 175

TQM doctrine, 38

Trump, Donald, 191

Tversky, Amos, 36–37

U

underconsumers, 128

unfair advantage, 3, 6–7, 8–19, 72, 126, 155, 174–175

characteristics of, 9–10

Unilever, 238–240

unique success formula, 32–33, 59, 68–69, 81–82, 105, 136

unsatisfied needs, 59, 70–72, 138–139, 144–145, 215

updating image, 11–12

V

VALS, 88

Vans, 188

Victoria's Secret, 92–93, 163

Virgin Atlantic, 47–50

Virgin Megastores, 46

Vision, 55–57

Vodafone, 158

Volvo, 46

von Furstenberg, Diane (designer), 51

W

Wal-Mart, 38

Walt Disney Company, 1

Warner, Ty, 203–204

WCRS (advertising agency), 160
what's feasible, 84, 107
what's next process, 66–67
what's now, 80–81, 107
Whirlpool, 122
Wieden, Dan, 182
Wife Swap, 191
Wolff Olins Company, 160–161
Woodruff, Robert, 42

X-Y-Z
Xplory, 124–125
Yagna, Al, 40
Yahoo!, 164
Yang, Jerry, 164
Zopa, 65

About the Author

Dr. Dan Herman is an Advantagizer, a globally renowned expert in identifying growth opportunities and creating competitive advantages for companies and for brands. He integrates winning competitive strategies with profitable business models and psychologically powerful branding. Dr. Herman is the co-owner and CEO of Competitive Advantages Ltd. Together with his highly trained team he serves worldwide clients ranging from local mid-sized companies to Fortune Global 500 corporations. Competitive Advantages often partners with local consulting companies in carrying out large scale projects.

In conjunction with his consulting practice, Dr. Herman is a conference speaker, seminar leader, workshop moderator, and is frequently interviewed by the media. Among his highly demanded topics for speaking engagements and for training are:

- Identifying opportunities to grow and devising growth strategies with the "What's Next?" process and Opportunity Scan (O-Scan) method.

- Creating successful off-core differentiation strategies that competitors will not imitate and turning them into a Unique Success Formula, a private monopoly.

- Predicting potential future consumer wants with the Consumer ForeSearch method.

- Achieving meteoric marketing successes with the Marketing Hit's Formula and the Short Term Brands (STBs) methodology.

- Creating a psychological and/or social instrumentality for a brand and applying the principles for creating emotional significance.

- Developing brands that click immediately with consumers' emotions using the just-on desire branding methodology.

- Bringing a brand to life with the brand drama method, the hypnotic branding principles and, the brand trance approach.

- Creating luxury or prestige brands, premium products, VIP services, upscale retail, elite places, exclusive organizations, etc.

- The Fear of Missing Out (FoMO) and other crucial phenomena for understanding the psychological makeup of today's consumer.

Dr. Herman is the author of two books in Hebrew, *Achieving an Unfair Advantage: Winning Strategic Management in a World of MBA Clones* and *The Brand Builder's Guide*. His book in Russian, *Birth of a Brand,* was published recently by Geleos and a collection of his articles, "I Want to Be a Brand," was published in Turkey by Alteo. Two other books in English, *Think Short! Short-Term Brands' Success and the Creation of Marketing Hits* and *Just-on-Desire Branding* will be published in the near future throughout the world. He has also authored numerous articles, textbook chapters, and e-books.

Dan is a devoted fan of gourmet food (in particular French, Italian, and Japanese cuisines), of fine wine, and of high quality alcoholic beverages (which he consumes moderately). He enjoys a good cigar every now and then, private dance parties, humor, world travel, and getting acquainted with people of varied cultures and lifestyles. He is a great lover of music (in particular classical, opera, jazz, and blues), modern dance, the cinema, storytelling, design, and architecture, as well as fine arts of all sorts. Dan writes poetry and draws, mainly with coal and lead. He is a qualified personal coach for the attainment of life goals and also a certified masseur.

Some of his major interests include: strategic thinking, the psychology of the intangible aspects of our reality, and altered states of consciousness (hypnosis and other trance states, interpretations of reality, imagination, positive illusions, fantasies, and emotions).

You can find out more about Dr. Herman or reach him via the web at *www.danherman.com* and *www.advantagizers.com.*